The Gunners of
August 1914

The Gunners of August 1914

Baptism of Fire

John Hutton

Published in association with Firepower, the Royal Artillery Museum

Pen & Sword
MILITARY

First published in Great Britain in 2014 by
Pen & Sword Military
an imprint of
Pen & Sword Books Ltd
47 Church Street
Barnsley
South Yorkshire
S70 2AS

ISBN 978 1 47382 372 3

A CIP catalogue record for this book is available from the British
Library

Typeset in Ehrhardt by
Mac Style Ltd, Bridlington, East Yorkshire
Printed and bound in the UK by CPI Group (UK) Ltd,
Croydon, CRO 4YY

Pen & Sword Books Ltd incorporates the imprints of Pen & Sword
Archaeology, Atlas, Aviation, Battleground, Discovery, Family
History, History, Maritime, Military, Naval, Politics, Railways, Select,
Transport, True Crime, and Fiction, Frontline Books, Leo Cooper,
Praetorian Press, Seaforth Publishing and Wharncliffe.

For a complete list of Pen & Sword titles please contact
PEN & SWORD BOOKS LIMITED
47 Church Street, Barnsley, South Yorkshire, S70 2AS, England
E-mail: enquiries@pen-and-sword.co.uk
Website: www.pen-and-sword.co.uk

Contents

Preface

In the minds of most people the First World War will always be synonymous with trench warfare and the mass slaughter inflicted by machine guns on the helpless but gallant infantry as they bravely struggled to break through apparently impregnable defences. There is good reason for the prevalence of this view of the war – it is largely true. Nothing in the history of warfare – before or since this titanic conflict – has ever compared with the ghastly ordeal and misery of a soldier's life in the trenches. And the German machine guns did indeed take a terrible toll of British lives. It is not entirely surprising therefore that the infantry's experiences over these four long years should continue to both fascinate and appal people today. It is no surprise either that most of the contemporary history of the war should be devoted to exploring and describing this terrible reality.

What often gets insufficient attention, in my view, is the role and contribution the artillery made to the prosecution of the war effort. It is not uncommon to read histories of the great battles of the war and see the role of the artillery sometimes reduced to a few introductory paragraphs describing a preliminary barrage. The actions of the infantry normally dominate the rest of the narrative. I have long felt that this has created a distorted impression of the reality of the First World War. No one can dispute the bravery and extraordinary heroism of the infantry in this protracted and violent struggle, and nor should their sacrifice ever be downplayed. That is not the intention of this book. If we are truly to understand the nature of the conflict then what needs to be struck is a better balance. The contribution of the artillery should be equally recognised.

The fundamental truth about the First World War is that the infantry and the gunners fought together – one could not succeed without the help and support of the other. This was true from the first shots of the war to the last. I hope this balance can be achieved therefore by telling the story of the war as the gunners themselves saw it. And they had a unique vantage point. The gunners may not have always shared the trench experiences of the infantry, but they were frequently the principal target of the enemy's guns, and the gun line was always a valuable prize and an objective for the attackers. So although the artillerymen may not themselves have always been physically present in the front line alongside the infantry (although for much of the early fighting they certainly were), they were always in the thick of the action. Success or failure, either in offence or defence, would very often depend on the performance and responsiveness of the guns.

I have chosen to focus this book on the first few months of the First World War. These iconic months of warfare would prove to be fundamental to the whole conduct of the campaign. To the surprise of many, and contrary to much strategic pre-war analysis, trench warfare, rather than a war of manoeuvre, soon emerged as the principal feature of the fighting. But the predominance of artillery as the primary weapon on the battlefield and the effect of concentrated fire in particular would also become equally fixed points of reference around which all offensive and defensive operations would be based. Firepower would prevail over manoeuvrability and it was the guns that would provide it. In these first few months of the war vital lessons about how to best use this firepower were quickly learned – lessons about equipment, tactics and strategy. These were the lessons that would lie at the heart of the eventual Allied victory four bitter years later.

Battles, of course, can only ever be successfully prosecuted if the material needs of the fighting men are satisfied. This is an often-ignored aspect of contemporary First World War history. The logistical effort involved in assembling, supplying and deploying the artillery, often in the most difficult conditions imaginable, also stands out as one of the most formidable achievements of British arms during the war. It was an effort that involved the gunners themselves, the infantry and the Army Service Corps, as well as industry back home, in a remarkable and resilient supply chain without which ultimate victory would have been for ever beyond reach. This aspect of the war serves as a poignant reminder of the hard physical labour involved in conducting military operations on the Western Front. No one knew this better than the gunners themselves. Victory would be a joint triumph – of labour as well as arms.

Wherever possible, I have tried to incorporate the personal testimonies of those who served with and supported the guns. In August 1914 this was a mix of regular soldiers, men from the reserves and some Territorials. Their accounts of the fighting provide a vital and fascinating insight into the colossal tragedy and drama of the First World War.

Here, in my view, lies the real story of the war. First and foremost, it was an artillery war. Driven by the enormous capacity of industry and science, the armies of all the belligerent states developed ever more powerful guns of increasing calibre, sophistication and range. It was these weapons that inflicted more damage, and killed and maimed more soldiers than any other used in the period 1914–1918. It was ultimately British guns that swept the Allies to victory in 1918 and exerted total dominance over the battlefield – not, contrary to popular mythology, the tanks, which, although a terrifying new weapon in their own right, were technically extremely unreliable and slow moving and thus highly vulnerable to anti-tank fire. It was not the advent of tanks that brought the war to its successful conclusion but the power and might of the artillery.

The history of the gunners in the First World War is, in my view, an inspiring tale of endeavour and achievement. By the end of the war the British in France had almost half a million men and nearly 6,500 guns serving with the Royal Regiment of Artillery – a mighty force. It was a far cry from the heroic but tiny contingent of gunners who deployed to France in August 1914. Each of the four infantry divisions of the original British Expeditionary Force in 1914 had a complement of 76 guns and about 4,000 gunners of the Royal Field Artillery. The cavalry went to France with only 30 guns and just over 1,500 men of the Royal Horse Artillery. Their guns were mainly light field guns designed to fire relatively small calibre shrapnel shells over open sights on a flat trajectory from uncovered positions – a strategy with which Napoleon and Wellington a century earlier would have been extremely familiar. Most of the guns at the beginning of the war were only equipped to fire shrapnel, which meant they were used largely as long-range shotguns. Only the howitzers (which were few in number) were provided with high explosive shells.

The small calibre of the guns was not a failure of planning or strategy. The size of the guns was effectively limited by the need for them to be transported around the battlefield by horses in what was mistakenly expected to be a largely mobile campaign. Four years later the Royal Regiment not only had a very different appearance, with enormous heavy tractors hauling much heavier guns that were used to destroy heavy defensive fortifications, but it employed starkly different strategies too, with greater concentration of accurate firepower under much more effective command and control, using vastly different techniques for identifying targets and with camouflage and concealment as basic concepts of deployment. This evolution in equipment, and the recognition of the need for heavier guns to neutralise both the enemy's own artillery and his defences, had its origins in the experiences of these first few weeks of fighting.

Artillery came into the modern age during the First World War and it was the British Army that led the transformation. The transition was inevitably a difficult one, confirming the truism that there is often no gain without pain.

The outbreak of war inevitably pitched the Royal Regiment into a sharp but often frustratingly slow learning process. It may have started the war less well equipped than its enemy and with less appreciation of the needs of modern warfare, but it ended the war stronger in every department than its opponents.

The evolution of British gunnery over these four cataclysmic years also belies another great popular myth of the War – that of 'lions led by donkeys'. Those who commanded the British artillery certainly made mistakes (as did their opposite numbers in the German and French armies), and men paid for them with their lives. Many of these mistakes would become apparent in the first few weeks of the war – the failure to concentrate the firepower of the guns, the failure of effective communication, and the inadequacy of equipment and supply. But these failures would act as a spur to a paradigm shift in thinking that led to the development of new technologies and tactics that were to transform the effectiveness of artillery and make it a crushing weapon of awesome power. In this sense, those in command and those who manned the British guns were able to turn the tables on an enemy who began the conflict with a clear superiority in both weapons and tactics over the British Expeditionary Force. It cannot therefore be said with any credibility that during the First World War the artillery was led by people who did not understand what they were doing. Quite the reverse, in fact. There were many outstanding and innovative artillery commanders and strategists. Few if any of them were to end the war as household names. They should have been.

The artillery war was, of course, fought on two fronts – at home as well as in the trenches. Industry eventually rose to the challenge of providing sufficient quantities of guns and ammunition to meet the requirements of the Army in France and Belgium. But here, too, the journey from insufficiency to plenty was far from straightforward. The enormous appetite for shells was driven partly by the nature of the fighting but also by the capability of the new quick-firing guns to consume vast quantities of ammunition. The former may not have been predicted with absolute accuracy in the run up to the war but the latter was well known and foreseeable. The munitions crisis of late 1914/15 stands out as perhaps one of the greatest and most reprehensible failures of wartime planning and supply. This initial failure of grand strategy to meet the real needs of modern warfare led to arguably the most impressive mobilisation of British and Allied resources in the entire war. However, it was only in the later stages of the conflict that these difficulties were fully surmounted, providing at that point the essential platform for the overwhelming firepower necessary for battlefield success.

In writing this book, the experiences of my grandfather, who served with the guns on the Western Front in 1915 and then subsequently in Salonika, has never been far from my mind. He came from a working-class family in Nottingham. Like many others of his generation, his early life had been hard. Fortune had not dealt him an easy hand. At the beginning of the war he was a warehouseman. But he was like millions of others who answered their country's call to arms during that extraordinary late summer of 1914. He would win no awards for gallantry. His service with the Royal Artillery was in no sense unique or exceptional, but he was, and is, special to me. It is impossible for me to either imagine or understand what he went through, the sights that he must have witnessed or the sadness he experienced with the death of so many of his friends. But I am so very proud of him and what he did all those years ago.

So, although this book is first and foremost a tribute to every man who served with the guns in the tumultuous last few months of 1914, it is dedicated above all else to 099109 Bombardier John Victor Hutton, A Battery, 117th Brigade, Royal Field Artillery. His service during the war and the physical hardships he had to overcome make my grandfather a great man in every sense of the word. I know that he drew enormous pride from the achievements of the gunners of 1914 and it was this pride which partly helped sustain him throughout his own years of service in the regiment. In the end it was people like him who helped secure in 1918 what was perhaps the greatest British military victory in our long and extraordinary island history. But for everyone who served with the artillery in the First World War, this eventual triumph of British firepower rested very heavily on the shoulders of those who fought with the guns in those difficult months of 1914. In these pages I hope I have been able to do justice to all of his comrades in arms of 1914. No fewer than 49,076 gunners died during the First World War and hundreds of thousands of others were wounded in the service of their country. Words alone can never do justice to their sacrifice, but without words we can never even begin to start.

I could not have written this book without the support of the Royal Artillery Museum at Woolwich, and without the energy and knowledge of Paul Evans, its archivist. I want to record my special thanks to him for his help, courtesy and advice. If you are able to, please visit and support the Museum and its mission, which is to keep alive the incredible story of the gunners. And there is one other person whose help and support I want to acknowledge: my wife Heather. She understood my passion to write this history of the gunners of August 1914, and without her encouragement this book would never have seen the light of day.

Maps

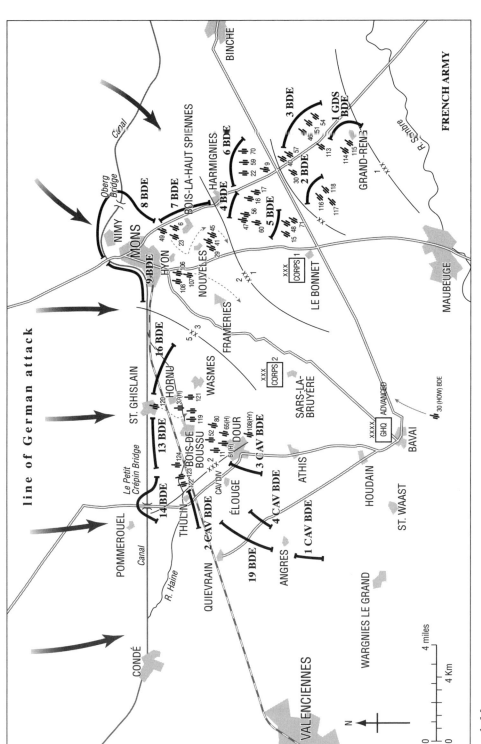

Map 1: Mons.

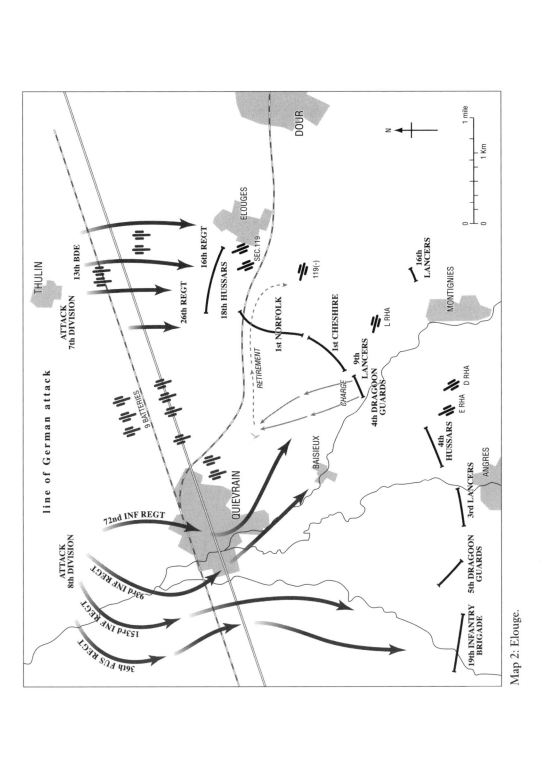

Map 2: Elouge.

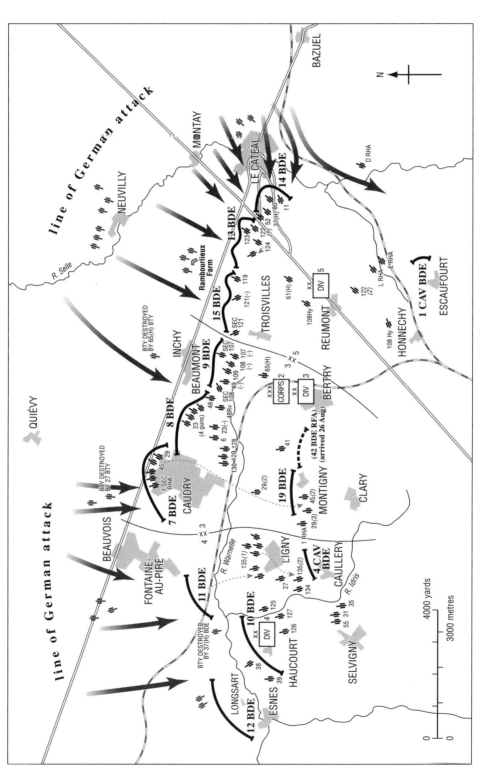

Map 3: Le Cateau.

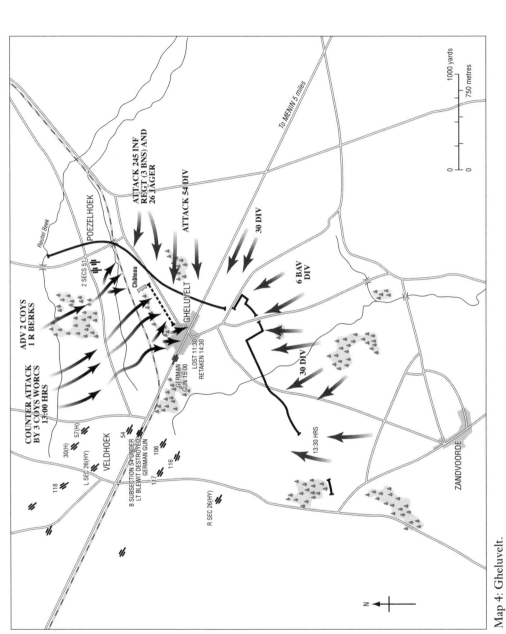

Map 4: Gheluvelt.

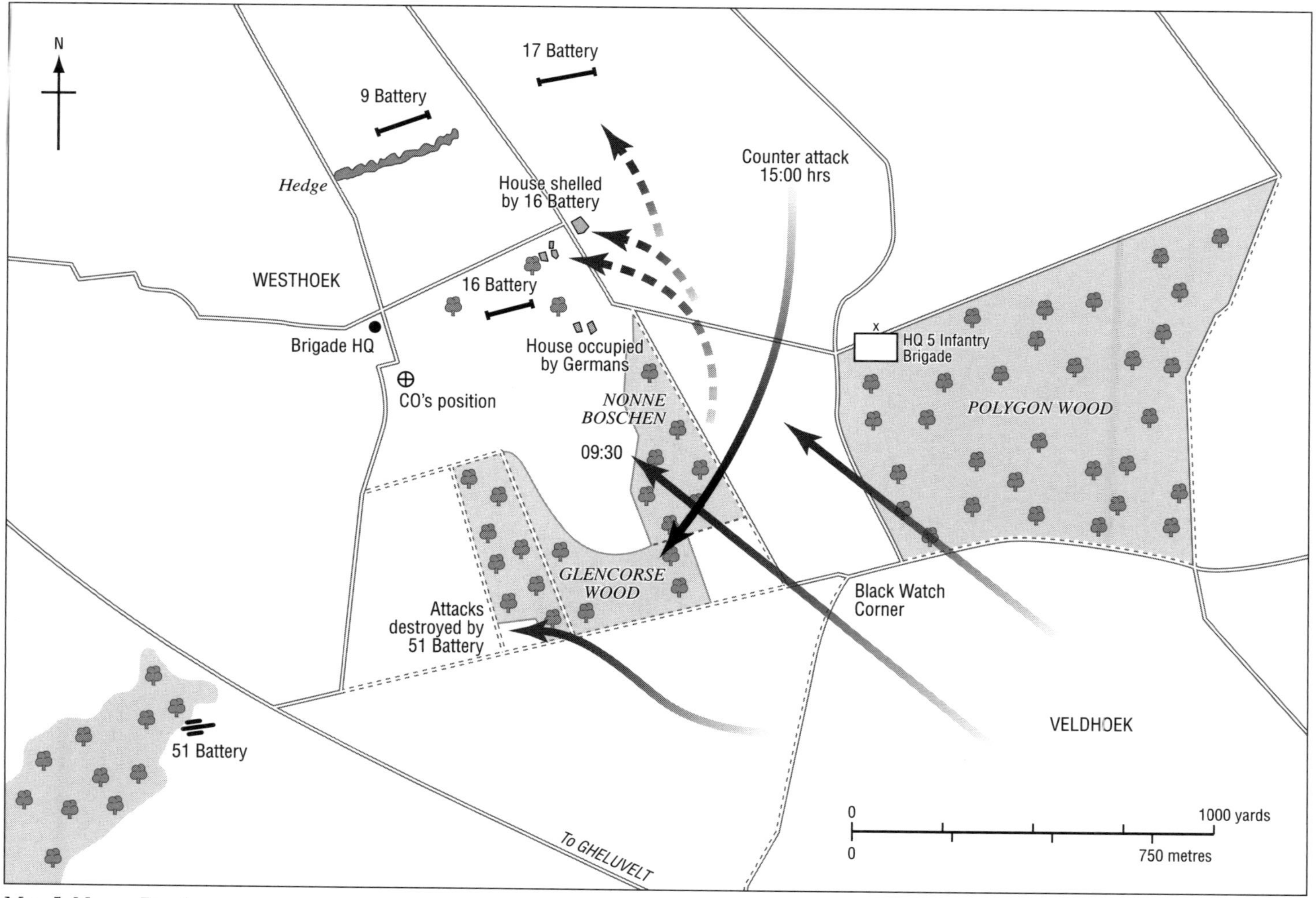
N
17 Battery
9 Battery
Hedge
House shelled
by 16 Battery
Counter attack
15:00 hrs
WESTHOEK
16 Battery
Brigade HQ
House occupied
by Germans
HQ 5 Infantry
Brigade
CO's position
NONNE
BOSCHEN
POLYGON WOOD
09:30
GLENCORSE
WOOD
Black Watch
Corner
Attacks
destroyed by
51 Battery
51 Battery
VELDHOEK
0
1000 yards
0
750 metres
To GHELUVELT

Map 5: Nonne Boschen.

Chapter 1

Mobilisation

'Everyone in good spirits and full of optimism. Germany has bitten off more than she can chew.'

Captain Mackie, 30th Brigade
Ammunition Column, 5 August 1914

In the late summer of 1914 the Great Powers of Europe finally stumbled into the war that had, for the best part of a decade, threatened to engulf them. The assassination on 28 June of the heir to the crumbling Austro-Hungarian Empire in Sarajevo by Gavrilo Princip, which appeared to most people in Britain as a deeply obscure act of political terrorism, lit a series of fuses that would explode with ferocious violence in August.

The British Army had at least contemplated the possibility of fighting a major war against Germany. Planning for such a campaign had been under way for several years as part of the Entente Cordiale. A small force of up to six infantry divisions and some cavalry would take up position on the left flank of the French Army as it advanced to meet the German enemy. Some of this planning percolated down the ranks. Driver Ryder, of E Battery, Royal Horse Artillery (RHA), recounted an eerie occasion in 1913 when the entire battery was paraded in front of its commanding officer, Major Forman, for a briefing: 'He had a board and an easel. On it he had chalked a map of France. He said perhaps not in my lifetime but definitely in yours we will have war with Germany. And he pointed to a place on the map in France.' When E Battery deployed to France the following year, Driver Ryder was astounded to find that 'the train took us to the same place in France as Major Forman had pointed to on his map'.

The growing military tension on the continent towards the end of July led to Britain's military forces being put on a heightened state of alert. On 28 July Winston Churchill, the First Lord of the Admiralty, ordered the First Fleet to proceed to its preliminary war station at Scapa Flow. The Navy had, fortuitously, already been brought up to full war strength for the Review at Spithead a few days before. The next day, army officers and other ranks were recalled from leave and furlough and the coastal defences were manned.

On this day, 29 July, Rory Macleod, a young lieutenant serving at the Curragh with 80th Battery, 15th Brigade, Royal Field Artillery (RFA), wrote home to his father: 'We are ready to mobilize at a moment's notice. All officers on leave have been recalled and no more leave is to be granted. We have been studying the mobilisation regulations so that everything will go off smoothly.' In fact, for several days beforehand, Britain had been firmly in the grip of a feverish, frantic, patriotic hysteria. A young bank worker, E.C. Powell, arrived in London from a trip to the country on the eve of war to find London in absolute turmoil: 'A vast procession jammed the road from side to side, everyone waving flags and singing patriotic songs.'

Osbert Sitwell, who would endure four bitter years of fighting with the cavalry on the Western Front, writing after the Armistice was signed, famously described these noisy crowds of August as 'cheering for their own death'. Enormous crowds began to gather in all of Britain's towns and cities. Outside the Houses of Parliament and in front of Buckingham Palace they gave voice to their support for war. In Newcastle upon Tyne the mood was, according to James MacKay, a young Methodist minister, a little more sober. On 3 August he had travelled with friends up the railway line along the Tyne Valley to Stocksfield, a few miles from the city centre: 'At every railway station on the way up a military guard is stationed. The whole community is alive with uniformed men. Several train loads of soldiers passed us on their way to the city.'

Two days later, as the reality of war began to sink in, the seriousness of the situation was apparent on Tyneside and elsewhere:

Great excitement and sorrow prevails in the city. All the volunteers have been called out as well as reservists. Soldiers have been leaving the city in great numbers all day. Went down to the town to see if I could see any soldiers. The sights were heartrending. Women weeping everywhere. There are no great demonstrations of enthusiasm. Everyone feels the awfulness of the situation and a becoming gravity prevails.

This mood of gravity was also shared by those being mobilised for war. Major John Mowbray, who would go to France as part of the artillery staff of the 2nd Division, wrote in a letter home from Aldershot on 4 August:

'We've had a black time of anxiety these two or three days. There is, of course, general animation here but I fear that people at home will be in for an anxious time. It will be a much more serious affair than we grasp in our moments of enthusiasm.'

On 2 August the British Government cancelled the orders for the annual Territorial Army training camps so that the Territorial forces could, if necessary, also be put on a war footing. This required them to be centred on their regimental depots. The War Office also cancelled the orders for annual army manoeuvres in order to ensure that the regular army was similarly prepared.

The British Army began its full-scale mobilisation for war at 4pm on 4 August 1914. Earlier that day two German cavalry divisions had crossed the frontier into neutral Belgium. Britain was the last of the major powers to mobilise. In the House of Commons the depressed but resigned Prime Minster Herbert Asquith set out the justification for going to war to tumultuous cheers from all sides:

I do not think any nation ever entered into a great conflict – and this is one of the greatest that history will ever know – with a clearer conscience or stronger conviction that it is fighting not for aggression, not for the maintenance of its own selfish ends, but in the defence of principles the maintenance of which is vital to the civilisation of the world. We have got a great duty to perform; we have got a great truth to fulfil; and I am confident that Parliament and the country will enable us to do it.

James MacKay had, in fact, been a witness to the careful and thorough planning that had gone into the possibility that Britain might one day have to fight a major continental war. The War Office plan for mobilisation, first published in 1912, was by now being put into speedy effect. The plan – known as the War Book – was a detailed encyclopaedia setting out the transition from peace to war time conditions. It identified in meticulous detail the means by which Britain would be ready to deploy an expeditionary force of up to six infantry divisions and a cavalry force to fight alongside the French against the expected common enemy, Germany. It involved an unprecedented marshalling of national resources – men, animals and equipment. Nothing had been left out. The railways, for example, came under government control in order to facilitate the movement of troops across the country, and the War Office was given extensive powers to requisition private property for army use. Each reservist had an identity document telling them exactly what to do now the war had begun. The document merely had to be presented at any rail ticket office and a travel warrant would be issued. Post offices, which would be required to stay open twenty-four hours a day, would hand over 3 shillings for expenses. The plans would proceed like clockwork.

In addition to preparing detailed mobilisation plans, for more than a decade the War Office had been focused on bringing the equipment of the British Army into the new modern age of warfare. Nowhere was this more necessary than in the case of the artillery. In the years leading up to the outbreak of the First World War, the artillery had been substantially re-equipped and reorganised after the humiliating inadequacies exposed by the fighting in South Africa during the Boer War. At the start of the Boer War the artillery was equipped with the ancient 12-pounder breech-loading light field gun with no on-carriage recoil system. It benefited from a rifled barrel that improved its accuracy and was fitted with a breech-loading mechanism to speed up its rate of fire, but the absence of any on-carriage recoil system meant that every time the gun was fired it had to be re-laid onto its target. It was no match for its Boer counterpart. The Boers were using the newly manufactured Krupp's quick-firing guns which were far superior in every department to the guns in use with the British Army. These Krupp's guns incorporated all of the latest developments in artillery science and technology. They reflected the principal design features of the new generation of artillery weapons that had been pioneered by the French in 1897 with their revolutionary quick-firing 75mm gun. They made full use of built-in recoil systems and new breech mechanisms that allowed the guns to maintain a very high rate of effective fire. They would transform the concept of artillery.

Given the clear weapons superiority enjoyed by the Boers, the Director General of Ordnance General Sir Henry Brackenbury was forced into ordering 105 15-pounder quick-firing guns from Krupp's arch rival, Erhardt of Dusseldorf, ushering in a new dawn of modern gunnery in the British Army. The purchase of the German guns met the immediate needs of the artillery, but national pride required a British quick-firing gun to be designed and procured as quickly as possible. As soon as the Boer War ended, the War Office formed a committee to draw up specifications for a series of new guns for the artillery. These would be British in design and manufacture. The result was the adoption in 1904 of the 13-pounder quick-firing gun for the RHA and a new 18-pounder quick-firing gun for the RFA. Both were highly effective weapons and a huge improvement on what had gone before.

The 13-pounder was of 3-inch calibre (76mm) and could fire its 12.5lb shrapnel shell a distance of about 6,000 yards. By the time war was declared in 1914, there were 245 of these guns available. The 18-pounder gun fired a larger shrapnel shell (3.4-inch or 84mm) a distance of around 6,500 yards. The shells had a powder-burning fuse set by hand which would detonate above and in front of the intended target, sending nearly 400 red-hot steel balls flying through the air. Firing this kind of ammunition, the 13- and 18-pounder guns were effectively a kind of giant long-range shotgun.

Both of these new quick-firing guns used a simple pole-trail carriage which had the effect of limiting the elevation of the gun. Given the prevailing orthodoxy surrounding the use of artillery and the preference for direct fire tactics, this was not considered to be a problem by the army. As the war progressed and lessons were learned about the benefits of indirect fire, the guns would be designed to fire higher and further. In 1914, however, the 18-pounder was probably the best gun of its class in service with any of the belligerent armies. Well handled, this gun could fire 20 rounds a minute. By 1914 1,126 of these guns had been manufactured. However, only 600 or so guns were based in the UK and therefore immediately available for use.

The third new gun to enter service at about this time was the 1909 4.5-inch howitzer. Although not the most accurate gun in its class, it was a brilliantly designed rugged weapon and once the teething problems with the breech mechanism were resolved it would remain in service with the army until 1944. It fired a 4.5-inch (114mm) 35lb high explosive shell to a maximum distance of 7,300 yards. At the beginning of the war British high explosive shells used Lyddite as their filling – a substance named after the artillery training ranges at Lydd on the south coast. These shells were fitted with a direct action fuse that burst on impact. The principal design feature of the howitzer was its absolutely critical ability to fire at angles of up to 45 degrees, dropping shells almost vertically onto targets that were otherwise protected from direct fire either by fortifications or by the lie of the land. By 1914 192 of these guns were in use with the artillery, and 108 of them equipped the British Expeditionary Force.

The British field artillery – particularly the 18-pounder and the 4.5-inch howitzer – would prove to be highly effective weapons of modern war. Over the course of the war modifications were made to improve the range of these guns. They were certainly not perfect, but their defects were of secondary importance. There were problems with the recuperators, which proved to be overly sensitive and liable to break down, and the original springs were all replaced by air recuperators. There was also a lack of traverse, which became particularly apparent with the advent of the tank, as the gun needed to follow a moving target. But the basic design of these field guns was proven to be sound and they passed every test set for them on the Western Front.

The Royal Regiment of Artillery was, however, still in transition from the old era of gunnery to the new. In short, there were simply not enough of these new quick-firing guns to equip the whole of the regular army. A doctrine of 'make do' prevailed. Some of the regular batteries and all of the Territorial Army batteries were equipped with older, less effective weapons. The most prominent of these older guns was the 15-pounder gun purchased from Erhardt, and an even older 15-pounder breech-loading gun. The Erhardt gun was a good weapon. It had a comparable range to the new 18-pounder but maintenance and repair were highly problematic. Parts were not interchangeable and the original wheels had proved not strong enough for use in difficult field conditions and had been replaced by British standard artillery wheels. The 15-pounder breech-loading gun, which was the main equipment for the Territorials, was an altogether different beast – a halfway house between the old pre-quick-firing guns and the new modern weapons. It was a conversion from an 1883 design and suffered from a lack of range and other problems. It would prove to be wholly unsuited to the needs of the campaign. Early in 1915 one senior general, Sir Ivor Maxse, commented that the gun was 'absolutely worthless and cannot be put in the line at all'. They were quickly withdrawn from service and used largely as training guns. In fact, there had been a long-running argument within the army about the wisdom of equipping the Territorials with any artillery at all. Eventually, once the decision to do so had been made, an uneasy peace reigned, despite a certain lack of grace on the part of the Regiment. Territorial gunners were allowed to wear the Royal Artillery cap badge but with a blank scroll under the gun, where the regular gunners proudly bore their battle honour 'Ubique' ('Everywhere').

The Territorials faced other problems with their equipment. It was not just the 15-pounders that were out of date – so too were its howitzers and medium calibre guns. The Territorial artillery had been issued with the 4.7-inch quick-firing field gun. This weapon had been originally introduced in 1888 for naval and coastal defence purposes and would probably have remained in this role were it not for the urgent need for heavier guns during the Boer War. To meet this need some of the naval 4.7-inch guns were taken from warships and mounted on basic field carriages. They proved highly effective in the conditions that prevailed in South Africa. In France, however, they would prove to be highly unpopular with the gunners. They were difficult to operate and manoeuvre – they had no on-carriage traverse, for example, and were barely stable when fired. They too would eventually be withdrawn from service on the Western Front as soon as alternatives became available.

These guns were all designed to provide support to the soldiers in the field. In 1914 an infantry division was organised into four brigades of artillery, each with eighteen guns divided into three six-gun batteries. Each artillery brigade was commanded by a lieutenant colonel with an adjutant, an orderly officer and a small staff. Three of these brigades were equipped with the 18-pounder quick-firing field guns, while the fourth had the 4.5-inch howitzer. Each brigade of artillery had a signal section attached to it, which was capable of establishing line communications (wireless communications were not yet developed) to only two batteries at one time. The theory was that the brigade commander would always be close to the other battery. In total, the BEF would leave for France with fewer than 350 light, medium and heavy guns.

There was one immediate gap in capability: at the very beginning of the war the artillery deployed to France without any dedicated anti-aircraft weapons. The army possessed a mere thirty anti-aircraft guns in total, of which most were 1lb pom-poms, a light and largely ineffective weapon. They were deployed on the home front to protect the likely targets of German Zeppelins and would only be shipped out to France later. Dealing with the new threat from the air would eventually require a completely new approach and new equipment.

Heavy artillery was traditionally considered as useful only in conditions of siege warfare where the enemy had conveniently withdrawn behind the walls of a fortress that could be pounded with big naval guns loaded on trains. The Boer War had clearly shown the need for a more mobile form of heavy support artillery and in 1914 the first of these new weapons was introduced into the army. This was the 60-pounder, designed by the Elswick Ordnance Company in Newcastle upon Tyne. It had a 5-inch calibre (127mm) and a range of over 10,000 yards. The top carriage, cradle and gun could all be disconnected and the whole assembly pulled back across the trail for transportation, distributing the weight more evenly between the two gun wheels and the wheels of a separate limber that supported the trail end. In this way the gun could still be pulled by horses. Later versions of this gun would be designed with heavy traction wheels enabling it to be hauled by heavy tractors. A heavy battery of four 60-pounders completed the divisional complement of guns. The Territorial heavy artillery was made up of obsolescent 5-inch howitzers that had first seen action in the Nile Campaign of 1897–98. These had a limited range and would also soon be withdrawn from service and replaced by more modern weapons.

The Cavalry Division was less well provided for in terms of artillery. It had only two brigades of horse artillery with twelve 15-pounder guns each. The theory was that a reduced level of artillery firepower compared to the infantry was sufficient given the highly mobile nature of the cavalry force.

The artillery of each division was commanded by a Commander, Royal Artillery (CRA). He held the rank of brigadier general and was supported in his role by a Brigade Major, Royal Artillery (BMRA). Both of these roles had only just come into existence and in consequence there was little experience or precedent for handling artillery at divisional level. This was not made easier by the fact that the CRA had no dedicated communications link to his brigades. Instead he had to make do with whatever left-over resources the divisional signals company might be able to lend him, or rely on other forms of less effective communication – runners or horses. Neither was particularly conducive to the exercise of effective command and control.

In 1914 there was no structure at corps level to exercise strategic direction over the use of divisional artillery. There was a post attached to Corps HQ – Brigadier General, Royal Artillery (BGRA) – but the holder occupied only an advisory role and could not issue orders down to division or brigade level. This rather confusing and clumsy structure would be the cause of endless argument in the years ahead. It impeded the effective concentration of gunfire on the battlefield and undermined both offensive as well as defensive operations.

By 1914, therefore, the artillery had undergone a significant transformation. The regular army had much more effective and up to date weapons. But its tactics for deploying these impressive new weapons were still evolving and would change rapidly as the fighting in France and Belgium developed. There was as yet no proper concept of a preliminary bombardment or a rolling barrage – artillery techniques that would eventually become closely associated with the Western Front. Smoke shells to help camouflage attacking infantry and blind the enemy had also not been issued. The artillery possessed no mortars of any kind at the outbreak of hostilities. Some of these deficiencies might well be put down to a sceptical view of the value of artillery held by some very senior army commanders. Giving evidence to the Royal Commission set up to investigate the conduct of operations during the Boer War, General Sir Douglas Haig commented: 'Artillery seems only likely to be effective against raw troops.'

It would probably have required an astonishing prescience to have predicted just how powerful and effective artillery would become during the war, but even so this remark must surely rank as one of the greatest miscalculations in Haig's military thinking. He was, in effect, describing the old system of artillery, not the new emerging weapons of awesome destructive power.

In 1914 guns would be deployed in open or semi-open conditions; on the one hand this made it easier to bring down accurate fire, but on the other it meant that the British guns could be easily spotted by the enemy. New equipment (specifically the number 7 dial sight and number 3 director or survey instrument) had been introduced to allow the guns to fire indirectly onto their targets from covered positions out of sight of the enemy. The prevailing orthodoxy, however, despite the use of indirect fire tactics during the Russo–Japanese War, in particular at the battle of Sha-ho in September 1904, continued to stress the importance of a battery commander being able to exercise voice control over his guns from the observation post. This meant that, as the battery commander had himself to be able to see the enemy, the guns were normally deployed in either open or semi-open positions. The 13- and 18-pounders were thus fitted with a shield to protect the gun team from enemy rifle and gunfire. These shields were 'tested with a service rifle bullet at a range of 400 yards and should not be pierced, cracked or distorted'. Guns were also to be employed to provide close support to the infantry when they were attacking, and were to be fought to the last possible moment. The guns were also designed to be pulled by a team of no more than six horses and so in order to facilitate the maximum degree of movement could not weigh more than about 1,500 kilograms. This led to minimal design features and limited ranges of fire. Given the limitations on fire control at this stage, this was not perhaps such an obvious weakness.

The traditional approach to gunnery was well set out at the 1911 General Staff Conference by General Sir Lancelot Kiggell, who advocated a strategy of 'lines of infantry pressing forward, bayonets fixed to close with the enemy. Lines of guns would support them at close range.' This description conjures up a heroic imagery of the perceived nature of future warfare; the reality would turn out to be much grimmer. In the early days of the war these tactics would result in the loss of many guns to the enemy, particularly at the battle of Le Cateau. It would also generate extraordinary acts of bravery by the gunners themselves. Members of the Royal Artillery would win six VCs within the first fortnight of the war.

The army's core source of doctrine in these matters was the 1909 Field Service Regulations, which stressed the need to obtain fire superiority for any successful attack. The regulations stressed that 'the greater the difficulties of the infantry, the more should the fire power of the artillery be developed'. In the extreme conditions of the Western Front, theory and practice would take some time to come into full alignment.

On 4 August the challenge facing the British Army was a considerable one. To fully equip itself for war, the army (and the artillery in particular) would need an enormous number of horses, equipment and men. Six divisions of infantry and the cavalry would need to be brought up to war strength within days and sent to France en masse. Nothing on this scale had ever been attempted before in British military history. A horse census had recently been completed and as soon as mobilisation was ordered, animals were requisitioned to meet the army's requirements. Over 120,000 horses were needed, 14,000 of which would be required to complete the first stage of mobilisation. Under a scheme initiated by General Sir John Cowans in 1912, horse owners were able to register their animals with the Army Horse Reserve. In return for agreeing to allow their horses to be pressed into service, they would be paid an annual subsidy of £4 for each artillery horse and 10 shillings for any others.

Despite these financial inducements, parting company with their horses would be painful for many owners. Mary Coules, a young woman living in Sussex, recorded in her diary a few days after war had been declared a touching scene as one owner said goodbye to his horses:

> About the 9th August we went down to the Steyning Playing Fields to see the horses that had been commandeered. Poor beasties! Three magnificent hunters came in from Findon; it must have hurt someone to part with them. A rough looking man came in with two cart horses and stayed for about half an hour patting them and giving them sugar. It was very sad …

Once war was declared, the mobilisation of the artillery, along with the rest of the regular army, proceeded fairly smoothly. Those units deploying with the original British Expeditionary Force had absolute priority over everything else and were brought up to war strength quickly and efficiently, often at the expense of those units that were not being immediately deployed.

The Reservists were recalled to the colours by special telegram. One of these was artillery reservist Walter Harrison:

August 4th. Sitting in my kitchen with my wife and baby on the night of August 4th, we heard the postman knock. What I had been expecting – the green envelope and mobilization papers calling me to the colours, to report to No.4 Depot, Woolwich on August 5th for active service.

What a sight when I reached there. Thousands of troops all in civilian clothes. There was nowhere to put them. Some of them had come a long distance from Woolwich and could not return home that night. They had to sleep anywhere they could get – in the riding schools, on the common, on the square [the parade ground at Woolwich] …

August 6th. Going back to Woolwich. Saw the doctor from the other side of the square, passed fit for active service. Drew my kit from the mobilisation stores. I am sent to West Rear Range, Woolwich to join the 27th Battery, 32nd Brigade, Royal Field Artillery. Found a room to sleep in, food in abundance, and good at that. Nothing to do that day, went to bed. Sixty men in the room, not very comfortable …

Albert Reeve, a gunner in 16th Battery, 41st Brigade, RFA, supporting the 2nd Division, confirmed this rapid escalation to war readiness: '[We] got orders to mobilize which had been expected for some days. Immediately got busy and for the following four days didn't know whether we were on our heads or our heels. Had marching order in full war strength on Monday 10th August. Got promoted to Sergeant.'

The heightened tension since the end of July had helped many of the brigades to anticipate the order to mobilize, so when it came they were in a position to act quickly. This was the case with 71st Battery, 36th Brigade, RFA, at Ewshott in Hampshire. According to the author of its war diary:

6pm, Tuesday 4th August. Orders to mobilize received. As it had been apparent for some days that mobilisation was imminent a considerable amount of work had already been done. All men were medically inspected on 3rd August and a commencement had been made of marking and sorting horses.

But it was not all plain sailing for the 71st Battery: 'August 10th. Horses issued from the Remount Department. These horses were very inferior and in very poor condition. Instructions were given for 20 to be returned. A draft of men to complete our war establishment arrived from 1st Brigade, RFA, at Edinburgh.'

Other brigades were in a similar position. Lieutenant Edmund ('Mac') Robertson was a subaltern in the 70th Battery, 34th Brigade, RFA, stationed at Aldershot with the 2nd Division. In late July part of the division and two of its artillery brigades were rehearsing mobilisation procedures. Mac kept a diary of those fateful days:

29th July. We paraded at full war strength in The Square. It looked most impressive.

30th July. Paraded at full war strength and then marched for eight hours to Frensham where we bivouacked. I have now about seventy men and fifty horses in my section. Everything has worked very smoothly.

1st August. We began our mobilising in a quiet way to be ready when orders came. Checked clothing, harness and gun pack.

August 2nd. Stayed in barracks all day. Germany has declared war on Russia and is in a state of war with France. What will we do? Much anxiety in the Mess that the Government will be traitors and refuse to go to war. I only hope it isn't true.

August 3rd. Did several mobilizing things, had medical inspections in the afternoon.

August 4th. Orders to mobilise came at 6.30pm.

August 5th. First day of mobilisation. Most of the men went on fatigues. The mobilisation harness issued and put together in the afternoon. Lots of officers have arrived for the Ammunition Column. Everything worked smoothly.

August 6th. Met reservists at 6.30am and saw to their breakfasts. They were all posted to their batteries by 9am. Saw clothing of reservists in the afternoon. Fifty horses arrived from Edinburgh. The reservists seem alright – old soldiers mostly. This all seems like a dream.

August 7th. Up most of the night getting horse parties off to the Remount Department. This mobilisation is very fatiguing work.

August 8th. More horses arrived from the Depot. We are nearly complete. Spent all day posting NCOs and men and taming horses.

By 10 August 71st Battery was ready for battle.

At the outbreak of hostilities, Lieutenant Colonel Arthur Wilkinson was in command of the 35th (Heavy) Battery at Aldershot. He would later write in his diary:

> Our scheme for mobilization was very complete and we had everything arranged and rehearsed beforehand. Notwithstanding this, it required about ten days to transform a Battery on a peace footing to a Battery equipped, complete and ready for active service. A Battery on a peace footing was only about half the strength of a Battery mobilized for war.

Some of the brigades needed a great deal of strengthening before they were ready to deploy. The 37th Brigade RFA, attached to the 4th Division, received over 100 horses and 400 men between 6 and 8 August. However, by teatime on 8 August, three days after mobilisation, the brigade was up to its war strength. The 24th Brigade needed nearly 300 men and 8 officers to bring it up to its war establishment. The 40th Brigade reached war readiness by 11 August. Its commanding officer nonetheless managed to register a complaint about the work of the Horse Collection Parties – special groups formed to requisition horses on the spot in a manner almost reminiscent of the ancient press gangs – who arrived at his barracks with no headcollars. The 42nd Brigade was ready for war by the evening of 13 August.

On 4 August 2nd Sergeant William Edgington was stationed at Newbridge with D Battery, 3rd Brigade, RHA: 'Got orders to mobilize at 5.30pm [on the 4th]. 8th August – mobilisation complete. All ranks anxious to fight.'

Gunner Saville William Crowsley of E Battery, 3rd Brigade, RHA, which was also stationed in Ireland at the outbreak of the war, reported a similar experience: 'First day of mobilisation [5 August]. Hard work for all. Very busy.' The following day '70 horses joined from K Battery at Christchurch. Balance to complete Battery up to war strength (228 men) came from Belfast and the Curragh. Majority poor.' On 7 August the reservists joined the battery: 'Men sleeping on the floor. Hard task to get Reservists back to discipline.' By the end of the next day the situation had improved considerably: 'Mobilisation completed. Battery ready to move, all ranks anxious to move to the front. Mobilisation completed in three days – seven were allowed. Very good work all round.'

By 8 August the full complement of E Battery was 5 officers, 2 staff sergeants, 7 sergeants, 7 corporals, 11 bombardiers, 75 gunners, 75 drivers, 10 batmen, 2 trumpeters, 2 wheelers, a farrier sergeant and 6 shoeing smiths. In addition to its six guns, the battery had 12 wagons, a General Service Wagon, a water cart, 14 riding horses and 214 light draught horses.

Gunner Charles Burrows of the 34th Brigade RFA arrived at Aldershot on 6 August: 'Arrived at Aldershot and started mobilizing the column. Breaking horses into harness and vehicles. Very cushy time with bags of hope.' Things were also going so smoothly for Lieutenant Ralph Blewitt of the 39th Brigade RFA, attached to the 1st Division in Hampshire, that his focus was more on his domestic affairs than the need to prepare for war; on 5 August he wrote to his fiancée Denys Henderson in Henley-on-Thames: 'Well, we're at it in earnest I'm glad to say. Why don't you and Mrs H roll over some afternoon. Bring a tea basket and I'll give you tea. Well, cheer up. May the best side win. Don't leave the soap in the bath. God save the King.'

In the artillery, the ammunition columns that had the job of providing logistical support for the guns were particularly short of personnel. As a consequence, the Royal Garrison Artillery Militia had, in the run up to war, been turned into a reserve that could be used in the formation of these vital units, upon whose efficiency the combat effectiveness of the artillery was absolutely dependent. Even with these arrangements in place, the ammunition columns would struggle the most to get up to war readiness.

The 36th Brigade Ammunition Column was in the process of being assembled at Ewshott. The war diary of the unit described its first few hectic days as it got ready to go to war:

5th August. First day of mobilisation. Captain Haining and Lieutenant Vining arrived from 36th Brigade RFA to join the Ammunition Column.

8th August. Lieutenant Geldart arrived from Preston to complete officers of the column.

12th August. Men all arrived and most of the horses. Battery Sergeant Major Bradford from Edinburgh with trumpeter and a few NCOs. Remainder were regular and special reservists.

Lieutenant Cyril Brownlow had been posted to the 40th Brigade Ammunition Column at Bulford. It was hard work pulling everything together:

When I arrived the column consisted of the vehicles lined in rows in a sloping field, a few disconsolate men and a taciturn quarter-master sergeant who sat gloomily in the mobilization shed. During the next few days the captain, the second subaltern and the remainder of the men and horses arrived, the latter in batches and at odd intervals, often in the middle of the night. Then the work at high pressure began.

At the end of the week the whole column went out for the first time in marching order. Across the way a battery was quietly filing out to manoeuvre, but we started amid shouts and reviling and the crack of whips. One team in six jibbed, and three teams bolted across the plain and disappeared from view. The bakers' horses pulled themselves to pieces, the grass-fed horses sweated, sat back in the breeching and refused to move and the aristocrats from private stables kicked with indignation. The captain galloped back and forth blowing his whistle and threatening all and sundry, the sergeant major uttered curses in a harsh voice, the sergeants shouted in unison and the drivers worked hard with whip and spur.

Captain Mackie had been given the job of pulling together the 30th Brigade Ammunition Column at Bulford:

5th August. Reservists coming in all day. The barrack square is full of them – a wonderful sight. How well they have answered the call. Everyone in good spirits and full of optimism. Germany has bitten off more than she can chew.

Such a congestion in the Mess last night that we had to have two relays for dinner.

August 7th. Everything going like clockwork owing to very fine NCOs. The horses have all arrived and we will soon have our full complement of men. We have eighteen ammunition wagons, two General Service wagons for stores and baggage and one water cart. In the morning and afternoon we have twelve wagons out with teams. All the new harnesses have been received and teams and drivers worked well.

Have been hard at it but we are far advanced and by Sunday [9th] everything will be ready.

I cannot speak too highly of our men – old soldiers back to the colours, splendid fellows, hard working and no grousing.

August 8th. Started with a kit inspection at 7am. Owing to the Army being increased the clothing department has run short so all the men have to return their spare jacket and boots which means that they go off with little more than they stand up in. We are filled up to strength with horses and men. In fact we are a little over.

Not everyone was experiencing this same, smooth progress. There was plenty of grousing going on, and it was not confined to the other ranks. The commanding officer of the 61st Battery, 8th (Howitzer) Brigade, stationed in Kildare, had plenty to complain about. On 6 August he got in some first-class grumbling: 'The battery has suffered severely by promotions, losing two sergeants and the majority of the battery staff. It is important that in future the various grades of NCOs for the ammunition column should be maintained in peacetime.' Two days later he was complaining again, this time about the need to inoculate the men against the risk of enteric fever – an eminently sensible precaution. A day after being inoculated, the entire battery was sick and confined to their beds: 'This inoculation is a great nuisance to a battery as we cannot get the reservists or men out to work.'

Those units that were not attached to the BEF but were also being mobilised that month found things much harder. Harry Davson was an officer with G Battery, 5th Brigade, RHA, stationed in Ipswich, a unit that would eventually arrive in France with the 8th Division in November 1914. Dawson described his predicament:

The horses were unfit and untrained for draught work but the batteries had to be prepared to take the field.... all our experienced drivers had gone and many of the reservists who had taken their places had not sat on a horse for years. All the new trained signallers and gun-layers had been taken from us.

On the 20th another complication arose when 190 recruits arrived to be trained. Our batteries were in a state that would not have been tolerated a fortnight previously and most of the NCOs were so rusty in their drill as to be quite incapable of training a newly joined civilian.

Next day 242 horrible horses arrived from Market Harborough. The distribution of these and the placing of recruits took up the whole day. It now became evident that it was an impossibility to train both the batteries and recruits at the same time. It was decided to remove the recruits altogether, supply them with officers and NCOs and form six batteries of them. This arrangement took away my remaining officers and I was left to train the battery alone. I shall always look back on the month I trained G Battery alone as the most wearing of my career.

Sergeant Francis Miller, who on the outbreak of war was attached to 69th Brigade RFA, was in one of those units that were not going out to France with the original BEF; he himself would be needed in order to help bring another battery up to war strength:

August 9th. Received orders to move to Edinburgh. Entrained and moved off on the morning of the 10th. Gay and hearty were we; made preparations handing equipment stores and harnesses over. Left Edinburgh for Borden [in Hampshire] to join the 17th Battery, 41st Brigade. Took over a sub-section – strange men, some reservists who had been away from the colours for years. Didn't relish the undertaking but had to do it. Had to put up with a lot of messing about in general.

Lieutenant Edward Schrieber was a young subaltern in 115th Battery, 25th Brigade, RFA. On 4 August 1914 he was stationed at Deepcut Barracks in Surrey:

The next 12 days were busy ones for us. It all seemed so strange. Subalterns had never really studied mobilisation orders but everything appeared to happen without a hitch. Men and horses kept on arriving. It was good to see so many former men of ours, who had gone on the Reserve, returning to us. In some cases, men turned up direct at the Battery. It was a great experience for us subalterns to command a section of some 70 men and 70 horses compared to the meagre peace establishment to which we had been accustomed.

Inoculation for enteric was perhaps our greatest trial as the time was short and we were given the full dose at one sitting which bowled men over right and left. I myself collapsed on the afternoon on which I was done, while teaming my horses. This kept me 24 hours in bed. Luckily by then, most of the work of mobilisation had been completed …

On 4 August Private W Collins was a young soldier in the RAMC at Aldershot. When the order to mobilise came, he was sent off to join the medical team attached to the 7th Brigade, RHA, also at Aldershot. Many years later, when he came to write about his own experiences, one incident during this time stood out in his mind:

Preparations for active service went on apace in the 7th Brigade, RHA, and on the morning of the 15th, while the final packing and limbering up was being done, the Royal Artillery Band regaled us on the square with some lively music. At this distance of time I remember only one of the tunes; it was 'Destiny', the hit waltz of the day, by Sydney Baynes. Listening to it I wondered how prophetic it might be for some of us in the Brigade. That afternoon, the Brigade proceeded to Aldershot railway station siding, and guns, vehicles and personnel were entrained expeditiously and without incident …

Boy soldiers – those under the age of 18 – were not supposed to be sent overseas on active service. Not all of them appreciated this kindness. Jimmy Naylor, a boy trumpeter stationed at the Royal Artillery depot at Woolwich, was determined to go with his battery to France. He was only just 16 years old but had been with the guns for two years. Jimmy took a delegation of eager young trumpeters to petition the commanding officer for permission to go to war with his battery. The CO relented, as long as the boys' parents had given their agreement. Jimmy's parents were in India and it would take too long to get their confirmation. He forged his father's signature and went to France with his mates.

Artillery resources had been carefully and wisely husbanded in the years leading up to 1914. The general reserve of artillery had been carefully built up and by 1912 had nearly doubled in size from forty-two to eighty-one six-gun batteries. This careful husbandry of guns was not, however, matched by a similar stockpiling of ammunition – a mistake that would have far-reaching consequences for the effective conduct of military operations during the early stages of the war.

As the mobilisation of the army proceeded according to the plans laid out in the War Book, ministers began to wrestle with two other important decisions: first, how to deploy the BEF and what its role in France should be, and second, how best to raise additional forces to help prosecute the war effort. On the afternoon of 5 August the new War Cabinet met for the first time. Prime Minister Herbert Asquith was supported by his principal Cabinet colleagues, Edward Grey (Foreign Secretary), Haldane and Churchill. The BEF was represented by its newly appointed Commander in Chief Sir John French, his deputy Henry Wilson and Chief of Staff Archibald Murray, and its two corps commanders, Douglas Haig and John Grierson. Lord Kitchener, the newly appointed Secretary of State for War, took his place in the Cabinet for the first time.

A strange discussion took place. Only one man at the table had a full appreciation of the secret talks that had taken place between the French and British armies over what strategy to adopt in the event of war with Germany, and that was Henry Wilson. The French planned an audacious frontal attack *a outrance* on the German centre in Alsace/Lorraine. Based on these assumptions, the small British forces would take up a supporting position on the French left, working in cooperation with the French Fifth Army under General Lanrezac. Far from relegating the BEF to a minor role, events would place Sir John French's command at the heart of the fighting. The German offensive movement through Belgium would see three German armies descend on the allies' left flank. Kitchener in particular had grave misgivings about the soundness of the French war plans. There was every possibility of them walking into a trap, especially if the thrust of the German movement through Belgium developed into a major enveloping action. The safest option in his view was for the BEF to concentrate no further forward than Amiens, to wait and see what developed, and come to a new understanding if necessary with the French.

In total disregard of the understandings reached between Wilson and the French army, Sir John French, having broadly set out the basis upon which Anglo-French war plans had been developed by Wilson, blithely proposed that the BEF should instead land at Antwerp, to strengthen Belgian resistance and to threaten the right flank of the German advance. Churchill pointed out the difficulties the Royal Navy would face in defending such an amphibious operation in the open sea. It would also involve violating Dutch territorial waters. Haig also reacted strongly against such a plan, believing it posed the risk of comprehensive defeat by separating the British from their much larger ally. The wobble was short-lived. French's extraordinary proposal was, fortunately, strangled at birth.

The only plan capable of being implemented at this stage was the one that Wilson had brokered with the French, even if, as Kitchener expected, it ran the very real risk of exposing the BEF to a potential heavy attack on the Belgian border. Under these plans the BEF would concentrate around Maubeuge and Le Cateau before moving up with the French Fifth Army to meet the attackers. This strategy was finally agreed on 12 August.

The first meeting of the War Cabinet did at least agree on how many British troops should go to France. Instead of the six infantry divisions that Wilson had envisaged, and the French expected, the Cabinet decided to send four, holding back the 4th and the 6th in case of a German invasion of England. In addition, a cavalry division and a cavalry brigade would also be deployed.

The remaining issue was what to do about raising additional volunteers to serve with the colours for the duration of hostilities. Kitchener and Haig both predicted a long conflict that would require significant additional troops, over and above the reserves available. It was decided to raise a new army modelled on the regular forces rather than the Territorials. The following day Kitchener appealed for an additional 100,000 men. This first wave of recruitment would form part of an expansion to the army of 500,000 soldiers. This would form the basis of a new expeditionary force of six fresh divisions. On the first day of the appeal, 7 August, the crowds outside the Central London Recruiting Office in Great Scotland Yard were so large that mounted police were called in to control them, just as they would at football grounds. Recruitment rose steadily. By 15 August over 50,000 had enlisted. The highest daily record for recruitment was set on 19 August, when 9,699 enlisted. Some 63,000 joined in the week beginning 25 August. This record would be shattered on 3 September when a staggering 33,204 men joined the army. By the middle of September the number had reached nearly 500,000. Given the success of this initial recruitment drive, a second new army of six more divisions was announced on 2 September, followed by a third and a fourth by the beginning of October. By December over 800,000 men had joined up. In only three months Kitchener had laid the foundations for no fewer than thirty new divisions of infantry and their supporting arms. There was no precedent in British history for such an extraordinary explosion in patriotic endeavour. It was no exaggeration for A.J.P. Taylor to describe these few weeks in the autumn of 1914 as 'the greatest surge in willing patriotism ever recorded'. In one of Churchill's memorable phrases, this was indeed the 'rallying of the ardent ones'. And these new divisions would need artillery –

more than 120 new brigades and thousands of new guns. This would stretch to the absolute limit the ability of both the War Office and British industry to deliver.

Given the numbers of volunteers and the short timescale involved in their recruitment, it was only to be expected that difficulties would be experienced in training and equipping the new recruits. One of these new recruits was R. Elwis, who enlisted with the Royal Garrison Artillery (RGA):

> There was such a rush for fellows to go in the Army that they'd had to get quite a number of officers in to deal with all these recruits. Even so it was about two hours before my turn came. I was only eighteen and I didn't weigh very much – I didn't look very much like a soldier – I weighed 8 stone 11lb but I was passed. I was given a parcel of food and a railway warrant and we were taken down to Midland station and put on the train and instructed to report to the officer at Newhaven.
>
> Anyway we got down to Newhaven, it was between nine and ten and a party of soldiers came to meet us and we were taken up what seemed to me to be miles, up a long valley from the railway station. It was pitch dark and we didn't know where we were going. We got to a place where there seemed to be a lot of tents and we were taken into a great big one, a marquee with a long table down the middle and some forms … presently two fellows came with a big basketful of loaves which had been cut in two. Another two men came down with a big dixie full of herrings and they plonked one of these herrings on half a loaf of bread and slapped the other half on the top of it and that was my supper.
>
> As far as I could see in the night there must have been hundreds of tents and the sergeant counted us out. There were twelve men put into each tent and he shoved us in. He said 'there's some blankets there'. There was nothing on the floor, just the bare soil and so we got down as best we could.
>
> About six o'clock the next morning there was such a noise outside and then a fellow blew a trumpet and I had a feeling that must have been the reveille. We got up. None of us had bothered about undressing. Some sergeants came up then – 'Come on, fall in.' We didn't know what it was we'd got to fall into. It might have been the sea for all we knew.

Gunner Elwis's experiences would have been shared by the thousands of other new recruits to the Royal Regiment of Artillery that August. The sheer scale of the new volunteers coming in meant that all stocks of uniforms were quickly used up. The new soldiers would have to remain in their 'civvies' for months before they would begin to look like soldiers. Being in uniform was, however, an important aspect of becoming part of the army and some creative solutions were found to address the shortage of khaki. Some of the new units were issued with old and obsolete clothing, including scarlet jackets of Boer War vintage, old buff leather equipment originally issued in 1871, canvas fatigue overalls and a number of full dress tunics normally used only for ceremonial occasions. The uniform most widely issued to the New Armies was a blue Post Office uniform worn with blue field service caps. It was not very militaristic but it was better than nothing.

Housing the hundreds of thousands of new recruits was another enormous undertaking for which no thought or planning had been given. The accommodation in barracks was limited. By clearing out the families of soldiers from the married quarters, and using every square foot of space, it was possible for just over 250,000 soldiers to be squeezed into existing military premises. Room had to be found, however, for another 800,000 men. Herbert Smith of Chartham Hatch near Canterbury was only 17 when he joined the RGA on 28 August. He too was posted to Newhaven in Sussex, where his experiences would have been not entirely untypical:

This was the start of two months' uncomfortable proceedings at this place. What with leaving home and our place of accommodation things were not so pleasant as the picture painted by the Recruiting Sergeant. We were marched from the station to the schools which had been accommodated for the arrival of recruits who were so rapidly pouring in from all parts of the country. We were eventually taken to our sleeping quarters which happened to be on a farm on the outskirts of the town. We were in a barn which had a floor covered in straw so as to make sleep a bit more comfortable. But as the nights went past I can tell you that our sleep was often disturbed by those little animal rats!

But the biggest problem affecting these new recruits to the artillery was the lack of equipment on which to train. Would-be gunners needed to get their hands on some real guns if they were to become proficient at their new profession. Unfortunately, once the immediate needs of the BEF and the Territorial divisions had been satisfied, there were precious few guns to spare. Large orders for new 18-pounders were placed almost immediately war was declared – 2,338 were contracted to be delivered by June 1915. A lack of industrial capacity meant that only a fraction of these new guns would be delivered on time. By October 1914 the first of the new Kitchener divisions each had a few 18-pounders to train on, as compared to a total requirement in each division of fifty-four. The second wave Kitchener divisions only began to receive their first guns in February 1915, initially on the ratio of one gun per battery. The artillery units of the newly formed 15th Division were training at Aldershot in September 1914 with an improvised gun made up from a log of wood mounted on the camp funeral gun-carriage. Things improved a little when an ancient 9-pounder brass muzzle-loading gun was borrowed from the Officers' Mess. Some early French breech-loading guns – some twenty years old – were also made available. When the 18-pounders eventually arrived, they were delivered without their dial sights – a vital piece of equipment. Dial sights did not become available in sufficient quantities until the summer of 1915, only a few weeks before the first of the new units would be sent on active service. The tribulations of the 15th Division gunners would have been replicated in each of the new artillery brigades during the first few months of the war. Many of their skills as gunners would be developed on the battlefield rather than on the training grounds of Salisbury Plain.

The experiences of the trainee gunners of the 33rd Division, raised in early January 1915, were very similar to their comrades in the 15th Division. Based at Dulwich in south-west London, the eager new recruits had to make do with dummy loaders and three of the ancient Boer War 15-pounders for the first six months of their training. It was only in July 1915 that four 18-pounders arrived for the whole divisional artillery to train on. The brigade would only have a few weeks to train with these guns before it would leave for France as a fighting unit.

Second Lieutenant John Leigh was one of the officers who formed the nucleus of a new heavy battery of the RGA in early September 1914. Even those batteries that had limited access to proper weapons were not finding things very easy:

Six officers and two hundred men proceeded to Fort Fareham and Fort Nelson to train. The only guns available were the 4.7s of the Wessex Territorials and these were placed at the disposal of each of these units for two days a week. However, after a week the guns were ordered to Woolwich and training became a farce.

A young Treasury civil servant, Harry Siepman, was given a commission in another of the new artillery brigades formed at the beginning of the war, and was sent to Preston Barracks near Brighton to begin his training:

> The class consisted entirely of officers but we were, of course, put through the drill of all ranks in the battery. As gunners we manned the guns and as drivers we rode out in the early morning with the teams onto the Downs, wearing our leg irons and learning the duties of each position in the team. We were called upon in turn to take command of a battery or section and carry out the manoeuvres, by whistle and gesture, which the drill book prescribed but which we were never again to practise. We were under the orders of a corporal who knew all about gunnery but was more coarse-grained than anybody I had ever come across. He seemed to take an obscene delight in teaching these young toffs what life was like without any of its amenities and decencies.
>
> After a couple of months I was sent on a course to Shoeburyness, where the treatment was different. We were there taught the mathematics and the mechanism of gunnery. The mathematics gave me no trouble and I delighted in the intricacies of map reading.

After he had completed the basics of training, Harry was posted to the 169th Brigade RFA, which had been raised in St Anne's in Lancashire. There the gunners had trained on the sands with tapes marking the places of imaginary guns and horses. The training routines had to be made up as they went along.

Lieutenant John Pearce Wills was another of the new gunner officers to join the army that August. He was posted to the 61st (Howitzer) Brigade at Weedon in Hampshire, a unit made up largely of a tough crowd of miners from South Wales and Lancashire. The brigade formed part of the artillery of the 11th Division – one of the first of the Kitchener units:

> Throughout September/October 1914 there were upwards of 2,000 men crowded into the barracks, without any uniforms or other clothes than those they stood in. Fortunately the weather was dry throughout or they would have suffered badly. There were no guns or equipment or harness of any kind, nor were there more than about a dozen horses per battery and a few officers' chargers. Gun drill was done by drawing chalk lines on a concrete floor and the drivers were given as much riding drill as was possible with the few horses available. Three old 5-inch

howitzers arrived for the brigade and with them a few ammunition wagons towards the end of October.

The 61st Brigade would only get its hands on the 4.5-inch howitzers in February 1915, but they came without any gun-sights and so effective training on their war equipment would be further delayed.

George Milward was barely 17 when war was declared but was quickly given a commission as a second lieutenant in the artillery and joined his new battery at Rollestone Camp on Salisbury Plain. The men had only one 18-pounder gun to train on and a few horses of variable quality. Milward's horse turned out to have a surprising pedigree:

> I was given a nice looking pony, but not [told] his history. He was circus trained and would do quite unexpected things on hearing a whistle blow or certain bugle calls. On the latter he reared and danced, which, however entertaining to watch, was disconcerting. A day or so later we were joined by a rather pompous older subaltern and we arranged for him to ride the circus pony and for a bugler to perform when signalled. We enjoyed the disappearance of pomposity.

Gunnery training for Milward and his men was rudimentary in the early days:

> We only had the one 18-pounder and the instructor took it to pieces, then re-assembled it, naming each part as he did so. When the weather wasn't too foul we went through the drill pretence of firing the gun, taking it in turn to do each job of the sub-section.

Public schoolboy Julian Tyndale-Biscoe was at an OTC camp on Cannock Chase when war broke out and had high hopes of joining his cousin Victor's regiment, the King Edward's Horse. However, the regiment was already up to war strength and so he made use of another family connection – his uncle Albert was a major in the Royal Artillery at Woolwich. After a rudimentary interview, Julian was given a war commission and joined a new battery being formed at Deepcut Barracks. He was in for a shock:

> Where were the guns and horses? All I could see was a large crowd of men in their civilian clothes marching unendingly to the voice of various

sergeants, on a gravel square, much to the detriment of their boots. The Major said 'Here is the Battery – I want you to train these men.' When I told him I had no artillery training he said 'Oh that doesn't matter, you just watch the others do it, and do it yourself.'

After a period training at the artillery depot at Woolwich, Julian was posted to another New Army battery at Aldershot. His new battery commander appeared to be more interested in horses than gunnery, and took a rather old-fashioned view of gunnery skills and tactics. Julian was informed by him that: 'I don't believe in all these angles and things. What I say is gallop up to the top of the hill and poop off.'

The shortages of equipment were not confined to the New Army. The Territorial artillery units were finding it hard going as well. The 1st (North Riding) Heavy Battery was originally dispatched to Monkseaton for coastal defence duties but, with the threat of invasion disappearing, it soon found itself attached to an infantry division to provide its heavy artillery. The battery war diary revealed that:

No equipment (other than for current needs) was issued until the week before embarkation. Training was a good deal interfered with, principally in driving owing to shortages in harness and in telephone work. Moreover the Battery was requested to lend to the Durham Heavy Battery 2 guns, 2 wagons and 17 horses with their harness, and for a long period – early September to March 15th – the Battery only had available harness for 2 guns and 2 wagons and had only 2 guns for training purposes. With this material, training of the large population of recruits had to be carried out as well as possible.

Alfred Walker, who worked as a typist in the offices of the advertising agents Laughton & Co. in the Strand in London, joined the Royal Artillery in the spring of 1915. Even then, shortages of equipment were still being experienced:

For the first six months we did our service living at home and reporting each morning to Headquarters in St Leonards Street in civilian clothes as there was a shortage of army uniforms. Meantime we used to march to Victoria Park [in Hackney] for physical jerks or simulated gun drill manoeuvres on foot or alternatively if weather was bad we used to muster in the playground of Cowper Street School for drill. When a consignment of uniforms and kit arrived the next problem was instruction in horsemanship. We had no horses in our Brigade, but Liptons the tea merchants had a stable at the corner of Bethnal Green Road with a supply of horses and our Brigade had a contract with them for the loan of a number of their animals for riding instruction …

The manpower of the Empire and its Dominions was also being mobilised. In early August 1914 young Canadian reserve officer Ormsby Allhusen had just completed summer camp with 14 Company, Canadian Army Service Corps at Calgary:

News of the declaration of war reached Calgary about 5pm (Canadian Mountain Time) and the wildest enthusiasm ensued. Nobody seemed to know what to do but most people were anxious to raise regiments of roughriders, apparently thinking that this war would be like the South African war again.

Allhusen sailed to England on 13 August and was quickly posted to a brigade ammunition column being formed to support some London Territorial artillery batteries:

The first months' training was the hardest work I have ever done in my life. We were all out by 6am and after working hard all day, in a very hot August and September, generally went to bed about 10.30pm. Our equipment of wagons and harness was all impressed civilian stuff and was not at all suited to carting ammunition.

In addition to raising new armies to bolster the war effort, it was also decided to bring two divisions of the army back from India with their attached artillery units. One of these was the 20th Battery, 14th Brigade, RFA, which received its orders to mobilize on 9 August. It would take some time before the battery would get on the move. Austin Anderson was its commanding officer:

A long and weary period of delay followed and it was not until 4th September that the Battery got orders to entrain for Bombay which was reached on the 7th. The journey was a hot one and the only noteworthy incident was the very enthusiastic reception we got in passing through Baroda on the morning of the 6th September. Several Ministers, military officers and Grandees of the State were on the station platform to greet us. Tea was provided for officers and men, a band played selections and we finally steamed out of the station amidst warm cheers and the strains of the National Anthem.

As the British Army in India prepared to return to join the fight, and Kitchener's recruitment drive began to deliver the urgently needed men of the New Armies, most of the original BEF crossed the Channel to France. Between 12 and 19 August they left England and disembarked at Boulogne, Rouen and Le Havre. During this period more than 1,800 special trains were run to transport the men and their equipment to Southampton, which was the principal port of embarkation. J.F.C. Fuller was a young staff officer working to ensure the dispatch of the BEF went as smoothly as possible. It would be an extraordinary operation. Only a single set of lines connected the railway station at Southampton to the docks. At the height of the deployment a train arrived every four minutes:

> The result was remarkable for during August we had to deal with hundreds and hundreds of trains coming in from every part of the kingdom, and in one period of twelve hours, eighty, and yet there was never a delay, never a mishap and when the first six divisions had left this country the sole casualty was one horse killed – it kicked itself out of its slings whilst being embarked.

Lieutenant Cyril Brownlow dis-entrained his men and equipment at Southampton docks at noon on 18 August:

> Within half an hour the train was empty and had departed. The men and horses were collected in one part of a great shed while the vehicles, heavy with ammunition, had been run by dock hands to the quay side and were being whisked into the air and dropped into the bowels of the great ship. At fixed intervals of time other troop trains arrived and poured forth their living burdens until the whole quay was congested with a mass of men, horses and vehicles. All through the day and far into the night the work of loading continued amid the shouts of men, the stamp of horses and the hiss and rattle of winches and electric cranes.

The die was now cast and the scene set for the first encounter between the British and German forces. The Royal Regiment of Artillery was ready for war. Supporting the Cavalry Division and the 5th Independent Cavalry Brigade were the 3rd and 7th Brigades, Royal Horse Artillery (D, E, I and L Batteries) and J Battery respectively. Attached to the 1st Division were the 25th, 26th and 39th Brigades, Royal Field Artillery, the 43rd (Howitzer) Brigade and the 26th (Heavy) Battery, Royal Garrison Artillery. The 2nd Division was supported by the 34th, 36th, 41st and 44th (Howitzer) Brigades, Royal Field Artillery, and the 35th (Heavy) Battery, Royal Garrison Artillery. Serving with the 3rd Division were the 23rd, 40th and 42nd Brigades, the 30th (Howitzer) Brigade, Royal Field Artillery, and the 35th (Heavy) Brigade, Royal Garrison Artillery. The 5th Division had the 15th, 27th and 28th Brigades, Royal Field Artillery, the 8th (Howitzer) Brigade and the 48th (Heavy) Battery, Royal Garrison Artillery. These units and their men were the gunners of August 1914.

Sir John French had been sent to France with clear instructions from Lord Kitchener:

> The special motive of the force under your control is to support and co-operate with the French Army against our common enemies. The peculiar task laid upon you is to assist the French Government in preventing or repelling the invasion by Germany of French and Belgian territory and eventually to restore the neutrality of Belgium on behalf of which, as guaranteed by Treaty, Belgium has appealed to the French and ourselves. These are the reasons which have induced His Majesty's Government to declare war and these reasons constitute the primary objective you have before you.
>
> It must be recognised from the outset that the numerical strength of the British Force and its contingent reinforcement is strictly limited and with this consideration kept steadily in view it will be obvious that the greatest care must be exercised towards a minimum of losses and wastage. Therefore whilst every effort must be made to coincide most sympathetically with the plans and wishes of our Ally, the gravest consideration will devolve upon you as to participation on forward movements where large bodies of French troops are not engaged and where your force may be unduly exposed to attack. Should a contingency of this sort be contemplated I look to you to inform me fully and give me time to communicate to you any decision which His

Majesty's Government may come to in the matter. In this connection I wish you distinctly to understand that your command is an entirely independent one and that you will in no case come under the orders of any Allied General.

The high courage and discipline of your troops should and certainly will have fair and full opportunity of display during the campaign but officers may well be reminded that in this their first experience of European warfare, a greater measure of caution must be employed than under former conditions of hostilities against an untrained adversary.

You will kindly keep up constant communication with the War Office and you will be good enough to inform me as to all movements of the enemy reported to you as well as those of the French Army.

I am sure you fully realize that you can rely with the utmost confidence on the whole-hearted and unswerving support of the Government, myself and of your compatriots, in carrying out the high duty which the King has entrusted to you and in maintaining the great tradition of His Majesty's Army.

It was a message dripping with caution and concern. Kitchener was fearful not just of heavy casualties to the BEF but of the ability of British officers to conduct this new form of industrial warfare with a technologically matched opponent. He was also not convinced about the soundness or otherwise of French military planning and operations. It would be hard to paint a more complicated and hesitant backdrop against which to wage war. Sir John French was ordered to cooperate with the wishes of our principal ally, but with strict limits as to how far this should be taken. Kitchener himself wanted a say in how the campaign would be conducted. Coalition warfare would, very quickly, become a highly charged and complicated issue.

For the ordinary soldiers, their marching orders were rather more humdrum:

You are ordered abroad as a soldier of the King to help our French comrades against the invasion of a common enemy. You have to perform a task which will need your courage, your energy, your patience. Remember that the honour of the British Army depends on your individual conduct. It will be your duty not only to set an example of discipline and perfect steadiness under fire but also to maintain the most friendly relations with those whom you are helping in this struggle. The operations on which you are engaged will, for the most part, take place in a friendly country and you can do your own country no better service than in showing yourself in France and Belgium in the true character of a British soldier.

Be invariably courteous, considerate and kind. Never do anything likely to injure or destroy property and always look upon looting as a disgraceful act. You are sure to meet with a welcome and to be trusted; your conduct must justify that welcome and that trust. Your duty cannot be done unless your health is sound. So keep constantly on your guard against any excesses. In this new experience you may find temptations both in wine and women. You must entirely resist both temptations and while treating all women with perfect courtesy, you should avoid any intimacy.

The Kaiser's mandate to his troops, sent on 9 August from his headquarters at Aix-le-Chapelle, was more direct and threatening:

It is my Royal Imperial command that you concentrate your energies for the immediate present upon one single purpose. Address all your skill and all the valour of my soldiers to exterminate first the treacherous English and walk over General French's contemptible little army.

The soldiers of the BEF were fighting fit and confident of victory. Many foresaw a short, one-sided campaign, with the Allies triumphant and home by Christmas. Not everyone shared this rosy view of what lay ahead. On the eve of departure from their depot at the Curragh, Lieutenant Rory Macleod was attending a farewell dinner given at the officers' mess. The dinner was to say thank-you to the locals for their support during the battery's stay:

There was an officers' club at the Curragh at which we used to entertain to tennis, dinners and dances the people who had been so kind to us. After mobilisation we were allowed there for one last dance before we went abroad. This was our Waterloo Ball. Captain 'Cully' Buckle [the battery captain], who seemed to have second sight, told Miss Honner that few of the officers dancing that night would return alive, and foretold ill-treatment of our prisoners by the Germans …

Chapter 2

The Gunners Arrive

'For mile after mile it was the same. Hands waved, hands kissed.'

Major John Mowbray, 2nd Division Artillery Staff

The BEF was given an ecstatic reception in France. Men, women and children lined the docks and quays of Le Havre, Rouen and Boulogne to give the British soldiers a hero's welcome. The streets and houses were festooned with British and French flags. Past rivalries were forgotten as the two countries united in their common stand against the invading Germans. Everywhere the troops went they were followed by crowds of well-wishers, civic leaders and marching bands. Younger women showered the British soldiers with affection. Children sought souvenirs. A carnival-like atmosphere prevailed. The warmth of this welcome left a powerful impression on the newly arrived soldiers.

Lieutenant Cecil Brownlow of the 40th Brigade Ammunition Column disembarked in Le Havre on 19 August:

As we passed through the lock the quays on either side were crowded with French people cheering, crying and waving handkerchiefs, and the troops lining the ship's side shouted and waved in reply. It was a wonderful moment, the first meeting of the English soldiery and the French people.

Major William Strong was commanding 128 Battery, 30th Brigade, RFA. His battery arrived at the port of Le Havre that same morning, 19 August, and sailed up the river to disembark at Rouen. 'We had a great reception all along the river,' he recalled in his diary. Sergeant William Edgington of D Battery RHA landed at Le Havre and his diary recalled how the local population 'smothered us with flowers and kisses'. The entente cordiale would be taken to unusual lengths. Gunner John Allan of L Battery RHA needed to use the toilet on the dockside at Le Havre, and 'was very surprised when a woman attendant carefully wiped the seat for me. That's something I'd never seen in Glasgow.' Charles Burrows, with the 21st Battery RFA reached Rouen on 19 August and remembered the 'great reception' they were given. Likewise Lieutenant Mac Robertson, landing at Boulogne on the 18th with the 70th Battery, recalled 'the French people received us with cheers'.

Gunner Reeve of the 16th Battery RFA landed with his comrades at Le Havre a few days earlier, on 16 August. It took many hours to safely off-load all their kit and stores as Le Havre was not then a well equipped or modern port. Once this job was completed, they marched to a large cotton warehouse to billet for the night. The following day, when Reeve and his mates went for a walk through the town, they were met with warmth and friendship from every quarter. It was almost as though they were tourists on holiday: 'We got an enthusiastic reception from the inhabitants. Everyone shaking hands and wanting souvenirs, cap badges, belts, etc. Had a 5 cent ride on a tram. French beer very pale and light.'

Two days later Lieutenant Edward Schrieber of the 115th Battery, 25th Brigade, RFA, also berthed at Le Havre. The enthusiasm for the BEF was still at fever pitch:

It was a triumphal procession which I headed through the town. I remember being full of pride leading my command, so much larger than any which I had ridden at the head of before. Little did I realise that behind me, what I imagined was a smartly turned out show, was turning rapidly into a carnival scene. I had to ride in front to find the way and I remember my horror when, near the end of the march, I dropped back to let the column file past. Very few men had cap badges or titles on their shoulders and even buttons had gone. Every man was bedecked with flowers and even the horses had them in their brow-bands. It was months before badges and buttons could be replaced ...

Lieutenant Cecil Brownlow, with the 40th Brigade Ammunition Column, recounted a similar set of problems unloading at Le Havre:

The means of unloading the ship were inadequate, for the French cranes were unable to lift our guns and wagons so that all the vehicles had laboriously to be unshipped by winches and derricks on the ship itself. All through the night we toiled by the blue white light of sizzling arc lamps. Hour after hour passed and ever the noise of shouts, of commands, of stamping horses and of rattling winches along the wharf side and ever men hurried up and down the gangways or heaved at vehicles on the quay.

Gunner William Crowsley left Dublin for Le Havre on 15 August on board the SS *Pancras* with the rest of E Battery RHA. They steamed into port on the 17th:

Very pretty sight entering Havre, throngs gathered at the docks cheering, children scrabbling for biscuits and souvenirs etc. Landed at 3.30pm and commenced to disembark, horses first, the guns and wagons very slowly coming up from the hold owing to the difficulty of getting the steam crane to work and the ship's staff going on strike. Unloading finished at 10pm and we marched to rest camp passing all through Havre on to a very high ground, arriving there about 1am. Enthusiastic reception by French population who smothered us with flowers and cheers ...

After settling in overnight, Crowsley and his pals went to explore the town: 'Not much to be seen as all the shops were closed. French girls seeking souvenirs; we had to more or less keep badges and buttons under cover. Had supper at a cafe. Could not get on at all well with the language. Returned to camp at 10.15pm.'

Some of Crowsley's friends in the RHA found a simple solution to the language problem. When they went into town to buy eggs at a grocery store near the docks, they failed to get anywhere until one of the men drew an egg on the counter and tried to cackle like a hen.

Others attempted to get round the language barrier by resorting to personal experiences gained through their Empire service. Many of the regular soldiers who had served in India used a mixture of English and Hindi to try to get their messages across to their new French friends, with varying degrees of success. French was seldom used by the Tommies but it did not matter very much either way. No one bothered whether they could make themselves understood or not. The point was that they were there, on French soil, to help France repel the German invader. That was enough.

The gunners did not stay long at the ports. They would soon leave on enormous trains, the guns and wagons packed onto open carriages while the men crammed themselves into carriages that were designed to take either eight horses or forty men each. Lieutenant Cecil Brownlow described the heavy lifting involved in getting his unit ready to move:

> Entraining in France was a far more laborious process than in England because owing to lack of platforms the vehicles had to be pushed by hand up unwieldy wooden ramps on to the trucks. For the third night in succession, the men, sleepy and tired, toiled at heavy ammunition wagons and struggled with obstinate horses.

Conditions for the men were rudimentary, and even the officers had to put up with cramped and crowded conditions. Nearly 150 special trains, dispatched at 10-minute intervals, would be needed to move the BEF from the ports to their designated areas of disembarkation. The lines were heavily congested and the trains moved very slowly, often at a snail's pace.

Captain Mackie of the 30th Brigade Ammunition Column RFA recalled the 'Awful train … it stops every now and then and re-starts with awful jerks. I feel sorry for the poor old horses. They must get some nasty shocks.'

Gunner Crowsley and E Battery left Le Havre on the 19th, on a balmy summer's evening:

> Battery entrained at Havre in one train about 500 yards long. Started about 7pm and travelled all night via Rouen, Amiens to Hantmount I rode outside with the gun as the carriages did not look very comfortable. Splendid sight passing up country, could not keep very clean owing to being exposed to smoke from the engine.

Captain Cully Buckle of the 80th Battery RFA, who would be killed in action on 26 August, was travelling on the train with the rest of the 15th Brigade. He and his fellow junior officers had to clamber along the running boards as the train gathered speed in order to join the senior officers for lunch. The silver cutlery was laid out on linen tablecloths. The fare might have been a little more spartan than in peacetime conditions on Salisbury Plain – the officers ate fresh French loaves with sardines, bully beef, eggs and cheese, washed down with port and brandy. The men had to make do with bully beef and biscuits. But these basic rations were supplemented at every stop along the route as the local inhabitants turned out in force to wish the Tommies bon voyage and provide them with copious amounts of coffee and food.

Sergeant Philip Hillman of the 123rd Battery, 28th Brigade, RFA, entrained at Le Havre on 19 August:

We were given black bread which was as hard as bricks, bully beef, emergency rations and some impure meat. We were in the train for 20 hours and had a tiring journey. But while en route we had a good reception – we were given coffee, wine, biscuits, flowers, cigarettes, French colours and fruit in plenty. The French people were mad after our badges and numerals …

Major John Mowbray was on the headquarters staff of the 2nd Division artillery. In a letter home written on 21 August, he described what it was like during those first few days in France with the BEF:

The days fly past, being full. It is difficult to break away from the sensation of a gigantic picnic. The men certainly haven't. Their welcome has been so warm. I came a considerable distance by road – everywhere the population was out en masse and they would throw flowers at us or come forward with loaves, bottles of wine or beer, or little charms or fruit or try to catch us as we passed. Vive les Anglais! Vive l'Angleterre! Vive l'Entente! For mile after mile it was the same. Hands waved, hands kissed. Presently the men began to jump out when the trains got to a halt and embrace the nearest good-looking girls. A veritable Entente.

Mac Robertson, with the 70th Battery, 34th Brigade, RFA, left Boulogne on 20 August:

The train took the whole Battery. We were received with great enthusiasm all down the line and supplied with drinks by the people. Stopped at Amiens and Arras and watered the horses. The journey took 10 hours. Arrived at Wassiguy and had to go on to Mesnil. Unloaded in the dark and bivouacked in a field near the station. Bed by 2am.

Lieutenant Colonel Wilkinson and the men of the 35th (Heavy) Battery left Boulogne the following morning:

The train journey was one of the most extraordinary journeys I ever experienced – the train travelled very slowly and stopped at every station. The stations were packed with civilians who were shouting, waving flags and bringing food and drink to our men. It was as much as we could do to restrain the men and keep them in their carriages. They had never had such an ovation in their lives and went perfectly mad. Many of them parted with their badges and buttons as souvenirs. Poor fellows – they did not realise where the train was taking them to …

The reception given to the British soldiers as they moved further inland was every bit as warm as it had been in the ports. Bombardier Harry Sprotson, serving with the 68th Battery, 14th Brigade, RFA, remembered 'a splendid reception by the people of the villages we passed through. They gave us great bunches of flowers, eggs and wine and as much fruit as we can carry.'

Lieutenant Brownlow of the 40th Brigade Ammunition Column recalled a similar experience: 'At every village we went through the inhabitants would flock into the streets begging for souvenirs. In many of them the windows were decorated with flags and strips of cloth hung across the streets bearing such mottoes as "Welcome to the British".'

Despite the numerous acts of kindness from the civilians, Driver Ryder, serving with E Battery RHA, recalled the privations the men experienced on the move:

We had three days and three nights forced march. We had very little sleep and very little to eat, only hard rations. Sometimes when we passed through a village some of the ladies would give us a piece of bread and jam. Being in the lead I got an egg. Broke it on the saddle and managed to swallow it. If we got the order to halt and there were potatoes in the field we would go over and help ourselves, clean them as best we could and eat them.

We would get the order when it was dark to halt and dismount. As soon as you sat down you went to sleep. One night as it was getting dark I could see everybody in front going from one side to the other in the saddle. I saw my lead driver fall off his horse's near side. Had he [fallen] off on the off side I feel sure he would have been trodden to death because the horses were like us – they were walking in their sleep.

The trains were taking the troops to the concentration area that had finally been selected for the BEF around Maubeuge and Le Cateau, close to the Belgian border. There had been a serious disagreement amongst the senior

British military commanders about whether it was right for the small British force to position itself so far forward. They ran considerable risks in doing so. Kitchener, expressing a profound mood of caution, had favoured an area much further behind, at Amiens, as the point of concentration. From here the BEF would have more time to see how the campaign was developing and avoid overstretching itself along extended lines of communication. Sir John French's deputy, Henry Wilson, who had been closely involved in the pre-war planning discussions which had assumed that the British army would take up a position on the immediate left flank of the French Fifth Army, favoured sticking to the original plan of action. Anything less than this might call into question the commitment of the British to their new allies. The Cabinet in London had effectively given the final say over where the BEF should be deployed to the French. They wanted the British troops to join Lanrezac's Fifth Army, strengthening the Allied line in the north. This would effectively ensure that the BEF would be in the thick of things.

The concentration area was a narrow strip, 25 miles long by about 10 miles wide, spreading from Maubeuge in the north-east to Le Cateau towards the south-west. The Cavalry Division was gathered around Maubeuge, with the 1st and 2nd Corps in echelon behind it. This concentration was complete by the late evening of 20 August. The five infantry battalions making up the hastily formed 19th Infantry Brigade, the troops guarding the lines of communication, would make their way separately towards Valenciennes, to the west of Maubeuge. On the immediate right flank of the BEF was the French 18th Corps, and on its left the 84th French Territorial Division. General Lanrezac, the commanding officer of the French Fifth Army, had ten divisions under his direct command; combined with the Belgian and British armies, this gave the Allies a combined strength of twenty-one divisions to deal with the expected German flanking attack through Belgium.

There was a lot for the men to take in. Brownlow described the new sights and scenes his men were confronted with on these burning hot days marching up to Mons:

> The march through the rich French country was full of beauty and interest. The men forgot their fatigue in their excitement at the unfamiliar scenes about them – the patter of the French tongue amused them, the strange country carts, the absence of hedges, the pruned trees, the cobbled roads, the shutters on the windows, the gendarmes' uniforms and the people's dress aroused their interest.

Notwithstanding these abundant bucolic pleasures, things were not going well for the Allied cause. While the BEF was girding up its loins for the first contact with the enemy, French plans to carry the attack to the Germans were already beginning to fall apart. By 16 August General Joffre, the French commander, was sure that the main German attack was coming through Belgium. He was right. Germany had assembled seven armies on her western borders under the overall command of Generaloberst von Moltke. Three of these armies, the First, Second and Third, would be tasked with executing a giant encircling manoeuvre in an attempt to outflank Joffre's forces, which were concentrated in the centre. Joffre had placed Lanrezac's powerful Fifth Army to the northern flank of his front to deal with the German advance through Belgium, but he had stripped it of some of its key units in order to strengthen his forces to the south, where the remainder of the French Army would be dispatched to deliver a powerful counter-punch. The units replacing Lanrezac's crack troops were a rag-bag of reserve divisions and some recently arrived African troops. To counter the German movement through Belgium, Joffre planned to deliver a strong attack by the French Third and Fourth Armies through the Ardennes. This would cut the German lines of communication and strike at the flanks of the armies to the north and south before they could wheel to meet them. This main advance would be supported by a secondary attack by the First and Second Armies through Lorraine, designed to hold the German defenders in their positions and prevent them reinforcing their comrades to the north. General Joffre's strategy was to break the enemy's centre and then to use all his available forces to break up the German armies moving through Belgium, which would, if all went well, be cut off from their supply lines. The general advance was to take place on 20 August. The plan was simple enough; the problem would lie in its execution.

The French tactics unravelled very quickly, with serious consequences for the BEF to the north. The attack through the Ardennes ended in bloody failure. The massed ranks of French infantry hurled themselves dutifully and bravely at the German machine guns with predictable results. The French encountered powerful concentrations of German troops, who were well dug in and expected to be attacked. The two French armies leading the offensive were forced to retire after suffering enormous losses. The attack in Lorraine fared no better. The troops were tired after days of forced marches, and the French attack was heavily defeated by concentrated artillery and machine gun fire from strongly fortified positions. Here too the French were forced to retreat in the face of their equally severe casualties. The attempt to smash through the German centre before the encircling movement in the north could be completed ended in abject failure.

In Belgium things were also not going well. The six divisions of the Belgian Army had put up stoic resistance but had been steadily pushed back by the overwhelming tide of invaders. By 21 August virtually all of Belgium was under German control, Brussels had been captured, most of the Belgian troops had retreated into Antwerp and the advancing Germans were bearing down steadily on the BEF and the weakened French Fifth Army. Lanrezac's forces were themselves already in a salient with strong German forces advancing rapidly on either side of them. It was an inauspicious beginning, but things were about to get much worse.

Notwithstanding these terrible setbacks, Sir John French, in the absence of clear intelligence and in pursuance of Joffre's original plan, issued orders on the afternoon of 20 August for the BEF to move northwards the following morning. Operation Order No. 5 ordered the BEF to move north of the River Sambre. Over the next three days the BEF would advance on the left of the French Fifth Army through Soignies in the general direction of Nivelles. The intention was clear: the British Army was to go on the offensive. It would advance to Mons, execute a wheel to face north-east and then deliver a powerful blow into the flank of the advancing Germans. However, intelligence about the precise whereabouts and strength of the enemy was still sketchy at the time French ordered the advance. Operation Order No. 5 promised that 'information regarding the enemy and allied troops will be communicated separately'. This did not happen, because there was not much information to pass on.

Chapter 3

Advance to Contact

'It was crazy, but we spent an hour actually in front of the leading
company of the Royal Scots Fusiliers.'

Gunner Pursey, 120th Battery, 27th Brigade, RFA

On 21 August the weather made aerial reconnaissance difficult. At dawn
there was a thick mist and the pilots of the Royal Flying Corps were unable to
get airborne. Cavalry patrols had been informed by local people that strong
German forces were in the vicinity. The 2nd Cavalry Brigade crossed the
Conde canal to the east of Mons and sent out patrols from the 9th (Queen's
Royal) Lancers and the 4th (Royal Irish) Dragoon Guards; these sighted
German forces near two bridges to the east of Mons. Local intelligence
gathered from residents suggested significant German forces moving
southwards from Soignies. In the afternoon the cloud cover cleared and the
RFC was able to send up spotter planes, which reported large columns of
enemy cavalry, artillery and infantry south-east of Nivelles.

In fact, no fewer than eleven German Army Corps were heading towards
the BEF – over 700,000 men comprising the First, Second and Third
Armies, a combined force of more than thirty-four divisions. Sir John
French took a rather more optimistic view of the forces ranged against him.
In his diary entry for 21 August he wrote: 'Lanrezac says that eight German
Army Corps and three cavalry divisions are now north of the Meuse. I doubt
if there are more than six; but time will show.'

The war became a practical reality on that day for Private William Collins,
on the medical staff of the 7th Brigade RHA:

On 21st August we were in Harmignies, a village near Mons and that
afternoon I saw my first signs of the war. There in the village square
was a pile of German saddlery smoking and smouldering. It seems
that early that morning our cavalry had clashed with some Uhlans and

captured two of them. They had unsaddled their horses and set fire to the saddles and bridles, taking the horses with them …

On 22 August cavalry patrols covering the British left flank made contact with the Germans at Obourg, just to the north of Mons. C Squadron, coming across a German piquet, opened fire on the enemy and drove them down the road. At 11am that morning the artillery fired their first rounds of the First World War. They were the first of over 170 million rounds fired by the artillery at the enemy. E Battery RHA, commanded by Major A.S. Forman, came into action near Bray, 4 miles north-east of Harmignies, in support of the 3rd Cavalry Brigade. No. 4 gun of C Section performed the Royal Artillery's first hostile act of the campaign, firing a few rounds at the enemy although to little effect. The German guns replied, wounding one horse. William Crowsley would later recall this momentous event:

> The Battery came into action just clear of the village, fired at German guns and infantry. Range found to be too long to be effective. We had not been in action long before a German aeroplane came hovering over our position, dropped a time fuse, giving the range to our guns and returned to its own lines. Then came our first experience of being under shell fire as their first round fell in the ground about 15 yards from me.

Captain Francis Adams was commanding the section of E Battery's guns that fired these first British shots of the war:

> [We] engaged German guns and infantry but the range was too long. This was our first smack at the enemy. The 1st and 2nd Sections retired, leaving my section in action, which was eventually shelled by the enemy, the shell bursting behind my gun limber wounding one horse. This was the first casualty in the Battery.

Further to the east, cavalry from the 5th Cavalry Brigade fired on German Uhlans in the area around La Louviere and reported German forces of all arms marching from the north. They also noticed that French infantry units were retreating back across the River Sambre on their right flank. Lanrezac's forces were under great pressure from two corps of the German Second Army under General von Bulow. Instead of moving up alongside the BEF, the French were, by the evening of 22 August, in full retreat. The

BEF, however, was fully committed to its movement forward and by the afternoon of the 22nd had taken up positions along the Mons–Conde Canal. At this point they were 9 miles in front of the nearest French troops, the 18th Corps, on their right. On their left there were a few scattered elements of the French reserve divisions. The position of the BEF was becoming increasingly untenable.

All talk of the BEF launching an offensive was quickly dropped at a conference of commanders chaired by French at Le Cateau on the evening of 22 August. The retirement of the French Fifth Army had put paid to any such prospect. In a note to the British commander, which arrived later that evening, Lanrezac made one last plea to order an attack against the German forces that were advancing against him on the Sambre. French rightly refused. It would have courted disaster for the BEF to have attacked across the front of the three German armies pouring down from the north. French instead promised Lanrezac that he would hold his positions on the canal at Mons for another 24 hours in order to provide some flank protection to the French Fifth Army.

The BEF now had to defend a difficult position against vastly superior opponents. The British position at Mons was vulnerable to attack on both flanks. The First Corps under Douglas Haig had already taken up a position to the south-east, as part of the original plan to wheel eastwards and attack the Germans in the flank. From here they could at least provide some protection to the right flank of the Second Corps. The Second Corps, now under the command of Sir Horace Smith Dorrien after the sudden death of Sir John Grierson from a heart attack on 17 August, was stretched out along the line of the canal to the west of Mons, with its right positioned precariously in a small salient at Nimy guarding the bridge at Obourg to the north-east. This was the position from which they too were expecting to turn to the east. The position at Mons was therefore a position that French never thought he would be required to defend as it was only occupied originally as a staging post for the planned attack on the Germans. The canal itself did not pose a very formidable barrier. At best 20 feet wide and 6 feet deep, it was crossed by eighteen bridges in the section held by Second Corps.

French's earlier confusion about the whereabouts of the enemy was echoed by the German High Command's lack of appreciation about the movements of the BEF. An ominous cloud of confusion hung over both sides. If anything, the German commanders were even more in the dark about the forces opposed to them than the British. General von Kluck, commanding the First Army, thought that the BEF had landed at Ostend, Dunkirk and Calais. French counter-espionage measures were so effective that no hard and fast intelligence about where the BEF had actually landed had reached the Germans. A message from the German Supreme Command that arrived at von Kluck's headquarters on the evening of 21 August gave a completely false impression of both the movements of the BEF and the size and strength of the forces that had been deployed: 'Disembarkation of the English at Boulogne and their employment from direction of Lille must be reckoned with. The opinion here, however, is that large disembarkations have not yet taken place.'

The Germans had spotted the presence of British cavalry at Casteau, a few miles to the north-east of Mons, on 22 August. This was the only information about the BEF that von Kluck had passed on to his divisional commanders on 23 August when the two belligerent forces eventually slammed into each other. What von Kluck feared most of all was an attack on his exposed right flank by British cavalry and infantry. The Germans had picked up information about enemy troops de-training at Tournai on 22 August. Believing this might indicate the BEF's arrival in force, von Kluck halted his troops and prepared them to turn westwards to face the new threat he believed was massing on his flank. In fact, the troops at Tournai turned out to be a French infantry brigade, which was actually in the process of retreating into Lille and posed no danger to the German advance. The mystery concerning the whereabouts of the British continued until the early hours of the morning of the 23rd itself. German cavalry, pressing on towards the numerous bridges over the Mons–Conde Canal, met rifle fire from 'invisible' infantrymen. Even at this point, as he propelled his forces onwards, von Kluck had no idea at all of the strength of the opposition in front of him. Other advance patrols of German cavalry were reporting the ground clear of enemy soldiers.

What he actually encountered were British forces positioned along a stretch of the Mons–Conde Canal. Only on the front held by the First Corps did the artillery have good fields of fire, over the open but undulating ground. The artillery of the 1st Division, commanded by Brigadier General Findlay, was deployed in open positions close to the infantry front line. The nearest guns were about a mile behind the infantry. On their left the guns of the 2nd Division, under Brigadier General Perceval, were deployed in a similar fashion. The 50th and 70th Batteries of the 34th Brigade were in semi-open positions just behind the infantry firing line. If the Germans had advanced towards the front held by First Corps, they would have met strong fire from the gunners, but in fact the German attack developed against the line held by the Second Corps.

The ground held by the Second Corps was completely unsuited to artillery and this put the defenders at a substantial disadvantage, given they were vastly outnumbered by the attackers. The Belgians called this part of their country 'Le Borinage' – the Black Country. It was a conglomeration of heavy industry, mines, giant slag-heaps and terraced houses all jammed together and crisscrossed by canals, ditches and watercourses. The field artillery found it difficult to establish effective forward observation and the guns could not fire round the slag-heaps and other obstacles that lay in their field of fire. In theory, the slag-heaps might have been expected to provide important observation posts, but, as Gunner Walter Pursey of the 120th Battery RFA found, there was only one problem with this: 'My Forward Observation Officer looked at the slag heaps and thought they were God's gift to an observation officer. We set off to climb one and within a couple of minutes our boots were sizzling and down we came. No more slag heaps and precious little observation.'

As a consequence, for much of the ensuing battle the artillery was blind and unable to contribute effectively to the engagement. The few guns that did take an active role in the battle would find themselves right up with the infantry and firing opportunistically at targets over open sights. There was no opportunity therefore for the Second Corps artillery to develop a coherent overall strategy to support the infantry. The guns would be merely accessories to the infantry rather than strategic assets. Kiggell might have been impressed, but in the circumstances there was no other option open to the gunners. It was the best they could do in the conditions in which they found themselves. As a result, the Battle of Mons would, from the British perspective, turn out to be fought primarily with rifles rather than artillery. There was, in fact, a better line on higher ground to the south, several miles behind the canal, that offered a better prospect of being successfully defended, but Smith Dorrien had been ordered to push his force right up to the canal.

The 3rd Division was on the right flank of the corps front and it was here that the first German blows would land. The 3rd Division covered the salient at Nimy and a short stretch of the canal as far as Jemappes. The 8th and 9th Infantry Brigades held the front line, with the 7th Brigade in reserve around the village of Ciply. The 9th Infantry Brigade held the line from Nimy out to Jemappes to the west along the line of the canal. The ground on the right of the division's firing line was dominated by the mass of the Bois la Haut, a steep, partly wooded hill offering good observation to the north-east – the line of advance for many of the German troops. The hill and part of the dangerous salient at Nimy were defended by the 8th Infantry Brigade. The troops were thinly spread out, holding a series of outposts rather than a continuous line. One battalion, for example, the 4th Middlesex, held 2 miles of the line between the Bois la Haut and the apex of the Nimy salient. The 4th Royal Fusiliers of the 9th Infantry Brigade was the other infantry unit in the salient. The men had barely enough time to construct some rough entrenchments by nightfall on the 22nd, and these were unfinished by the time the fighting began the following morning. The hill itself presented particular difficulties for the guns, as, although it sloped gently from the north and east, it rose very sharply on the western and southern edges, making it hard to position the guns effectively, given the flat trajectory of their barrels. Brigadier General Wing, the commander of the divisional artillery, placed the 40th Brigade on the Bois la Haut position itself. The 6th Battery was in covered ground on the eastern shoulder of the hill facing the north-east. The 23rd Battery was in the semi-open on the top of the hill itself, facing directly east. At this point the guns were only a few hundred yards behind the infantry. The 49th Battery had one section of guns facing to the north and two sections facing north-east. Once battle commenced, these guns would engage the enemy infantry at quite short range. The rest of the 3rd Division artillery – the 23rd and 42nd Brigades RFA, together with the 48th (Heavy) Battery – was held in reserve to the north and east of Ciply. The 30th (Howitzer) Brigade was not on the battlefield in time to take any part in the action, only arriving at Bavai from Valenciennes at 3pm on 23 August. Captain Mackie, travelling with the 30th Brigade Ammunition Column RFA, remembered the journey and hearing the first sounds of battle: 'Disentrained safely and did a long march, all the villagers treated us to beer, fruit etc as we passed along. Battle raging close to us. 130th Battery reported to be in action. Bivouacked in a hay field. May move at any minute.'

The reserve artillery brigades prepared positions at Nouvelles.

The 5th Division held the rest of the front line. The 13th Infantry Brigade held a 3-mile section on the left of the 9th Infantry Brigade. On the left of the 13th Infantry Brigade, the 14th Infantry Brigade held the line from the railway bridge at Les Herbieres westward towards the Pommeroeul road bridge, a distance of 2.5 miles. Small groups were positioned on the north side of the canal to protect the approaches to the bridges. The 5th Division artillery was under the command of Brigadier General Headlam. Four guns of the 120th Battery, 27th Brigade, RFA, took up a forward position right along the tow-path of the canal at St Ghislain with the 1st Battalion, Royal West Kents on their left and the 1st Battalion, Royal Scots Fusiliers on their right. Gunner Pursey was with these guns as they came into action on 23 August: 'It was crazy, but we spent an hour actually in front of the leading company of the Royal Scots Fusiliers.'

General Headlam concentrated his guns in order to provide as much support as possible to the infantry firing line. He kept two of his brigades – the 15th Brigade and 8th (Howitzer) Brigade RFA – in reserve north-east of the village of Dour on the left, where it was hoped the guns would be able to deal with any German flanking movement to the east. The 28th Brigade RFA was deployed to support the 14th Infantry Brigade on the left, and the 27th Brigade RFA, minus the 120th Battery but with the addition of the 37th (Howitzer) Battery, was ordered to support the 13th Infantry Brigade on the right. It was, however, an enormous challenge to find suitable battery positions – even for single guns – along the 5th Division front. The Official History, in a masterful understatement, described the difficulties as being sufficient to 'baffle the most skilful and sanguine of gunners on the British side'.

This gloomy assessment of the challenge faced by the artillery at Mons was confirmed by Lieutenant Rory Macleod of the 80th Battery, 15th Brigade, RFA, who provided a vivid personal account of the difficulties his battery experienced in finding a suitable position for the guns:

About 10 o'clock Major Birley [Battery commander] and Mirlees [Battery adjutant] rode off to reconnoitre a battery position to support the infantry on the canal bank on the left flank of the 5th Division. They were the King's Own Scottish Borderers and they were having a very warm time of it. The Germans were shelling them and they had pushed up a field gun behind a hedge within 500 yards of a house the KOSB were holding. They were pounding it to bits. The Major went right through this shelling looking for a suitable place for the guns. There wasn't one! The country was absolutely flat, cut up by ditches. No cover at all. The party came back very despondent.

The infantrymen faced their own problems. They were stretched out in a long line of small outposts with poor fields of fire and in improvised positions that provided minimal levels of protection. It was hardly surprising, therefore, that Smith Dorrien had already begun to consider and prepare a better position in the rear of the canal to which his men might retreat if necessary.

Chapter 4

Mons and the Start of the Retreat

'We thought of Sunday in England and of our friends ... and we all
envied them.'

Sergeant George, 120th Battery RFA

The morning of 23 August began with light rain and mist hanging over
Mons and the surrounding area. People wore their Sunday best as the
church bells summoned the faithful to mass. But six German infantry
divisions were now on a collision course with the Second Corps and as
dawn began to break their advance elements started to come into contact
with British patrols. Early in the morning the mounted troops of the 1st
and 2nd Divisions encountered enemy patrols as they scouted north around
Binche, Obourg and Bray. At 6am German cavalry began to engage the 4th
Middlesex. Further to the west German patrols were ambushed by British
infantry. The German divisions were attempting to complete a wheel from
east to south, which would take them directly through the British line
held by Second Corps. By 9am German artillery was in position on the
high ground to the north of the canal, and shells soon began to fall thick
and fast in the Nimy salient. One German battery coolly rode up to within
a mile of the salient, unlimbered their guns and opened fire on the 4th
Middlesex, but they were soon forced to retire by the Middlesex machine
guns. German infantry began to press on strongly, attacking all sides of
the Nimy salient. The attackers met a hail of rifle and machine gun fire
from the British infantry, which inflicted heavy casualties on the Germans,
halting them in their tracks. British musketry skills had been finely honed
in peacetime. Soldiers were expected to be able to let off fifteen rounds
of aimed rifle fire a minute from their new short magazine Lee Enfield
rifles. For the Germans it felt as though they had walked into a storm of
fire from dozens of machine guns. The German artillery, however, kept
up a powerful fire on the Middlesex and Royal Fusiliers, and this would

eventually force the British to retire, initially to better positions around Frameries and Nouvelles, 3 miles to the south.

For the British artillery the next few hours of battle would be a time of extreme frustration. The difficulties over sighting the guns meant that most of the British batteries would not come into action at all and were able to provide no protection to the infantry as wave after wave of Germans steadily began to overwhelm them. On the 3rd Division front, for example, the 42nd Brigade did not manage to fire a single round during the day and the 23rd Brigade was unable to contribute much. Four guns of its 109th Battery came into action on the outskirts of Mons and its remaining two guns joined in a little further behind, but the fire from these guns could only provide token cover.

It was the guns of the 40th Brigade on the Bois la Haut that saw most of the action on the 3rd Division's front on 23 August, and these guns were firing at targets at quite close ranges – between 1 and 2 miles at most. The guns of the 49th Battery on the Bois la Haut were the only guns firing directly to the north, the main line of advance of the attacking German infantry of the 17th Division. Here the range between the guns and the enemy was less than a mile. In artillery terms it was a close–quarter battle.

Lieutenant Cyril Brownlow, 40th Brigade Ammunition Column, was tasked to replenish the ammunition for the guns of the 23rd Battery on the Bois la Haut:

[At about 2.30pm] I was sent forward with four wagons of ammunition for the 23rd Battery on Bois la Haut. We moved across a couple of meadows and up a road, which skirts the left flank of the hill. Coming down this road were three horse ambulances crammed with wounded men, dusty and torn and swathed in blood-soaked bandages ... as this company of suffering humanity moved slowly by they left behind them on the white and dusty Belgian road a scarlet trail of English blood.

Suddenly I heard a whistling in the air which grew to the shriek of a soul in torment and ended in a terrific double crash and a hundred yards to my left there appeared two oily clouds of smoke.

To reach the Battery it was necessary to go to the northern end of the hill and then to follow a rough track which doubled back to the crest in rear. Leaving the road, we swung at a trot through a gate on the right and up a sandy track. On the left, fifty yards away, were trees and undergrowth where shells were bursting continuously. The noise and concussion of the explosions were terrific; trunks, branches and leaves were cut down and splinters and bullets struck the ground about us with deadly smacks ... [on] the higher south-eastern part of the hill sheltering alongside a copse I found the Battery wagon line while two hundred yards away was the Battery in a clearing among the woods. As the ammunition was wanted at once I took my wagons direct to the gun position. The six guns, each with an ammunition wagon alongside, lay in line just below the crest. The detachments were grouped about each piece, the muzzles of the guns were lifted towards the enemy and on the ground were heaps of empty brass cartridge cases which flashed in the sunlight.

While my wagons were being unloaded I spoke to the Captain, who said 'It's quite quiet now, but they have been shelling us periodically. Luckily they have not done much damage.'

Under the sheer weight of the attack, the 8th Infantry Brigade defending the Bois la Haut began to retire, exposing the Nimy salient to attack from the rear. By mid-afternoon the salient had to be abandoned. As the British moved back through Mons in the afternoon, the guns on the Bois la Haut became exposed to the German infantry. The 109th Battery became engaged at this point, providing some cover to the retiring British soldiers.

However, the tide of advancing Germans was now impossible to resist. A party of German infantrymen worked their way around Mons to the south, directly threatening the retirement of the artillery from the Bois la Haut. As the 23rd Battery left its positions on the hill, it encountered German infantry moving along the road to Hyon. The front horses and drivers were all shot down. The gunners had no choice but to become infantry themselves, alongside the Gordon Highlanders tasked with escorting the guns. Engaging the Germans with their rifles, they drove the enemy back into the village. After further skirmishing later in the evening, the guns would be got safely away after dark from within 200 yards of the enemy.

The 6th Battery also had a narrow escape. For most of the early evening they expected to be attacked by enemy infantry. The guns were placed in a semi-circle and defended by parties of Royal Irish, Gordon Highlanders and the gunners themselves facing to the north, west and south. The attack never came. Just before midnight the guns were man-handled to the foot of the Bois la Haut, the teams hooked in and the battery made good its escape, taking with it two temporarily abandoned 18-pounders.

Young Jimmy Naylor, a trumpeter serving with the 3rd Division artillery, remembers the moment the guns of his battery had to be withdrawn. The gunners depended on the infantry in front to give them the necessary time to get the horse teams and limbers up to the gun positions. Jimmy could hear the officer commanding the infantry giving the fire orders to his men:

He was saying 'At four hundred … at three fifty … at three hundred. The rifles blazed away but still the Germans came on. They were getting nearer and nearer and for the first time I began to feel rather anxious and frightened. They weren't an indeterminate mass any more, you could actually pick out the details, see them as individual men, coming on and coming on. After the officer, still cool as anything, was saying 'at two fifty … at two hundred … and then he said 'Ten rounds rapid'. And the chaps opened up – and the Germans just fell down like logs. I've never seen anything like it, the discipline, the fire discipline of those troops. I've never forgotten that, I was so impressed. As a boy of 16 I was simply astounded. I thought 'What a marvellous army we are!' The attack was completely repulsed – long enough for us to get the guns away. It saved us.

Further to the west the German attack along the canal developed momentum as the day wore on. Just before midday German shells began falling in Jemappes and German infantry began to advance against the British outposts on the north side of the canal. These parties were gradually withdrawn but the enemy was met by heavy fire all along the canal and was not successful in crossing the waterway. The 120th Battery came into action during the morning and suffered a number of casualties from very heavy rifle and machine gun fire.

Sergeant Albert George was with the guns of 120th Battery when they came into action at St Ghislain:

In St Ghislain the people were going and coming from the different churches and the scene was very peaceful. At 10am we put our gun in action behind the Mons canal on a small hill about 500 yards to the right front of the town hall. All the gunners were busy barricading and digging gun pits and about 11.15 when they were almost finished the order 'Action' came down and everybody went to their different duties, and also we were very pleased to have a go at the Germans. About 11.20 four shells came whizzing through the air and all four dropped in the town, terrifying the people, who started screaming and running in all directions and a panic started but our presence soothed them a great deal. At 11.30 our battery opened fire and the war began in earnest.

All the while the German shells were dropping all around us but they could not at first find our battery. At 12 noon the Germans found a good target, the town hall and church spire, and we counted over a dozen holes in the dome of the town hall and half a dozen through the church, and as the church was in the middle of the town the Germans could not help hitting a house or something. At about 12 noon also the German infantry were advancing upon us and things were beginning to look unpleasant as we had to fire alternately at the infantry and guns as our infantry had not arrived. At about 12.15 the German gunners found our battery and things were beginning to get very hot for us but not causing serious damage, only ploughing up the ground and killing civilians. The Germans were advancing so rapidly that we were firing at the low range of 600 yards and every shell killed dozens as they were advancing in close order.

At 1pm, seeing that the only way to save the Battery from being captured or killed, our Major ordered us to get ready to retire and at 1.15 we retired into the town behind the town hall. The civilians came out of their houses and shops and they readily gave us wine and sandwiches, fruit, boiled eggs and bread and butter but we refused most of it as we felt too sick and down-hearted to eat. Some of the men were drinking beer to try to drown their miseries but our Captain fell the battery in and threatened to shoot the first man he saw taking wine or beer from the villagers. This order might seem severe, but he said, 'It might be drugged or poisoned and that we must not disgrace the British Army'.

Second Lieutenant Robert Thornhagh-Foljambe was commanding one of the sections of the 120th Battery at St Ghislain:

[At] 11.30am heavy rifle fire and thick columns of German infantry advancing within 2,000 yards. Fired hard and the Major reported afterwards that we had done a lot of damage. Two batteries opened onto us and I had a direct hit on the parapet in front of one of my guns. Fortunately I had put up two steel plates with 3 feet of stones between them and this stopped the shell. Things getting very hot so we ran the guns out by hand under cover of buildings.

Once the guns had withdrawn from their position on the tow-path, one section managed to come into action on the side of a slag-heap during the afternoon. Sergeant George described what happened next:

> At about 2.30pm our infantry had taken up their position and as the firing had died down somewhat our Major resolved to have another go at the Huns so we went into action again. All that afternoon we kept the Huns at bay although they were about ten to one. It was an awful ending to an awful day. We thought of Sunday in England and of ... our friends in England and we all envied them.

It was here that the battery commander, Major C.S. Holland, was killed by a gunshot wound to the head. As the retirement from the salient at Nimy took effect, the troops along the line of the canal had little choice but to conform, and their withdrawal began in the middle of the afternoon. The guns of the 120th Battery were in danger of being cut off from the rear, and the gunners came under rifle fire from this direction. The battery was finally withdrawn but had to leave two of the guns behind. The 119th Battery was briefly in action near the Bois d'Hamme, where it fired on enemy infantry and attempted to engage enemy batteries. It was assisted in this task by the division's heavy battery, the 108th Battery RGA under Major de Sausmarez, from a position near Dour. One of the shells fired by this battery hit a stockpile of German ammunition, causing a gigantic explosion in the enemy's lines. Later that evening the 52nd and 124th Batteries were ordered forward to provide help but by this time it was too late – the retirement was now general across the whole corps front. These were the only guns of the divisional artillery to see any action that day. The infantry of the 5th Division moved back to a new line 2 miles behind the canal.

Rory Macleod, serving with the 80th Battery moved back with his guns to Dour at about this time:

> There was a field in the middle of the village close to Dour church and we left all the vehicles there, dismounted the gunners and marched through the village and turned into a turnip field with a railway running at the bottom. Here we started preparing a battery position along the only possible cover, behind a hedge bordering the railway. It was on a forward slope and somewhat to our surprise it was facing north-west.

Macleod's guns were being positioned not to provide help to the beleaguered infantry defending the canal, but to check any possible flanking attack coming from the west that would threaten the BEF's withdrawal. The line on the canal itself was beyond help:

> At the top of the slope was a factory with a tall chimney we could use as an observation post. We cut gaps in the hedge and dug the gun pits so that the top of the hedge would be level with the tops of the gun shields. And we made gaps in the hedge on the other side of the railway line and filled in the ditches on each side with logs so that the guns would be able to roll forward smoothly when the time came to advance. We had no doubt that we would advance.
>
> We knew the infantry were falling back from the canal bank because we could see them digging in along the hedge 500 yards in front and soon others came even further back and started digging in just in front of us along the hedge on the other side of the railway track. All the while the sound of the gunfire and the rifles and machine guns on our right front to the north of us was getting heavier and heavier – and there wasn't a blessed thing we could do about it.

On the far right wing of the BEF front only a small part of the line held by the First Corps came under any attack and that was the section immediately adjacent to the 3rd Division around the Bois la Haut. In the afternoon German guns opened fire against the left of the 3rd Infantry Brigade holding the ridge at Haulchin. The 22nd and 70th Batteries, which had only just arrived on the scene, were unlimbered at Vellereille le Sec and came briefly into action when they spotted German cavalry moving across the British front. Mac Robertson, with the 70th Battery, described what happened next:

> We came into action on a ridge behind Vellereille le Sec and dug for an hour. Suddenly, about 3.30pm the Major ordered us to be ready to fire (we were behind the crest of the hill and couldn't see to the front) and we fired our first rounds. No sooner than we had fired about 6 rounds than the German guns started on us from near Vellereille St Ghislain with high explosive shrapnel. At first they were all over but they gradually got closer and closer to the guns till finally they burst right over us and all round us. They got the wagon line till we had to stop firing and crouch under the shields – several men hit – it wasn't pleasant. Then

they switched off us and we opened fire on their infantry. At once their guns turned on us and gave us hell for an hour. We had to stop firing again. More men hit. I got hit four times, all slight, on shoulder, head, and left leg. At dusk we were able to withdraw the guns.

Lieutenant Edward Schrieber of the 115th Battery witnessed this action as his unit was halted on the road from Rouveroy to Croix le Rouveroy. From the hill he had a perfect vantage point:

Here we were on high ground and could see Batteries of 2 Division in action behind a crest about 2 miles to the north. We saw a German shell burst for the first time. Our Batteries appeared to be having a very bad time. Time after time salvoes of shrapnel and air burst high explosive appeared to obliterate our guns and we waited anxiously to see the effect when the smoke cleared. Great was our relief to see the flashes of our guns as they continued their fire apparently unharmed. Air burst high explosive had never been seen by us before. We nicknamed these shells 'woolly bears' because of the peculiarly woolly looking smoke of the burst. The noise of the explosion was perhaps the worst part of them as they burst with a most terrifying crash.

Their actual effect was fairly innocuous. I remember that morning seeing a salvo of woolly bears burst right over a wagon line halted in the valley in front of us. We expected to see a tangle of men and horses; all that happened was that the teams quietly trotted to a new halting place some three hundred yards to a flank – there was not a single casualty …

The artillery of the Cavalry Corps, which was itself scattered about the battlefield, saw little action on 23 August. The Cavalry Corps was in position protecting the far left flank of the British line but no German attack developed on this side of the British line. But J Battery RHA did see action that day. A young NCO serving with the battery, E.J. Cummings, provided a graphic account of the day's fighting:

We rose at 3.30am. It was a glorious morning and little did we dream that ere nightfall we should have fought what was perhaps the greatest battle in the world's history. Soon after noon the battle started and our convoy was heavily shelled when passing down a road for about 3 miles.

Hot, tired and dusty we dropped into action about 3pm. Our commander chose an admirable position with 3 or 4 false crests in the ground line and though it took us some considerable time to range our enemy it was as hard for them. Our guns were almost red hot, our mouths were parched and the heat hung in mists before our eyes yet the order came through with a monotonous regularity 'Two rounds rapid battery fire – repeat'. And like machines we repeated.

William Collins was with the 7th Brigade RHA at Quievrain on the morning of 23 August:

It would have been about noon that Captain Scarlett [7th Brigade Adjutant] called me over and gave me a written message for the CO of I Battery some 200 yards away down the village street. That afternoon we moved forward and later on, approaching a wood, I heard my first shell burst some 50 yards ahead. It was shrapnel, a high burst, a cloud of white smoke and then a sound like a hundred shrill whistles as the pellets spread around. No one was wounded but the shrill [sound] of the shrapnel bullets lives with me still …

By contrast, Gunner Crowsley of E Battery RHA, despite the battle raging a few miles to the east, had a quiet day attending to his horses: 'The Battery rested [at Quievrain] until 8.30pm. This was the first chance we had of attending to the horses; was able to unharness and groom them – this they sadly needed. Tried very hard to buy some salt from a small store but found it very hard to make ourselves understood.' It would be a different story in the morning.

During the early hours of 24 August the British line at Mons moved back to higher ground on a line south of the River Haines. It was the first movement of a retreat that would last a fortnight. Nevertheless Field Marshal French had reason to feel quietly satisfied with the day's events. British losses had been around 1,600 men killed, missing or wounded, but German losses were thought to be far higher. His plan was to consolidate the new position and repel any further German advance, and orders were issued to this effect during the evening. Whatever confidence French felt earlier in the day, his plan rapidly disintegrated in the light of fresh intelligence concerning the retreating French Fifth Army on the right. The French Fourth and Fifth Armies were pulling back after being heavily attacked. Lanrezac intended to pull his left flank back another 15 miles to the south-east of Mons. The gap that already existed between the French and British forces was about to widen dramatically. At 1am Field Marshal French decided that his troops should begin a general retirement and take up a position from La Longueville (to the west of Maubeuge) through Bavai and beyond to the village of La Boiserette. In all, this would involve a retreat of about 8 miles from the line at Mons. French ordered the First Corps to cover the retirement of the Second. The order of retirement was to be settled by the two corps commanders. First Corps managed to get away with very little trouble as the main enemy advance continued to focus on the western flank of the BEF, but a series of running battles took place on 24 August as the Germans tried to outflank the retreating British from the west. Once again, it was the troops of Second Corps who would face the main onslaught. Casualty figures on 24 August would exceed those of the day before as German infantry and cavalry threw themselves at the British with extraordinary bravery and an almost complete indifference to losses. As dawn broke, the guns of the 23rd Brigade came into action around Frameries, supporting the rearguard units of the 1st Battalion, Lincolnshire Regiment. All three batteries of the brigade were in action, firing on enemy guns and infantry. The enemy attacks failed. The guns and the 1st Lincolns retired at about 10am, although the guns were forced to provide covering fire as they moved back to their new positions at Bavai. There was little other artillery action on the front held by the 3rd Division.

Captain Hill, serving with the 109th Battery, was seriously injured during the early morning fighting at Frameries. Later that day he would eventually be taken prisoner:

I was wounded in the early morning of 24th August at the village of Frameries near Mons. I was first dressed by a captain RAMC attached to the Lincolnshire Regiment and succeeded in walking back to where a section of my battery was already in action. I was then carried by stretcher bearers, by order of the doctor, to the local hospital. My right arm was removed by a Belgian surgeon and I was put to bed. About mid-day I think a German officer entered the room where I was lying, followed by an orderly with a fixed bayonet. Having called us to attention he proceeded to read us a notice in English to the effect that we were prisoners of war, that anyone found in possession of arms or ammunition would at once be shot. I remained at Frameries where

I was operated on and cared for entirely by Belgians until 8th September. During this time I never saw another German.

Captain Hill was eventually released and returned home from prison camp in the early summer of 1916.

The main action on 24 August would take place further to the west at Elouges. Here the main German thrust would fall on the infantry of the 15th Brigade: the 1st Battalion, Bedfordshire Regiment, and the 1st Battalion, Dorset Regiment, at Hornu and the 1st Battalion, Cheshire Regiment, and the 1st Battalion, Norfolk Regiment, at Elouges. One section of the 121st Battery, 27th Brigade, RFA, was in the firing line with the Dorsets. Once again, the field of fire was poor as the ground was covered with industrial buildings, slag-heaps and terraced housing. Soon after dawn the guns, under the command of Lieutenant H.C. Chapman, opened fire at very short range – a mere 750 yards – and inflicted very heavy casualties amongst the German soldiers, silencing their machine guns. Chapman himself soon came under enemy artillery fire and had to withdraw one of his two guns. The remaining gun, firing in front of its own infantry, stayed in action until 8am, when, under the weight of fire, Chapman decided to disable the gun and manhandle it to safety behind the walls of a burnt-out cottage. Despite coming under direct small arms fire, Driver Bruskett then rode up with his team of horses under the noses of the German attackers and led the gun away to the safety of the British lines.

Elsewhere along the line of retreat of the 15th Brigade, other guns were also in action. The four remaining guns of the 120th Battery, 27th Brigade, RFA, were firing in support of the rearguards alongside the howitzers of 37th Battery, 8th (Howitzer) Brigade, RFA. Private Kennedy of the Dorsets was astonished to find three howitzers 'firing away at close range as if they were machine guns'. These high explosive shells tore the enemy infantry to pieces. Later in the afternoon a staff officer of the 14th Infantry Brigade arrived on horseback to tell Lieutenant Colonel W.H. Onslow, commanding the 27th Brigade RFA, that orders had been issued for the brigade to retire. Onslow refused to comply unless the order was given to him in writing. In a powerful display of solidarity and courage, soldiers of the 1st Battalion, Manchester Regiment, and the 1st Battalion, King's Own Yorkshire Light Infantry, stayed with the guns, under heavy and persistent fire, until the written orders duly arrived some time later.

Two miles further to the west the 28th Brigade RFA was dug in around the Bois du Boussu. The German advance here was a little slower to develop. Most of the guns were withdrawn around 10am and so when German infantry did eventually begin moving forward at midday, they were met by ineffective gun fire that was not able to inflict very much damage. The guns of the 122nd Battery were, however, able to silence an enemy battery that had come unwisely into action in open country.

Second Lieutenant Robert Thornhagh-Foljambe, commanding a section of the 120th Battery dug in around Champs des Arts, experienced the inevitable confusion of a rapidly developing action, which created a significant challenge to effective communication:

> We fired a good deal of shielding fire in front of our infantry but had few visible targets. As usual, we had no orders. At 3pm the infantry were practically back to the line of the guns and were holding on until we got them away. We walked away under a heavy but inaccurate fire ... all the German shrapnel burst far too high and I don't think there was a single casualty.

The Cavalry Division, together with D, E and L Batteries RFA, was also in the vicinity further to the west, seeking to provide some further flank protection. The British rearguard had taken up an excellent defensive position, with a wide field of fire on high ground facing west towards Quievrain. D and E Batteries took up a position just to the east of the village of Angres, with L Battery coming in to position behind the Norfolks just behind a railway embankment north of the village of Audregnies.

The German attacks began just after noon and came from the direction of Baisieux and Quievrain. Two divisions of the German Fourth Corps, supported by nine batteries of artillery, began the attempt to outflank the British Second Corps. The meagre rearguard force of two battalions and four batteries of artillery were all that stood in the way. It would prove to be the critical engagement of the day. As the enemy infantry began their attack, the 4th Dragoon Guards and the 11th Hussars launched a bravura charge over open ground to try to take the enemy in the flank. The men and horses came under a withering fire from rifles and artillery, and the attack broke down without achieving very much.

Shortly after the cavalry mounted their attack, the guns of L Battery came into action. They fired with tremendous effect, bursting their shrapnel

shells low over the advancing infantry of the German 8th Division. Major
Tom Bridges of the 4th Dragoon Guards recalled seeing the six guns of L
Battery drawn up behind the railway embankment north-east of Audregnies
firing 'according to the drill book as if they were on range practice'. Gunner
John Allan of L Battery RHA was too busy helping keep the guns in action
to notice the effect the battery was having:

> Bombardier Perrett and I were busy bringing up ammunition and it
> was a very hot day in every sense. I don't know how long the action
> lasted but I remember a staff officer galloping up and shouting 'Good
> old L!' On our way back a farrier who was an old South Africa man told
> me we had fired more shells in one afternoon than during the whole of
> the Boer War!

In fact, L Battery fired about 450 rounds at Audregnies.

The German attack crumbled under the combined fire of L Battery, the
machine guns of the Norfolks and Cheshires, and supporting fire from two
guns of the 119th Battery. These two guns came under very effective enemy
shell fire and Lieutenant Preston, in command of the section, was forced
to withdraw to safer positions. They became entangled with the retiring
British cavalry but managed to come into action again at extremely close
range, engaging German cavalry and infantry. Once again the guns had to
be withdrawn under very difficult conditions. Losses amongst the section
were heavy. At one point in the fighting Preston had been ordered by his
commanding officer, Major Alexander, to take up a position near a wood at
Thulins. Lieutenant Preston described the action that day:

> I took up a 'half-cock' position north of the Wiherries–Audregnies road.
> The enemy commenced shelling the road and the factory immediately
> behind my guns as we got into position. I then found there was such
> a row going on that I could not command the section by voice control
> – even with a chain of orderlies – so I determined to shift my position
> and called up the teams. By this time the shelling was pretty heavy and
> we had several casualties.
>
> When the teams were hooked in I moved along the road in the
> direction of Audregnies – in full view of the enemy and heavily shelled.
> The Cheshires were lining the embankment of the road but gradually
> withdrawing.

We came into action in the open just alongside the end house of the village where two field tracks met in a fork – heavy ploughed land. From here we could see the field grey uniforms swarming towards us and we let them have it. When the ammunition wagons were getting exhausted and the ground [was] littered with empty cartridge cases, I sent for the teams to come up. By this time the enemy had worked forward and was playing very prettily on my section with machine guns. I had several casualties but got away both guns and one ammunition wagon. I then hurried after my teams to catch up the guns and got a bullet through my knee while doing so but managed to clamber on to an ammunition wagon …

A few hours later Lieutenant Preston was taken prisoner by the Germans. Ten of his men had been killed and many others wounded.

The remainder of the 119th Battery was engaged in an artillery duel with two German batteries near Quievrain, which it succeeded in silencing. There was a desperate struggle to get the guns away after they came under enfilade fire from a German battery. Only the battery commander, Major Alexander, and three men were left standing to pull back the guns by hand, one at a time. Captain Grenfell of the 9th Lancers, witnessing this unequal struggle, dismounted and lent his assistance, and that of his squadron, to the exhausted gunners. The enemy were within 300 yards of the battery position but the guns were eventually got away safely to a railway embankment in the rear. Alexander and Grenfell would both be awarded the Victoria Cross for their actions on 24 August. Alexander's citation read:

Major Alexander handled his battery against overwhelming odds with such conspicuous success that all his guns were saved, notwithstanding that owing to heavy casualties they had to be withdrawn by himself and three other men – all that were left available. This action enabled the retirement of the 5th Division to be carried out without serious loss. Subsequently, Major Alexander rescued a wounded man under heavy fire with the greatest gallantry and devotion to duty.

This was the first of eighteen VCs awarded to men of the Royal Regiment of Artillery during the war.

Further to the left the guns of D and E Batteries were in continuous action throughout the afternoon. For Gunner Crowsley of D Battery, it was a day of high drama and danger:

Marched out from bivouac at Bassiens at 4am with the cavalry division
to cover the left flank of the 5th Division. The right section under
Lieutenant Maxwell took up a position north-west of Audregnies
and engaged German infantry advancing, hosts of them, and did
great execution. The Battery then retired further back and took up
a position in a cornfield, got heavily shelled, difficult to get out of
action. [We took up] another position at Angres. The centre section
under Lieutenant Palmer [was] ordered to retire to cover the retreat of
the other 4 guns, this was done. I was sent as signaller to this section
and to get into communication with the remainder of the Battery
which was a difficult task. I had to climb the house of the gate keeper
at a level crossing and sit aside the gable of the roof before I could
be seen by the other signallers. After an elapse of about 20 minutes,
[we] received a message from the Battery for the section to 'limber
up and prepare to advance at any moment'. I repeated this order to
Lieutenant Palmer, who thought they must be mad, but carried the
order out when the signal was given, to move forward with the 16th
Lancers to get round the German right flank. The two guns were
halted in rear of the village. I had to assist Lieutenant Palmer to select
a position, [leaving] our horses in rear of a large house with his horse
holder. I cut down a wire fence in a few places so as to make it easy
to get away, should he decide to move that way. We were spotted by
German artillery which sent two ranging rounds at us. One fell at
our heels as we managed to just get clear at the corner of the wall
surrounding the house. We then went back to the rear of the house
and saw the colonel in charge of the cavalry. Lieutenant Palmer was
observing the fire of the German artillery which was sweeping the
fields thinking they were scattered with our infantry. No such luck for
them – another waste of ammunition. I went back to my horse and as
shells began to fall near the house found cover on the bank of a ditch
near the wall. Lieutenant Palmer told the colonel he would bring
his guns into action at the top of the village, left me to bring orders
should there be any. He did not stay in action long before the German
artillery sent a very heavy fire at the guns so they had to retire to the
rear of the village as it was impossible to stay in action.

The position we were in was getting too hot so the colonel in charge
of the cavalry decided to move. Before doing so he said 'You men, get
on your horses and go for all you're worth to the rear of the village, you

are in the hottest corner you can ever possibly be in. Don't go together, but about 25 yards distance. Good luck to you, off you go.'

Having received these orders I soon made myself scarce. A heavy fire soon followed us but fell short. I hadn't gone far before a five-strand wire fence was in front of me. Didn't like the idea of my horse jumping it owing to it being a difficult obstacle at the best of times. I decided to stand the consequences and made for a gateway 150 yards along, fully exposed, making a good target. Either my horse was too fast or the Germans too slow, but I got safely back to Lieutenant Palmer and the guns.

The right and left sections went into action in the open near Angres and, being completely missed by the fire of the German artillery, did great execution against an infantry advance. After a time the left section under Lieutenant Walwyn was moved to the left to cover a valley and some dead ground on our left, firing with great effect, completely checking for a time a strong infantry advance up the valley. The right section under Lieutenant Maxwell was then moved still more to our left doing some good work against cavalry and infantry. The two sections between them fired 350 rounds with good effect. The whole battery was then withdrawn at 6pm and bivouacked at Wagnies le Grand after a very heavy day.

The small rearguard had succeeded in checking the advance of a force six times larger than itself. Losses were, however, high. The Norfolks lost over 200 men. The order to retire did not reach the Cheshires at all, although it was sent to them three times. They continued to hold their ground until they were completely surrounded and had exhausted their supplies of ammunition. Only 200 men from the battalion strength of over 1,000 would make it back to their own lines that evening. An even more powerful blow might have been landed on the German Fourth Corps if it had been possible to concentrate the firepower of the 3rd and the 5th Division artillery. As it was, four artillery brigades did not fire a single shot between them, even though they were within a few miles of the action at Elouges. Poor communication was the critical factor in this failure to muster the maximum strength of the divisional artillery.

The 80th Battery, 15th Brigade, RFA, came into action to support the 2nd Battalion, King's Own Yorkshire Light Infantry, to the west of the village of Wasmes. The 37th (Howitzer) Battery of the 8th Brigade RFA was also level with the infantry. Rory Macleod described what happened:

The KOYLI were holding a slag heap about 2,000 yards to the north of us. We could tell our troops by their round flat-topped caps which appeared white in the sunlight. We could see the KOYLIs firing at something beyond them and German shells were bursting among them with a greenish smoke. Nearer was another slag heap with a high conical mound on which was one of our machine guns. We couldn't see much beyond the KOYLIs but they were obviously in the front line and hotly engaged so we opened fire beyond them at a range of 2,400 yards. One of our howitzer batteries was also assisting the KOYLI by dropping shells beyond the slag heap. We had been firing a few minutes when the Germans replied, but most of their shells fell twenty to thirty yards to our left in an open field. Soon after this the KOYLI began retiring by small detachments at a time and they finally took up position along a bank about 1,000 yards away. We kept up our shelling but no Germans appeared to follow up the retirement.

A motorcyclist now appeared but would not come up to the guns because he said he did not like the sound of the guns firing. I think he must have been a university man who had joined up at the beginning of the war. I went back to him and he gave me a signal ordering me to retire. I quickly limbered up and trotted out by a lane which led round a copse in our rear as the main street was still being heavily shelled. We had to cross about fifty yards of open ground which we did at a trot, and although in full view, not a shot was fired at us.

The retirement continued the following day. The First and Second Corps began to drift apart as they followed separate routes to the south. The plan was for the two corps to take up a position around Le Cateau and fight the enemy here. By the evening of the 25th, however, the two formations would be about 9 miles apart – a gap that would once again threaten the ability of the BEF to withstand the German onslaught. Haig's First Corps had to go the long way south, around the eastern edge of the Foret de Mormal on roads crowded with French refugees and French troops also making their way back. They made slow progress. Given the circumstances, there was little prospect of the two corps joining hands at Le Cateau.

On 25 August there were a few minor clashes between the British and German forces. The First Corps had minimal contact with the enemy. There was a short, sharp action at Landrecies when the 3rd Battalion, Coldstream Guards, was ambushed by the advanced guard of the German Fourth Corps.

Sporadic and confused fighting continued until midnight, when a howitzer of 60th Battery, 44th Brigade, RFA, was brought up by hand and quickly silenced the German field guns. The howitzer was commanded by a young lieutenant, Harold Willcocks. In a letter written to his parents on 29 August, he recounted the whole episode:

> I was sent off in the middle of the night to support some infantry who were being pressed in Landrecies. I came up the street in a perfect hail of bullets with shells bursting overhead. No one was touched and I got into action. I first set a house on fire with Lyddite in the enemy's position and laid onto the flash of their gun which I could just see. Popped a shell right on top of one that was bothering the infantry and I heard later had turned him over in the ditch. Later on I took the gun right up to an advanced post of the infantry and came into action in the open, just behind them; went on firing until the German fire stopped altogether.

Francis Miller was serving with the 17th Battery, 41st Brigade, RFA, attached to the 2nd Division at Landrecies:

> [We] marched to Landrecies. We had just got the horse lines down and taken the harness off the horses, a little grooming while a little refreshment was got ready. I had not had a shave for a week and was just preparing when I heard two civilians yelling out 'Allemands!' A little excitement prevailed. We had been surprised by a German flying column – they came on our flank in motor lorries …

Confusion reigned everywhere during these first days of retreat from Mons. Lieutenant Colonel Wilkinson, commanding the 35th (Heavy) Battery, recalled the night of the attack at Landrecies:

> Everyone was by this time in a horrid state of nerves and uncertainty – we knew the enemy was pressing closely on us and we had lost touch with our own troops. It had a comic side, however, and the left section of the Battery never lost the opportunity of chaffing the right section for firing round after round into an empty wood at close range. The night which followed [24/25th] was simply horrible. To start with we found a civilian lurking about the wood and in our horse lines – he was undoubtedly a spy so we tied him up.

About midnight the most appalling noise began – the fierce rattle of musketry and the crash of artillery and the whole sky lit up with flashes and the glare of burning houses. This was the German attack on 4th Guards Brigade at Landrecies. We knew nothing of what was going on …

On the line of retreat of the Second Corps, a stray shot from a gun of the 61st Battery caught a platoon of German infantry crossing a viaduct, causing very heavy loss of life, but on the whole the 5th Division was not disturbed on its journey down the Roman road to the west of the Foret de Mormal. The 3rd Division was lucky to avoid a very difficult day as it was by now on the western flank of the retreat and thus directly in the path of the German First Army. The Germans were not, however, pressing home their attacks with any great vigour.

In the meantime much-needed reinforcements in the form of the 4th Division had arrived from England. The divisional artillery (14th, 29th, 32nd and 37th (Howitzer) Brigades RFA) had taken up positions around the village of Ligny on the western flank of the Le Cateau position. The divisional heavies (31st (Heavy) Battery RGA) and the ammunition column were still en route to join the rest of the division.

During the evening of the 25th Field Marshal French had decided that rather than stand and fight again at Le Cateau, the BEF would in fact continue its retreat on the 26th, this time by a further 15 miles to the south-west. This would allow the BEF to keep in step with the retiring French armies. Orders were issued to both corps to this effect. The situation facing the BEF was, however, much more menacing than French had appreciated. The Germans were closing in, and a considerable force was gathering on the BEF's right flank. The Cavalry Division, which was supposed to be providing flank protection to the Second Corps, had instead become widely scattered around the battlefield, and as a consequence was completely unable to act as a rearguard in the way French had intended. Continuing the retreat under these circumstances ran the risk of the BEF being caught in the rear without any effective means of defence. This danger had already been increased by the fact that many of the units of the 3rd and 5th Divisions had been held up during the night and were in no position to begin the next phase of the retreat at the allotted time of 7am. By that time the Germans would be upon them and a rout seemed highly likely.

Against this dynamic background, in the early hours of the morning of 26 August General Smith Dorrien made one of the most significant command decisions of the war. Resolving to postpone the retreat, instead he decided to stand and fight on the line Second Corps presently occupied. In doing so he had to ignore the orders he had received from GHQ. The idea was to land a stopping blow on the Germans that would enable his battered force to make good its escape later in the day. It was an unconventional tactic that pre-war training had never envisaged being attempted by an army in the field. Le Cateau would become the first major artillery battle of the war – a duel fought by the British against overwhelmingly superior forces. The notion of a 'duel' in these circumstances was more than mere metaphor – it accurately describes the way in which the opposing forces would line up against each other. By and large the British guns were sited in the open and engaged German targets at very short range. The first great artillery battle of the new century was therefore largely a rather Napoleonic affair. The gunners of Waterloo would have been in their element at Le Cateau.

Chapter 5

Le Cateau – the Stopping Blow

'The Germans kept moving forward, forward, until they were actually shooting at us with their rifles.'

Second Lieutenant Hodgson, 122nd Battery RFA

The British line at Le Cateau can best be described as taking the shape of an inverted 'L'. The 5th Division was on the right around Le Cateau, covering the town itself and the approaches to it from the south, and then stretched for a couple of miles along the Roman road leading to Cambrai. The 3rd Division held the centre of the line from Troisvilles to Caudry. The 4th Division held the left flank from Caudry to Esnes. In all the line was about 13 miles in length. Unlike at Mons, here at least there was good all-round visibility. The guns this time would have plenty of opportunity to engage the enemy troops approaching across the gentle, undulating hills. It would not, however, be plain sailing for the artillery. The order to stand and fight did not reach some units until the battle had started, causing confusion about tactics and targets as well as disrupted logistics. There was also little time to reconnoitre the ground properly. Many batteries took up extremely exposed positions, particularly on the vulnerable right flank, on the mistaken assumption that the First Corps was in close proximity to the east and would be able therefore to cover the flank. This was not the case. The First Corps was already retiring and would provide no help to Smith Dorrien's forces. The gunners were also working under the assumption that this was going to be a fight to the finish. Many batteries were dug in right alongside the infantry in the front line.

On the right flank the guns of the 11th, 80th, 37th and 52nd Batteries of the 15th Brigade RFA took up what would prove to be an extremely dangerous and exposed position in open fields behind Le Cateau itself, under clear observation from high ground to the north-east. They did so to provide the maximum possible support to the infantry front line a few hundred yards in front of them. Just after 6am the German artillery opened up on them as the prelude to a massive infantry assault.

Rory Macleod was with his section of 80th Battery on the exposed right flank of the line:

> We came into action in a turnip field in front of a field of standing corn and one hundred yards behind the crest of a low ridge. The ridge dipped in front of 37th Battery and 11th Battery on our right was on slightly higher ground so we seemed to be the best off for concealment. Captain Bartholemew, the staff captain, rode along the position and told us there was going to be a big battle and there would be no retreat.

Captain Bartholemew was relaying this news to all the 5th Division guns. To Macleod's left the guns of the 28th Brigade were in position alongside the Roman road running from Le Cateau to Reumont. Second Lieutenant Clarrie Hodgson was serving with the 122nd Battery:

> He [Bartholemew] came, dismounted and stood up on one of the limbers and looked out over all the chaps who'd gathered round and told us what the situation was. He said that it was very, very serious and he was depending on us. He left us in no doubt as to what we were expected to do when we went into action. He said it was up to us, that we'd done well and he knew we'd do well again and wouldn't let him down.
>
> I felt terribly elated. I was terribly young and quite inexperienced and I felt that this was something really exciting, that something was really going to happen in my life. I wasn't scared or apprehensive at all. Oddly enough, I thought more about my brother – my twin brother Victor. He was in 124th Battery and I hadn't seen him at all though their battery position wasn't far away from us.

The 15th Brigade opened fire soon after 6am. Rory Macleod provided a full account of the ensuing action:

> We opened fire about 6am and registered a few targets including the railway embankment. When the mist lifted we saw that the high ground on the opposite side of the valley beyond the embankment was crowded with Germans. We opened on them with battery fire 20 seconds at 4,000

yards gradually reducing the range as the Germans advanced and for two hours we kept up 'battery fire 5 seconds' at a range of 2,400 yards on the line of the embankment they were trying to cross. They suffered severely.

The German artillery soon opened frontally on the trench in front of us. The fire became hotter and hotter and several 'overs' fell among our batteries. One of our first casualties was Lieutenant Coghlan of the 11th Battery on our right. He was killed and I saw his body being taken to the rear on a stretcher to the back of our position to a sunken lane. We continued to fire at the German infantry. Some of them came within rifle fire of our infantry and were wiped out.

More and more German batteries came into action, a big concentration of them [at] Rambourlieux farm which was now visible on our left flank and from there they could enfilade our position. A German aeroplane came overhead about 9am and started dropping stuff like streamers of silver paper over our trenches. Whenever he did this the German guns opened up on the spot he was flying over. He came over our Brigade and did the same. A ranging round fell near the 11th Battery from a German battery enfilading from the left. Salvoes then began to fall on the 11th Battery and their casualties started mounting up. We could hear them calling for stretchers and many shells also fell on the 37th Battery on our left knocking out some guns and detachments. We, behind our low ridge, were more fortunate and only had comparably few shells on the position.

Driver Job Drain was serving with the 37th Battery at Le Cateau on 26 August:

There was little cover or hiding place and when the battle began there were 18-pounder batteries on either side with a siege battery to the rear. Terrible shells came over in sixes and were bursting all over the place and over the tops of our guns and wagon lines with plenty of bullets flying about. Man after man was becoming wounded and horses were being killed and batteries were being smashed to pieces. I just don't think there was a man on the field who did not say his prayers for a general retirement to be ordered …

As the hours went by, the British position on the right rapidly deteriorated as overwhelming numbers of enemy infantry pushed forward under heavy supporting artillery fire. Pressure was also mounting on the 28th Brigade on Macleod's left. Lieutenant Hodgson, based with the signallers in a small foxhole just behind the guns, described the scene as the fighting wore on:

I noticed that our two flank batteries [123 and 124] had swung back and were pointing at right angles to the original line of fire so that the whole regiment formed an open square just like the Napoleonic wars! This indicated, even to a rookie like myself, that things were not going too well – and subsequent events proved that this was putting it mildly!

By then we'd had about half a dozen guns knocked out and a lot of casualties in the gun crews. Then there was a lull but still we were getting casualties. We couldn't understand it. We were still firing of course but there wasn't much coming back and yet men suddenly dropped dead at the guns. Then we realised what was happening. We couldn't see into Le Cateau itself from where we were but we could see the spire of the church through a slight dip between the high ground in front and the high ground on our right. It suddenly struck us that there was a machine gunner in the church tower. So we ranged on the spire, put a few shells on it and put him out of action pretty quickly.

But it gave us a nasty turn because it was only then that we realised that the Germans had occupied Le Cateau – and it was only a matter of a few hundred yards away.

Lieutenant Lionel Lutyens was serving with the 122nd Battery of the 28th Brigade and provided a vivid account of the intensity of the battle:

One of my No. 6 detachment was shot dead with a rifle bullet in the first half hour and there were a good many whizzing about. Quite a number lodged in the little bank in front of my pit and I could hear them zipping all the time I was passing orders.

I suppose the Germans started shelling us at about 9am and it went on consistently, shrapnel and high explosive. My own Battery was very fortunate indeed. We were just under cover and the enemy couldn't see us …

Lutyens described what happened to the 123rd and 124th Batteries:

The other two batteries suffered terribly. They were practically bang in the open and had a lot of men killed and wounded, limbers set on fire and guns knocked about… . they had a really awful time. Miller told me their gun shields were a mass of silver where they were riddled with bullets and several guns received direct hits.

Macleod's battery had also swung some of its guns around to face the attacking infantry swarming forward on its left and began firing practically over each other at targets less than a mile away. Macleod himself was seriously wounded by shell fire in the head and arms, and took shelter in the shallow trenches the gunners had prepared behind the guns.

All along the British line the heavy fire of the German artillery was concentrated on finding and destroying the British guns. Major William Strong, commanding the 128th (Howitzer) Battery of the 30th Brigade RFA, had arrived with his guns at about 5am and had taken up position just in front of the railway line behind the village of Caudry, on the left centre of the British line: 'We were tremendously shelled, but little harm done. My haystack in which I climbed to observe was the object of much attention …'

In the centre of the British line, around the village of Audencourt, the guns of the 6th Battery of the 60th Brigade RFA were providing fire support to the troops of both the 3rd and 4th Divisions. Sergeant Albert George, serving with the 120th Battery near Troisvilles, had a bird's-eye view of the action on this section of the front line:

We woke at dawn eager for the fray and by 9am we were in action with our Brigade but our shells were falling short so our Captain received orders to pick up a new position. At 1pm we started for our new position about two miles away and while we were advancing shells and rifle bullets whizzed all around us but our Captain said 'Follow me, men' and we couldn't refuse. We got into action with the 3rd and 4th Divisions about 1.30pm just as the Huns were getting the range of the 6th Battery, several shells hitting the guns and wagons and killing most of the gunners. We found that for about two miles to our right and left was British artillery and we knew then it would be an artillery duel. Every gun of our army was firing as fast as possible and by reports we did awful damage but the German guns were 10 to 1 so you can imagine which had the best chance. All our gunners stuck to it as long as possible but we were being gradually beaten by force and numbers.

Commanding another section of the guns of the 120th Battery to the right of Sergeant Reeve was Second Lieutenant Robert Thornhagh-Foljambe. He confirmed the harsh predicament the Battery found itself in:

> ... told to take up position to draw fire from 6th Battery which was being heavily shelled. Came into action but found we could not clear the crest (ahead of us). Ran the guns up by hand. Opened fire and after some trouble with trees in front got effective fire onto edge of wood occupied by Germans. Fired 550 rounds in two hours from our four guns with considerable effect. A hail of bullets flying just overhead and heavy shelling by some small howitzer firing high explosive. Their shells landed left and right, twenty yards in front and behind but never hit us. The 6th Battery close on our left were knocked out and lost all their guns and many horses in the wagon line a few hundred yards in rear.

The guns of the 108th Battery were dug in just behind the village of Inchy, in positions on the forward slope of a hill covering the ground to the west of the village. Their experience of the battle was very different. Lieutenant Eric Anderson was in command of one of the battery's sections:

> About 6.30am our guns opened fire at enemy infantry in the distance, just to slow them up a bit. About 9am firing from guns behind us became fairly continuous. They did really very pretty shooting against infantry trying to get into Inchy and also against a long belt of trees round our left flank, range about 2,500 yards. [The enemy] had not spotted any of our guns but were plastering where they thought the guns ought to be. They did not do much damage.
>
> Our role was close defence so we had to remain quiet and not give ourselves away until the infantry became dangerous. Consequently there was nothing to do but sit still and listen to the shells whizzing overhead, eat some bully and biscuit and sleep.
>
> The men treated the whole thing as a joke and were only too glad of the opportunity for a little much-needed rest. I was rather surprised at the cheery way they behaved, trusting as we did to the turnip tops for our protection. These we had planted very carefully on every newly turned patch of soil and on the wagons and gun shields. It was only by artful hiding in this way that we could hope to be of any use at

the critical moment because to be discovered prematurely meant to be knocked out before the moment arrived …

The men trying to supply the guns also had a grim time under this crushing weight of German artillery fire. Sergeant George described the violence they endured in their efforts to keep the guns firing:

> We could see the ammunition wagons trying to replenish getting about half way to the gun then a couple of shells would burst blowing the drivers and horses to smithereens, it was a terrible sight but the last two days had made us used to it. At about 3.30pm the Germans were advancing upon us so rapidly that the General Staff could see it was useless trying to stop the furious advance so a general retirement was ordered and it was every man for himself.

In the early afternoon Lieutenant Brownlow, serving with the 40th Brigade Ammunition Column, described his impression of the battlefield at this critical time:

> I was standing on the northern edge of Bertry. To my front lay the open Caudry ridge which showed the dark line of trees along the Cambrai road. I could see our batteries strung out in an irregular line and all were in action firing hard. Shrapnel flecked the whole landscape and in the village of Audencourt heavy high explosive shell was bursting on percussion among the houses. But the din of battle was dominated by the throb of noise from our right flank. We all looked instinctively in the direction of Le Cateau where the Montay spur was overhung by a bank of white and yellow smoke punctuated by angry flashes.

At around this time Macleod and his comrades were forced to abandon their position before the guns were overrun:

> About 2.30pm I saw all the brigade teams racing up at a gallop from the wagon lines led by Major Tailyour, the Brigade Major and ours by Captain Higgon. Shells were bursting all round them. It was a magnificent sight. Now and again a man or horse or whole team would go down from the fire directed on them. Balaclava over again! My No. 6 gun team had only a pair of wheelers left and No. 5 gun team

a leader, a centre and two wheelers. Major Tailyour helped to limber up No. 6 gun before going to the OP where he was captured. I helped to limber up No. 5 gun. There was no centre driver so, assisted by a gunner, I mounted the centre horse and we galloped out of action. Luckily the German fire was not now so intense, so there were few casualties going out of action and we got five guns away. Our No. 1 team was destroyed so the gun had to be left but the breech block was removed.

We entered Reumont village and I dismounted at a dressing station set up in a convent with a large red cross flag outside. Here I sat down, and my revolver [was] removed and put outside as no arms were allowed in the dressing station. I was given a cup of Bovril and a doctor probed the wound in my head and the hole through my arm and clean dressings were put on. Nuns came round and gave us cigarettes but I could not smoke. 'Cully' Buckle came in soon after and was put in a bed close to me. He had a bad wound in the back. On taking off my breeches I found that a bullet had gone through them and had grazed my leg. Perhaps it was when I was mounting to drive out of action.

Macleod would face a moment of decision later that afternoon:

About 4pm, a very tired Lieutenant Colonel of the RAMC came into the ward and called out that all who could walk must leave immediately as the Germans were expected to enter the village at any moment. I never felt less like walking in my life, but an infantry officer in the bed next door to me whose arm had been broken by a bullet said that he intended to go and persuaded me to make the attempt too. I said that I did not propose to leave unless Cully Buckle left too. He couldn't walk but an RAMC officer said that he would very soon be carried out on a stretcher and put in a horse ambulance which was at the door of the dressing station. As I left the building I saw it, but I never saw Buckle again and he shortly afterwards died in German hands. Shells were now falling round the building and in the streets outside …

Macleod made it back to England and in the new year would be back at the front again.

Second Lieutenant Hodgson, in the 122nd Battery just to the left of Macleod, suffered an equally violent time in extracting his guns:

The Germans kept moving forward, forward, until they were actually shooting at us with their rifles. Then the order came down – 'Save the guns.' And the gun teams came dashing down over the hill right through the middle of this carnage. The Hun opened up on them – artillery, machine guns, rifles, everything! The horses were silhouetted against the skyline and they made a perfect target. It was absolute slaughter. Men and horses were just blown to pieces. One team of four horses and a limber managed to reach one of the guns, limber up and drag it over the high ground behind us. Our colonel, adjutant and two battery commanders had been killed and many of the men and the place was a shambles. Then, to our intense relief, down came the order – 'Every man for himself. Destroy the guns.'

Lionel Lutyens added:

Our own bad time did not come till nearly three o'clock. I was sitting in my pit wondering how long it would go on and when we would get a shell right into us when I heard the pop-pop-pop-pop-pop of a machine gun and a perfect hail of bullets started coming over. The Germans had pushed a machine gun or a couple, up onto the knoll – 5–600 yards to our right front – and had turned straight onto the Battery.

   We couldn't save the guns now so I got what gunners I could on the limber and sent it away. When the limber was gone I ran to my horse. My groom had been standing waiting all the while with my two horses on the bank behind. Peel [Lutyen's groom] came galloping past as I tried to get on. I was so trembling with excitement and funk by now that I couldn't get my foot in the stirrup. I ran backwards trying to reach it and expecting Bronco [the horse] to be shot at any moment. However, he was not and I got up and let him go down the road as hard as he could gallop …

The achievement of getting the guns of the 37th (Howitzer) Battery away under the very noses of the advancing German infantry would see three Victoria Crosses won on 26 August. Unable to remove all the guns of the battery simultaneously, the men had initially withdrawn to Reumont, leaving two of the howitzers on the battlefield. Having discovered two horse teams at Reumont, Captain Douglas Reynolds asked for volunteers to help him return and rescue the guns. Two young subalterns, Lieutenants Earle and

Morgan, together with Drivers Cobey, Luke and Drain formed one of the volunteer teams. They galloped up to the guns under a hail of rifle fire and shrapnel and within 100 yards of the approaching German infantry hooked up the guns and began to make good their dramatic escape. Driver Cobey was almost immediately shot dead on his horse but the gun was saved. The other team, under Lieutenant Earle, failed to extricate the remaining howitzer. The horses were shot and killed and the gun had to be abandoned. For their heroism that day, Captain Reynolds, Driver Job Drain and Driver Fred Luke were awarded the Victoria Cross. Lieutenant Earle received the DSO, and other members of the rescue team received the DCM.

The 28th Brigade RFA would lose sixteen of their eighteen guns on the battlefield of Le Cateau.

Second Lieutenant Hodgson remembers the rush to get away from the forward positions now that the Germans were almost within shouting range of the guns:

Everybody was running the same way – everyone who was left! We'd just got to the crest when Gunner Major tripped and fell forward flat on his face. At least I thought he'd tripped and I went back to help him up. Poor chap. There was blood coming out of his back. He'd been hit by a sniper's bullet and killed outright. There was nothing I could do but grab the breech and run on over the hilltop towards Reumont with the rest of them. Just over the other side on the left of the road there was a farmhouse and of course it had the usual cess-pit in the courtyard. So I heaved the breech into the middle of this foul-smelling muck and I remember thinking 'Right – no ruddy Hun will ever find that one anyway!'

Over on the left flank the guns of the 4th Division were trying to fend off an enemy encircling movement. Gunner Walter Harrison was in action with the guns of the 27th Battery, 32nd Brigade, RFA, near the village of Ligny:

In the village of Ligny where we halted by the roadside … everybody was shouting 'the Bosch are here'. They were just outside the village. We retired through the village, turned to the right and came into action in an open field. [We waited] half an hour and received the order to open fire at one thousand yards range over open sights on a German battery at about 800 yards. [We] finished that battery off. Smashed them right up. We increased the range to 2,400 yards. Here we fired all our shells. Whether we hit what we wanted I cannot say as we were firing with the dial sights at an invisible target. All this time we were getting shelled; the shells came in to us like rain from the clouds …

General Snow, commanding the 4th Division, witnessed this heavy fire directed at the guns around Caullery, just to the south of Ligny:

I was watching one of our Batteries near Caullery. It was under fire from about 12 guns. The enemy was firing salvoes and each salvo looked as if it must have annihilated our Battery. Directly, however, the last shell of the salvo burst, bang! bang! bang! bang! bang! went the guns of the Battery and you could see lanes being driven through the dense masses advancing on Ligny. Nothing could shake the defence of Ligny whose garrison mowed down the attacking Germans literally in thousands …

Once the right flank began to give way, the left and centre had no choice but to fall back. The main purpose of the action – delaying the German advance – had been achieved. But getting the guns out would be just as hard for the gunners of the 4th Division as it was for those of the 5th. Walter Harrisson of the 27th Battery, 32nd Brigade, RFA, described the desperate measures taken to save the guns from being captured by the remorseless advance of the German infantry. The guns of Walter's battery had been temporarily abandoned under the weight of shell fire and after all the available ammunition had been expended. The detachments remained close at hand, under cover and awaiting instructions:

We ceased fire about 1pm. We had to leave the guns to their fate as it was death to stop there. The Colonel [M.J. MacCarthy] called the remaining gunners together and asked for volunteers [to rescue the guns]. Six of us gunners and two sergeants volunteered to save the guns … it was awful. Two gunners killed crawling up to get near them. It was here that I got my first slight wound. We ran [the guns] down the road on an incline. Put what teams that were left in and galloped away getting shelled all the way … This day I will never forget as long as I live.

Two of the guns had to be left on the field. Walter won the Distinguished Conduct Medal for his actions at Ligny on 26 August.

Harry Sprotson of the 68th Battery, 14th Brigade, RFA, was in action all day further to the west of the 32nd Brigade RFA, on the extreme left flank of the 4th Division. The battery had moved at 7am to take up a position just to the west of Haucourt village, where it came into action to support the infantry of the 12th Brigade defending the British line around Esnes:

> … we soon got into action, Germans only 1,600 yards away and as they came over the hills in front in their thousands our guns seem to mow them down. Still they seem to come and we are forced to retire to another position [near St Aubert Farm]. This we hold for about 6 hours until one of their aeroplanes discovers us and then we are forced to retire again as they are closing upon us. Our horses seem to have been the worst sufferers, for we lost about fifty … Passing through the village [almost certainly Selvigny] we see some of the destruction done by their artillery – wagons blown to bits and horses and men lying on the sides of the road dead.

At Inchy the orders to retire reached the gunners at about 3.30pm. Eric Anderson, with the 108th Battery, recalled what happened as his gunners tried to extricate themselves from their advanced positions:

> At 3.30pm the adjutant shouted for me and on going to him he told me a general retirement had been ordered. I was to cover the retirement of the infantry to my front. I was to wait until the last man had gone then leave the guns and clear out.
>
> We loosed off for all we were worth at the fringe of the village which was fairly strongly held and the return fire fell like anything. When the last line of infantry [1st Battalion, Lincolnshire Regiment] came past me, I ordered the guns to be dismantled. One gun had exhausted its ammunition and the other one was badly jammed. A Captain of the Lincolns had halted about 50 men in line with the guns and wanted to stay and fight it out. I told him the situation and what my orders had been and he agreed there was nothing to be done. So we very sadly collected all the kit we could carry and the mechanisms and the spares of the guns and then bolted for the hill top …

The Second Corps had succeeded in delaying the German advance long enough to allow the BEF to continue its retreat to the south. Thirty-six guns were lost at Le Cateau – the inevitable consequence of deploying the guns so close to the firing line. There was no doubt that their presence provided enormous moral support to the infantry, but the price was very high, and in many cases the firepower needed to repel attacks was reduced to a minimum at critical moments of the fighting. The artillery should have been distributed in greater depth. This was one of the early lessons of the campaign.

And the casualties had been high. Nearly 8,000 British soldiers were either dead, wounded or missing in action; many of these would become prisoners of war. Amongst those captured that day was young Gunner Alfred Gilbert of the 80th Battery. He had been sent to the church in Le Cateau to act as a signaller to the battery. He was captured early in the battle after receiving a flesh wound in the side and another in his right foot, together with a broken elbow. He remained at Le Cateau until November, when he was transported to a POW camp to Salzwadel in Germany; here he would sit out the rest of the war.

Major Eustace Jones, commanding the 37th Battery, 8th (Howitzer) Brigade, RFA, was wounded by shell fire at about 7am while at the brigade observation post on the exposed right flank of the British line at Le Cateau. A shell splinter entered his back close to the spine:

Our line was enfiladed, fired into from the rear and overpowered from the front. [Regarding my treatment] there was nothing to take exception to. A German officer gave me his water bottle full of coffee as he passed. Our party, the extreme right of the line, was marched to Le Cateau town after disarming and taking of field glasses. No other private property was taken to my knowledge. In the town of Le Cateau we stopped at a small German dressing station where very rough and ready dressings were applied to our wounded. Officers and men were now separated, officers going after some delay to the house of M. Seydown, a rich silk merchant. We were permitted to write postcards home by a German officer whom we met in the street. I believe that many weeks after some of these reached their destinations.

Major Birley, commanding the beleaguered 80th Battery, was also taken prisoner at Le Cateau and would spend over a year in captivity in Germany before being invalided to Switzerland, from where he would eventually make it back to England:

I was wounded sufficiently late in the afternoon to be left in the church at Reumont near by, after the ambulances had finally retired. I was wounded in the leg, shoulder and chest, all on the left side, and lay on a stretcher unable to move. The church, with over 150 in it, was captured by the Germans some hours later. We were left in medical charge of our own officers – Major Brunskill, Captain Kelly and another whose name I do not know. I should like to pay a tribute to the work of those RAMC officers. They had to conciliate the Germans, get food for the nearly 200 wounded in the church, to search the battlefield for men lying out and make arrangements for burying the dead. They then had to dress the wounds of the living as best they could in the dim light of the church. They appeared to be tireless. This lasted nearly three days.

But a breathing space had been secured. The Second Corps had succeeded in landing a heavy blow on the advancing German forces and the retreat would continue more or less undisturbed for the next fourteen days. The troops often moved during the night to avoid being spotted by German aircraft. The men were tired, confused and hungry. It would be a gruelling time, testing the men to the limits of their physical and mental endurance.

On 27 August Arthur Wilkinson, commanding the 35th (Heavy) Battery, remembered that the

weather had improved and was fine and hot. At 3pm we bivouacked … by this time our men and horses were thoroughly fagged out and I had to fall in the men and give them a serious lecture about keeping their end up… . the officers had a very hard time of it trying to get things done. At 6pm we received orders to take up a position of readiness as the enemy's cavalry was reported close at hand. The orders were very vague and the direction of attack uncertain. We came into action in a beetroot field and after much arduous labour got our guns into position about midnight. The men were so done that they practically refused to work and to make matters worse there was a dense fog. One of our wagons went right over one of the men who was asleep under a corn stack and he took no further interest in the operations. All our labours were in vain as nothing happened. The day's march was about 15 miles.

Major William Strong, commanding the 128th Battery RFA, recalled his own sheer exhaustion, even at the beginning of this long retreat: 'August

28th. Went into bivouac at 8pm. Lay down on some hay and had 8 hours real sleep – having been on the go continuously without lying down for 66 hours …'

The experiences of Captain Mackie of the 30th Brigade Ammunition Column, recounted in his diary on 30 August, were typical of many during those long wearisome days of retreat:

Had my first shave for 5 days by the village barber. Will stay here until I hear something definite. Every staff officer contradicts the one I asked before! No one seems to know anything. Horribly hot and I haven't been out of my clothes for over a week – result rather horrible and smelly. They have forced us back further than was expected. I wish that we could collect ourselves and start advancing. The infantry are dead beat. They have had an awful time, poor fellows and many regiments have suffered heavily: still it is early, the real fighting has hardly begun …

Similar sentiments were expressed by Gunner Walter Harrison of the 27th Battery on 29 August: 'The retiring was playing on us… . no rest, men falling off their horses asleep simply dropping down, feet cut to pieces, the infantry all but asleep as they march. We hung on – retiring and fighting. Would it never end?'

For Albert Reeve of the 16th Battery the frustrations of the retreat were more humdrum. On 30 August he wrote:

March, march, march all the blessed day. Halt. Dismount. Mount. Then dismount. Halted long enough to get the water for tea all but boiling and then of course we got the order to shift! The irony of the thing was that after going half a mile we halted for an hour at a spot where we couldn't make tea …

Gunner Crowsley, with E Battery RHA, felt much the same. On 27 August his diary entry recorded: 'All ranks very much depressed owing not only to the fact of us continually retiring but at the total absence of any information, we appeared to be blindly driven back.'

For Edward Schrieber, with the 115th Battery, the retreat was characterised by an overwhelming desire to sleep:

By day we marched along apparently interminable straight roads under a boiling sun. Our main care was to keep the horses going. If the halting place did not supply [water or corn] every man except one at the heads of the lead horses threw himself down and slept. We officers, with the exception of the Orderly Officer, did likewise. To wake after 8 minutes of such sleep was most trying. One longed to sleep on and one woke up wringing wet with sweat.

Often the marches extended into the night. Then indeed it was difficult to keep awake. If one walked, one staggered along the road practically asleep: mounted, one slept in the saddle and woke oneself up by nearly falling off.

A few days later, with speculation rife amongst his comrades, Crowsley had developed a deep fear that calamity had struck the BEF:

We know that we are marching towards Paris, owing to the retirement of the whole army and we heard such rumours as the French Government had been shifted to Bordeaux, our base had been shifted to Nantes – which all seemed to point towards disaster. We were occasionally told that we were going back some distance to rest or to the base to be refitted but the way we were brought out of villages at the dead of night with such a rush, we all knew the Germans were too close to let us rest. Horses were suffering from improper rations, want of grooming, continual marching, sore backs and withers, galls, leg weary etc, men too, riding fast asleep in their saddles.

The physical suffering was not confined to the men. Horses are also sentient animals. Their tribulations during this long retreat were pitiable to behold. But they also had an instinct for survival, as Gunner Crowsley recounted when his battery came under enemy shell fire: 'To say a dumb animal has no sense is all rot, as my horse, quite on its own, got down in the ditch (which was not above a foot deep) and then on to the bank where I was sitting and crouched under the wall for shelter.'

For Sergeant Francis Miller, serving with the 17th Battery, 41st Brigade, RFA, the retreat would involve him and his mates in some heavy rearguard action, as the guns sought to protect the columns of retreating infantry from attack by the German vanguards. On 1 September, near Compiegne, his battery engaged enemy artillery:

We retired to Villers-Cotterets and came into action near the road. A German battery was reported coming into action, range about 1,950 yards. They had fairly got the drop on us: we started ranging, the first round alright, the second round alright but the German battery then let it rip. The telephone line got broken, we lost communication with headquarters. The fire of the German batteries [was] terrific, one mass of bursting shells above our heads – everybody gave us up. The General himself thought it was all up. We got our guns out of action one at a time. The Battery was exceptionally lucky. We got out of it safely but it was a near thing.

On the same day Albert Reeve's 16th Battery, 41st Brigade, RFA, were also in action at Boursonne:

As we halted behind the rest of the [4th Guards Brigade], the Germans opened heavy fire and we soon felt the bullets flying around. Many infantry shot alongside me. We got under cover in the trees and reversing, managed to get an oblique fire onto the enemy's guns and kept a heavy fire until it was getting dusk. Later I was told we were successful in smashing up 10 out of 12 of the enemy's mortar guns. We ourselves had no casualties.

The 27th Brigade RFA would also see action on 1 September. It had remained intact as a fighting unit during the chaotic conditions of the retreat from Le Cateau and together with the 13th Infantry Brigade was in constant action as rearguard to the 5th Division. Captain Josslyn Ramsden, Adjutant to the 27th Brigade, described in a letter home on 5 October what happened to him and his men on that day:

At about 4am, being again on rearguard with 13 Infantry Brigade, we got ready to march but were ordered to occupy positions at once as a considerable force of Germans were advancing. The Colonel, who seems to have an instinct for placing guns on splendid positions, took me forward with General Cuthbert [commanding the infantry] into the advanced infantry line. We had just stopped to speak to the officer commanding the left section of the infantry line on the Bethancourt–Crepy road, about one and a half miles north of Crepy, when Cuthbert's horse was shot under him, the first shot – then the game began and for an hour we sat where we were until it became evident that the enemy were in some force and surmised they had been sent on in large motors. The Colonel now sent me back for two guns of the 119th Battery which he had left behind a ridge. Earlier in the morning he had put the 121st in the centre and the 120th on the right before we went up to General Cuthbert.

Lieutenant Tennison (119th) brought up a section and we started firing into the Germans at about 1,400 yards over our own infantry about 100 yards in front! I believe we did great execution with these two guns which fired a marvellous lot of ammunition. Anyhow, their fire completely checked the enemy and although we withdrew about noon battery by battery to another position about five miles south, we were never attacked again.

We finished that night in a charming house at Silly Le Long, south of Nanteuil. The owner, a charming woman, was just off with all her servants to Paris. Poor people, how the Germans have looted the houses of absentees!

Organising the retreat of the BEF demanded some inspired staff work. The roads were narrow and congested, and units were all mixed up together. Order had to be restored somehow. This was often achieved by reliance on some very simple methods. Lieutenant Cyril Brownlow of the 40th Brigade Ammunition Column RFA recalled one such technique in the first days of the retreat (28 August):

Just before entering the town of Noyon, the road from Ham forks into two branches. During this afternoon, standing in the angle of the bifurcation was a blackboard on which was chalked in large letters directions as to where the various Divisions, 3rd, 5th and 4th, were to go for billets for the night. I have often thought that this use of a school blackboard to disentangle the retreating troops was, in its way, a little masterpiece of staff work, the outcome of a flash of genius. By no other means would it have been possible to give efficient directions to that moving medley of units from three Divisions. By the side of the blackboard stood a staff officer who looked cheerfully through an eyeglass at the passing streams of men and horses and who was ready to amplify the chalked directions.

The retreat, however well organised, took a physical and mental toll on the men. Later on during the retreat Mac Robertson, with the 70th Battery, 34th Brigade, RFA, recalled the events that took place on one of the baking hot days of the retreat – 2 September – in his diary:

> Orders at 2am to move at once to Betz, which we did. No breakfast. Marched solidly in burning sun, via Vincy, till 3pm. No food or rest. We were all quite dead beat. Got beyond Meaux and bivouacked there. All country deserted. No baggage, no news. This continual marching in hot sun very trying. Got a meal and went to sleep on some straw. What we are doing no one knows.

The day before, 1 September 1914, one of the most famous artillery engagements of the war was fought at Nery. It was of little military significance, but the action at Nery came to typify in the British national psyche the heroism and gallantry of the original BEF. L Battery RFA, attached to the 1st Cavalry Brigade, had bivouacked the previous night in a field to the south of the village and was under orders to be ready to resume the retreat at dawn the next day. Dawn broke with a heavy mist rendering movement impossible. The men settled down for a rudimentary breakfast. Suddenly a patrol from the 11th Hussars came galloping back into the village and warned the gunners of the proximity of strong German forces close by. Almost immediately L Battery came under heavy artillery and machine gun fire from little more than 600 yards away. The village was overlooked to the east by high ground, which had been occupied by the German batteries under the noses of the British picquets.

The German shell fire was accurate and effective. Casualties began to rise, and included Major Sclater-Booth, the battery commander, who was temporarily blinded and put out of action by a shell burst in the main street of the village. Three guns of the battery came into action very quickly and began to return fire. Captain Bradbury, who rallied the battery with the famous cry 'Come on – who's for the guns?', led the teams at the guns, assisted by Lieutenants Giffard, Campbell and Mundy and Sergeant Nelson. The ammunition wagons were some 20 yards to the rear, with the space between the guns and the wagons swept by deadly fire. Gunner Derbyshire and Driver Osborn had the task of keeping the guns supplied with ammunition. One gun was almost immediately put out of action by a direct hit. The other two kept firing in an increasingly unequal struggle.

After only a few rounds had been fired off, one of the remaining two guns was also hit, wounding Giffard and killing or injuring all the others. Captain Bradbury's gun, the only one left in action, appeared to enjoy a charmed life, escaping serious damage and enabling the battery to remain in action, despite the overwhelming force being directed against it. Bradbury was lent support by Battery Sergeant Major Dorrell, who came up to support him. Not only did they keep up a steady rate of fire, but managed to inflict serious damage on the enemy's positions.

Bradbury's solitary gun was now engaged by the firepower of three German batteries, all less than 800 yards away and enjoying a commanding position over the battered remnants of L Battery. Sometime after 7am, L Battery fell silent. Bradbury himself was killed, along with Campbell, while Giffard and Mundy were seriously wounded. Eventually I Battery and infantry reinforcements arrived to drive off the German attack. Many of the German guns were either destroyed or captured. Bradbury, Nelson and Dorrell were all awarded the Victoria Cross for their extraordinary bravery under fire. Theirs was not the only sacrifice. In total, fifty-four men of L Battery became casualties that day.

On 4 September E Battery RFA found itself engaging enemy guns near Le Hayet at Bois de Done. Gunner Crowsley recalled the next few hours of fighting:

We came into action ... and engaged two German batteries that were concealed behind a hill [Dove Hill], behind which stood a church, the Germans were using the belfry as an observation post. This was at a range of 4,600 yards. The Battery was only partly concealed and fired over 150 rounds at the above, searching the ground behind the ridge where the German guns were known to be. Major Horman, who was controlling the Battery, took great care not to touch the church, giving his guns proper deflection when firing right or left of the church. The whole time the Battery was in action both the German batteries were firing at us. The Battery staff were at the observation station which was quite in the open on the right flank, seven in all. I was one of the seven, all the cover we had was a small apple tree, about as much use as a blade of grass. When we were ordered to retire from this position, we did so under a much heavier fire, but strange to say, although they had the range to our guns and the shells were falling within a few yards of them, the Battery retired without a single casualty. Our cavalry patrols reported that we had disabled one of their guns and [we] did considerable damage to their gun and wagon teams.

The retreat carried on day after long hot day. E.J. Cummings with J Battery wrote on the 6th: 'Still retiring. We go into Chaumes which is really a suburb of Paris. We are all to put it mildly "fed up" with retiring and longing to have a rub at the Kultur Models.'

It was a long hard slog that took an increasing toll on men and animals alike. For Gunner Low of the 117th Battery the memory of these long, hot, dusty days would never fade:

That retreat was the only part that shook me up in the whole war and it was because we weren't getting any food and when there are no rations you have to put up with nowt. Oh it was chronic! We had to live on the land, get what we could from the farms.

We were going along this road and we had to stop now and again, because it got jammed up with the military and with civilians with all their little belongings in handcarts. We'd pulled up for something and I dismounted, and I thought my luck was in. I saw a biscuit – one of those hard army biscuits – fallen in the mud at the side of the road and I picked it up and when I looked at it, it was spread with marmalade. Well, that brought me down that did, because I really hated marmalade. But we were hungry! I managed to eat a bit of it, mud, marmalade and all.

Captain Mackie recalled the hardship the horses endured. On Tuesday, 1 September he wrote in his diary: 'Arrived at our bivouac at about 6pm. Had an awful job watering the horses. Water seems very scarce in this vicinity and the poor beasts have long intervals, sometimes all day, between drinks.'

Gunner Crook with J Battery RHA witnessed the desperation that men could be driven to:

Rations were very scarce. It was almost impossible for rations to reach us. We had to resort to looting. Most shops and houses had been evacuated and nearly every French family had a rabbit – so we had a choice of a rabbit in a hutch or a duck on the pond. Our trouble was being able to cook them. We had to form groups. Those that had done the looting had to share with those that had held the horses. We found our horses very useful. Grapes were very plentiful because quite often there were vines growing up the front of houses. Us gunners who rode single horses could ride up to the grapes and just pick a few bunches. For some time we done very well. Then came the sad order 'Looting must stop'. We had a very good officer commanding J Battery. Often if we were staying in a place for a few hours he would find the village baker and order him to bake bread for us.

In a letter home to his brothers Percy and Fred, Lieutenant Austin Bates of the 31st (Howitzer) Battery recalled a moment during the retreat which served to highlight the stress and physical strains experienced by the men:

Firstly, with regard to that retirement for nearly 150 miles. The chief impression I have left is the extraordinary amount of endurance the infantry showed even when some of them were so far gone that they scarcely understood what was said to them. When you take into consideration the fact that these men were ejected from a long train journey straight into a very tough show from which they had to undertake that march, you must realize what they did.

The gunners of course did not feel it nearly as much, but I have never before seen a whole column of artillery sleeping exactly where they stopped on the road. Horses hooked in and most of them lying down, men sound asleep on the hard high road, using the horses as pillows in some cases, all for a two hours halt only!

Personally my only trouble was in keeping awake when on the march. I found I could not keep myself from falling asleep on my horse and had to walk. It was a case of keep going or appear in the 'missing' column. We nearly always had enough bully beef and biscuits for the men and ourselves but the horses had a very thin time of it.

The retreat also, inevitably, affected morale. Lieutenant Ralph Blewitt of the 39th Brigade RFA, for example, wrote home on 5 September to his future wife:

About the 'romance of war' one hears such a lot. Do you know anything about it? Can't spot it here. One is usually too tired to think of anything except getting a few corn sheaves to doss down on. However, I suppose it exists somewhere … we have done no real fighting in the battle sense of the word, only some pretty dirty rearguard actions but we live in hope of a pukka show in a day or two …

Chapter 6

The Marne and the Aisne

The Battery Sergeant-Major put down his glasses and observed, 'Oh Sir! I can't look anymore; the carnage is too terrible.'

Lieutenant Colonel G.H. Geddes,
42nd Brigade RFA, 14 September 1914

Lieutenant Ralph Blewitt's sense of what lay ahead was almost prophetic. The British retreat from Mons would end on 6 September, when the Allied armies resumed the offensive at the Battle of the Marne. During their advance from Mons, a gap had opened up between the attacking German armies. The First Army, under General von Kluck, in an effort to close ranks with the Second and Third Armies, began to manoeuvre away from its planned route to Paris and instead marched across the front of the French and British lines, inviting an attack on its exposed flanks. Joffre was quick to spot the opportunity. The BEF, together with the French Third, Fifth and Sixth Armies, launched an advance that would halt the enemy invasion in its tracks and transform the whole course and nature of the conflict. It would also come to mark the end of what had been, up to now, a war of movement. Trench warfare would become the new order of the day, with a line of static defences that would stretch over the next few weeks from the Belgian coast to the Swiss Alps.

Despite their exhaustion, the mood amongst the gunners as the offensive began on 6 September was one of elation and relief. For Sergeant Edgington of D Battery RHA it was a time of 'great joy in the change of direction'. Bombardier Thomas Langston with the 114th Battery recalled that 'we are all fed up with the long retiring march and everyone is eager to get a smack at the enemy'. Even at a time of such great significance, the Army Chaplaincy's commitment to the pastoral care of its flock did not slip: after a church service in a swede field at dawn on the day of the advance, Gunner Crowsley had been warned by the padre to 'keep our hats on as the day was very hot'. Captain

Mackie with the 30th Brigade Ammunition Column recalled that his unit moved out at 6am and that 'we actually started advancing. The retirement is now, I hope, over and we shall once again take up the offensive'. On 6 September Mac Robertson of the 70th Battery 'got up, shaved and breakfasted by 6.30am and moved off north to near Fontenay. We are taking the offensive at last, after a fortnight's retreat in co-operation with a big French army.'

Over the next few days the BEF pushed the Germans 60 miles back across the Marne and up on to the steep banks on the eastern side of the River Aisne. E.J. Cummings recalled:

> D, E and J Batteries, working in conjunction with each other, managed to smash up a German convoy. Later we captured 2,000 prisoners. [On 11 September] we advanced over the battlefield and view with interest the damage we have done. Bodies, horses, wagons etc are scattered over the fields and we have to throw them into the ditches on either side of the road in order to proceed.

During the advance to the Aisne the main bodies of the British and German armies were not in direct contact. A few glancing blows would be struck, but the British were, in the main, chasing the retreating Germans as they tried to manoeuvre into better positions from which they intended to dig in and defend themselves.

Gunner Crowsley was acting as signaller with E Battery at Mauroy on the banks of the Marne on 8 September:

> The Germans were not long in finding the range to this position and fire from our right and left seemed to concentrate on E Battery. We had a very bad time. Shells were falling all around us in countless numbers cutting large trees down as though they were matches. And the noise of shells flying and bursting and our own guns firing made such a din – which is indescribable, in fact most hellish. Soon men began to fall. The first to go was Lieutenant Gough, shockingly wounded in the head. Major Gibson wounded in the throat, Corporal Elliot in the shoulder. Our two guns were still firing when the signaller at the guns signalled to me 'No more ammunition at the guns'.

The men took cover as best they could, being no longer able to return fire. Crowsley himself was seriously wounded during this action.

Gunner Albert Reeve of the 16th Battery, 41st Brigade, RFA, had a narrow escape from catastrophe in the advance to the Marne on 8 September:

> Got shelled on in column along the road but got into cover without any damage. Had several whiz around us. Dropped into action and got off a good many rounds. [We] advanced and caught the enemy retiring up the hill. Got under a heavy Maxim fire. Two rounds of 18-pounder ammunition were pierced through the cartridges by bullets as they were being handed across to the gun but miraculously nobody got hit ...

The Battle of the Marne marked a decisive turning-point in the war as the Germans were forced to halt their advance on Paris. But the battle itself consisted mainly of a series of thrusts and parries as each side began a complex series of manoeuvres designed to secure comparative advantage. All that would change on the banks of the Aisne when the Allied armies met the German forces dug in on the high ground overlooking the valley of the river. Cummings himself could sense the shift in atmosphere: 'Today, Sunday [13 September] a terrible battle starts. The artillery as usual are playing a part in it. The Germans have an almost impregnable position and are making a determined resistance.'

For the next fortnight intensive fighting raged as the British tried to scale the steep heights above the river where the German infantry, backed up by artillery, held out in strong defensive positions. Despite extraordinary acts of bravery and courage under fire, the British troops failed to dislodge the enemy. The Germans could not be moved. The British forces, weakened by the losses they had already sustained and short of heavy artillery, lacked sufficient weight to be effective against an enemy that was larger and better equipped than themselves, and who now enjoyed the advantage of defending a greatly superior position. Despite these massive obstacles, artillery tactics on the Aisne showed signs of early innovation, particularly in the use of spotter aircraft to help identify enemy targets that were hidden from the sight of forward artillery observers.

Much of the initial fighting was at close quarters – a lot of it hand-to-hand combat in circumstances of almost total confusion as the British had no real appreciation of the strength of the German forces or their intentions on the Aisne. In fact the Germans had been able to rush forward a new army to strengthen their position on the heights above the river. They were determined to hold their ground and cede no more territory to the Allies.

In the early stages of the fighting Field Marshal French and GHQ even believed that the enemy was still retreating and that they were still in pursuit of a defeated opponent. In reality the pursuit had evolved into a set-piece battle and the Germans held all the advantages.

For the gunners it was a grim experience, as they were exposed once again to the inherent weapons superiority enjoyed by the enemy, especially in larger calibre howitzers. On 13 September Lieutenant Eric Anderson, in command of a section of 18-pounders of the 108th Battery, described his first encounter with these awesome weapons:

> We all imagined that [today] we would be pushing forward as we had been doing. Here, however, we made the mistake of our lives. We were all on top of the Chassemy plateau waiting to move on when we suddenly heard a whistling noise that seemed to be high up in the heavens. This was followed by three others at one-second intervals. We had met these before, the day we crossed the Marne, and all knew what was coming. [We waited a few] seconds and then CRUMPPP – one after the other they plumped their 90lb of unpleasantness down in the valley about 100 yards to our left. Four great clouds of blackness came shooting up. There was no point in staying where we were for the enemy to complete ranging on, so we dodged behind a friendly wood …

The Germans had bigger guns and more plentiful supplies of ammunition, and the BEF simply did not possess the firepower required to shift the enemy from their hilltop fortress, which gave the defenders the added advantage of almost perfect observation over the British. The Germans were able to deploy on the Aisne some of the very heavy artillery pieces that were originally intended to lay siege to Paris. The British had no response to these highly effective, long-range weapons. The only British guns that could match these heavy German howitzers were the 60-pounders and these were too few in number to redress the balance. In any event, not all of the heavy batteries available to the BEF were in action on the Aisne. Some were still en route to the combat zone when the fighting erupted. As a result the German guns enjoyed an almost universal mastery of the battlefield.

Sergeant Francis Miller with the 17th Battery, 41st Brigade, RFA, at Vielle Arcy recalled what it was like to be under shell fire from the German heavy guns:

You hear one coming, you hear a terrible thud then an awful explosion which throws up a tremendous lot of earth, and when these pieces of earth come to the ground it sounds like a squadron of cavalry galloping along. The hole that one of those shells made – well you could put one of our wagons in it comfortably. Those shells had a terrible moral effect. I do not care how strong you are, you will feel it …

Finding suitable firing positions was another problem for the British. The best and safest positions meant that the guns were firing at the limit of their range and effectiveness. If they deployed across the river itself, there were few decent locations from which the guns could land accurate fire on the Germans on the heights above them. On 14 September, for example, a critical day in the battle, the 40th Brigade RFA, which had crossed the river at Vailly, could not find any position from which it could come into action at all.

On 14 September Captain Francis Adams of E Battery RHA experienced a similar set of difficulties as he tried, unsuccessfully, to get his guns into action in support of the 3rd Division:

Started at 5am and after a long halt at the chateau [Chassemy], ready to cross the river at Vailly, had to fall back under very heavy fire from big howitzers. Could only move slowly up the steep hill east of Chassemy as the road was bad and congested with J Battery and 3rd Brigade RHA ammunition column, also field ambulances. Just as we got on top of the hill my horse was hit in the shoulder and neck. This was the only casualty which was very fortunate as the 3rd Divisional artillery who were in action here were having a bad time of it, shells falling all around them. The fire was coming from German batteries behind Conde Fort. The Battery kept moving about from place to place under cover until we went into bivouac at Lime at 7pm, the men sleeping in a large corrugated iron shed.

The 1st Division crossed the Aisne on 13 September. The 25th Brigade RFA was the first artillery unit to cross the river at Bourg. On the 14th the guns of the entire brigade were drawn up in a quarry near Vendresse. Lieutenant Colonel Geddes was in command of the brigade:

The 2nd and 3rd Infantry Brigades were about 1,000 yards in front of them fighting their way uphill near Troyon and were hard pressed. Orders arrived to send a Battery to report to the GOC 3rd Infantry Brigade and the 113rd Battery was detailed. Major Ellershaw, the Battery commander, rode forward with his Battery staff. As he topped the hill he saw a strong German attack advancing at 1,000 yards distance. The Battery came into action at 900 yards range in the open and inflicted terrible slaughter on the Germans. The Battery Sergeant Major put down his glasses and exclaimed 'Oh sir! I can't look anymore: the carnage is too terrible'.

The attack was completely repulsed and two machine guns knocked out by gun fire. Major Ellershaw and the Battery staff rode forward to reconnoitre and fetch in the disabled guns. Coming round the corner they found themselves suddenly confronted by two officers and fifty Germans. Drawing his revolver, Ellershaw shouted 'Form line – charge!' The party of eight men, including little trumpeter Cockaday (who was unarmed), followed their major and charged into the Germans. Trumpeter Cockaday seized the helmet off the head of a big German and flourished it, shouting 'I've got his one'. The Germans at once surrendered and were disarmed and marched back under the Battery Sergeant Major and one man. Ellershaw went on and brought in one machine gun and destroyed the other.

Bombardier Tom Langston was manning one of the 18-pounders with the 114th Battery on the Paissy Ridge on 14 September:

We advanced at daybreak [and] are obliged to take cover as the enemy are heavily shelling the roads. Still under shell fire we take up the third position and open fire. The position is rather poor and it is marvellous how we got out without being hit for the poor infantry were falling all around us. In withdrawing, several guns and wagons toppled over the ridge. Owing to the heavy rain the ground is in an awful condition, making quick moves impossible. In this position, three bullets struck the shield directly in front of my head. Take up fourth position and open fire. Here again we are under heavy shell fire from the Germans for at least five hours. Fortunately no casualties occur at the guns.

The 114th Battery remained in action on the Paissy Ridge for several more days, supporting the beleaguered infantry around the village of Paissy. This advanced position would prove untenable, given the weight of enemy fire it attracted. There was hardly a moment when the battery was not under direct enemy fire. At 5.30am on 20 September the German infantry launched a major counter-attack and disaster finally struck:

> The enemy commenced to shell our position. The first round injured several of the staff who were on their way up to the observing station, the second round dropping under a tree directly in rear of No. 3 gun and killed 4 and wounded 7. Under great difficulty we managed to dress the wounded and bury the dead. Still the shells continue to fall around us and are doing great damage to the wagon line. Altogether the casualties number around 60. We are now ordered to withdraw – a very difficult procedure owing to the number of horses being injured. I assist in getting three guns and 1 wagon out of action …

Sergeant Reeves with 70th Battery, 34th Brigade, RFA, was supporting the crossing of the Aisne by the 2nd Division on 13 September:

> [We] marched at daybreak and the 22nd and 70th batteries came into action half a mile west of Dhuizel to cover the crossing of the river Aisne at Chayonne by the 4th Guards Brigade. The crossing was effected without much opposition. The 70th Battery opened fire on the enemy occupying the heights above Chayonne.

The following day the battery itself crossed the river via the pontoon bridge built by the Royal Engineers alongside the bridge at Pont Arcy, and came into action on the south end of the spur just to the north of Moussy:

> It was a very misty morning and did not clear until about 10am. The German gunners opened fire on us and we replied. During the afternoon the German heavy guns shelled the Battery and they also searched the back of the spur towards Verneuil and inflicted casualties on the wagon lines. The casualties in the 70th Battery were one officer wounded, five men killed and fourteen wounded and twenty-seven horses killed.

On 13 September Major H.W. Newcombe was commanding the 47th (Howitzer) Battery, 44th Brigade, RFA. His guns were also supporting the 2nd Division advance: 'We came into action near Vieil Arcy at 4pm and shelled a German counter-attack coming from Bray. Cease fire at 5.30pm. Got into bivouac near Dhuizel at 9pm. Very cold and rain at night.'

The next two days would see the battery engaged in heavy fighting:

September 14th. Left bivouac in pouring rain at 5.45am. Came into action at 9.45am north of Bourg and shelled heights east of Bray at 2pm. Fire very hot all the time. Blathwayte was killed by shell fire. Move to Tilleul, north of Verneuil. Move to Moussy at 5pm but went back into action near Verneuil for the night.

September 15th. Went up to observing station at Tilleul at 4.30am and remained in action all day. The whole of the hill was under fire all day from a high explosive howitzer and from quick-firing guns which we could not locate. Wagon line also under heavy fire. Very unpleasant day. Bivouac'ed where we were and spent a very uncomfortable night in the rain.

Clarrie Hodgson faced a dilemma on 13 September. The 122nd Battery – which now consisted of only two guns after the losses at Le Cateau – was desperately needed to provide covering fire for the 3rd Division attacks and his gun needed to cross the river quickly. The sappers had not, however, quite finished the job of getting the crossing ready:

They said we would be able to cross at any minute now so I had a talk to the fellow doing it and he said 'Yes, very well, if you'd like to risk it without side rails'. So off we started, trying to get across this river along the pontoon bridge. Well, just as the horses and the gun got half way across a German shell pitched into the river. It frightened the horses so much that they slewed off the bridge dragging the gun with them. Of course, with the weight of the gun they didn't have a chance. All the horses drowned. The drivers managed to jump clear and they were struggling in the water. Luckily they could swim and they made it to the bank and we dragged them out and saved them – but the gun was at the bottom of the river. And it was deep! The gun was completely submerged.

Well, we were very fed up! We'd wanted to have a bash at the Germans after they'd pushed us back like this but it was not to be. The question now was to try to get the gun. Sitting along the banks of the river were dozens if not hundreds of British troops waiting for something to happen. So one chap came forward and he said, 'Look, do you want us to save the gun? I used to be a diver ...' So I said 'Right, you're the chap. Come on!'

He dived and dived and after a number of tries he managed to tie some ropes round the gun and we got a dozen or so of these chaps heaving on the rope and eventually we succeeded in dragging it up on the bank. But it was no good! Water had got into the buffer so that was that. We were finished. We hung about for a bit with the Brigade but without a gun we were useless so as soon as things were established they sent us back to the railhead to wait for another one.

Bombardier Sprotson also saw action on the Aisne on 13 and 14 September at Bucy Le Long as the fighting on the Aisne reached its climax:

We advanced to the top of the hill where our infantry seemed to be under heavy fire. We put two guns into action to cover them but we had to retire, we could not show our heads over the crest and several German batteries opened fire at us so we were very lucky to save the guns apart from anything else as the Germans were only 800 yards from us.

During darkness we retired to a position just in front of the bridge which we had crossed earlier in the morning. During the night we dug pits as well as we could in preparation for the morrow. I did not care for the position myself – it seemed so open – and I knew the Germans had got the range to an inch. We had the order to advance and at the same time the enemy opened fire on us. We returned the compliment and from somewhere on our right one of their heavy batteries opened fire. After about two hours we were forced to leave our guns. The men were very downhearted at this but nothing could be done and it was only murder to stay there as we had lost four of the detachment out of six and one gun out of action.

We chopped down some trees and with some old corn sacks made stretchers to fetch our dead and wounded in. What a sight – some with legs off and [injuries] too awful to describe. I don't think there was a man in the Battery with dry eyes that morning.

Second Lieutenant Robert Thornhagh-Foljambe was with the guns of the 120th Battery at Ciry on 14 September:

Came into action on the far side of the village up a steep bank. An extraordinary escape from shells. They put salvo after salvo of shrapnel just over us, most bursting overhead. Only one man and some horses hit. The wagon line of the 121st Battery which was in the street was caught by the furthest shells and lost a good many men and about 20 horses. Opened fire on the enemy battery whose flashes could be seen in the edge of the wood in front of Conde Fort.

Mac Robertson of the 70th Battery, 34th Brigade, RFA, had a long difficult day on the 14th. His guns were supporting the vanguard of the 2nd Division as it advanced across the Aisne by the pontoon bridge at Pont Arcy:

Up at 3am, got off at 5. We were advanced guard battery. Crossed the Aisne by pontoon bridge. Rained all morning. Just past the river guns began to fire and we halted for two hours, then were ordered on to come into action, but the place we chose was under fire and we had to retire.

The Major selected another and we came into action. We dug in a bit, when rifle bullets began to whistle over and we heard the Germans were making a close attack. Infantry was hurried up from the rear and gradually the bullets stopped coming. We had got ready to have a go at them with fuse [very close range firing] and Bombardier Goodall was killed by a percussion shell. All afternoon we stayed in our pits, firing at intervals. A heavy howitzer battery opened fire [on us], high explosive coming at intervals, rather nerve straining. Had an awful disaster to our wagon lines. Thirty horses and four men killed and about ten wounded. We got back to the wagon line after dark. I was dog tired. Had to take charge of an out-lying picquet at night. It rained the whole time. We fired 500 rounds! Jelly was killed today, my best friend: the news knocked me out – he and I were real pals.

The following day was equally grim:

Up at 2.30am and did more digging. We have now got very good cover: a deep pit each side of the gun and thick parapets. Meals get sent up from the wagon line. It is very trying being stuck all day in one place. It isn't safe to leave the pits – we don't know the least what is going on. Aeroplanes are over a lot. The heavy German battery fired at us today and burst one right at the muzzle of the gun where I was. The shock was very great but no one injured. Rained all night. Supper in the rain. Slept up at the guns. It is a great strain this show. The German infantry losses have been very great. I saw some of our dead this morning – it wasn't pleasant. I hope this damn war will finish soon ...

Lieutenant Victor Walrond was a young officer serving with the 48th Battery, 36th Brigade, RFA, which was also part of the artillery of 2nd Division. His brigade had crossed the Aisne via the same bridge as Mac Robertson, hurriedly built by the sappers at Pont Arcy on the night of 13/14 September, and eventually deployed around the village of Moussy. He was anxious about the coming battle:

By this time it was becoming obvious that we were up against a bigger thing than was expected. The whole of the northern slopes of the Aisne form a magnificent position for defence, the steep banks rising sheer from the river. The slopes on our side of the river are neither so steep nor so high: so the Germans can watch and shell us from short ranges while we can neither see them nor shoot except from very long ranges south of the river.

We moved off towards Moussy, being told that we would probably come under fire just before entering the village. This proved correct and, the Major and Inchbald having gone forward to reconnoitre, Godman and I bore the brunt of this attempt at annihilation. Fortunately the gun fire they poured on us was a bit short, though the bursts were beautiful, and no harm was done.

It would be different in the morning. They had spent the night digging gun pits in anticipation of coming into action, but when heavy German howitzer shells began landing around their position at 1pm there was nothing they could do about it:

About one o'clock some infernal big guns firing high explosive started bombarding us and [for two hours] gave us their undivided attention. You could see them starting to place a row of shells about 200 yards short of us and gradually coming closer by 50 yards till they got to the Battery and then about 50 yards over and then back on to us by 25 yards and there they stuck, planking those great shells all around us, many of them falling within ten yards, but never one landed right on top of us, thank God. Meanwhile, three other Batteries had come up nearby – the

50th right in front with their observing station next door, the 47th just on our right and the 60th 200 yards behind.

About 3pm, 'Little Willie' as we called him, made himself more generally felt all over the hill. A gun of the 50th suffered a direct hit and poor J.E.L. Clarke was killed. The other two Batteries lost their Captains, Blathwayt and Furse, and many horses. The streets of Vermeuil were full of dead men and horses.

Major John Mowbray was serving as a staff officer with the 2nd Division's artillery headquarters under General Perceval (the CRA) during the fighting on the Aisne and provided this summary of the action on his divisional front on 14 September:

[A] misty morning. Sent up to order 41 and 44 Brigades and the Heavy Battery to move via Bourg aqueduct which is intact. We crossed at Bourg and 44 Brigade were immediately confronted with high explosive shell on emerging from cover of trees about Courtonne. Ordered to come into action there. Anxious afternoon. Ground all around pitted with craters by high explosive shell. The enemy have got the range precisely.

Lieutenant Colonel Lushington was commanding the 41st Brigade RFA as it entered the battle on the Aisne. The brigade had taken up positions near Vieil Arcy:

About the second or third day, we were spotted and ranged on by an aeroplane and then the fun began. I do not know the exact size of the weapon employed against us, but we were honoured with two hours' slow and solemn strafe. When we returned to the guns again (we were in action in a ploughed field) nothing was injured, but between three of the guns were single shell craters, each occupying the whole of the interval between two guns. Similar duck ponds to the number of about fifty were all around us.

Supplying the guns with ammunition was an especially hazardous business as all the main approach roads were under continuous German fire. Captain Mackie of the 30th Brigade Ammunition Column recalled one particular episode early on in the battle:

The road leading to 129th Battery was under heavy shell fire and the wagons sent up to replenish them could not proceed, so I took them round about and found another track along which, although fairly exposed, I was able to take them. Passed through Chassemy where a shell had caught two ambulance wagons. Road strewn with dead horses and men. Came back along the low road half a mile of which was under shell fire. Most exciting.

Lieutenant Austin Bates was serving with the 31st (Howitzer) Battery of the 37th Brigade RFA and his guns were also in action at Bucy Le Long on 15 September in an orchard in front of a large but abandoned chateau. The artillery duel was far from being one-sided:

About 8am we were much annoyed by 77mm shrapnel enfilading the Battery from the direction of Pont Rouge. A good many splinters were flying about and [Captain] Mahon got hit in the foot. At about 9am I was despatched towards La Montagne Farm to try and locate these guns. I climbed up [a haystack] and spotted a whole 6 gun battery complete with observation limber and two guns and an observation limber of a second Battery. These guns were on the Maubeuge road shooting between the poplar trees. After four rounds of Lyddite they pulled down the observation limber of the left battery and a few more stopped it firing. Peace now reigned.

But not for long. Later in the afternoon Austin Bates and his men came under heavy fire from a large calibre howitzer, causing the battery to take cover:

What had been a pleasant orchard was pitted with the largest shell craters I had yet seen. One or two dead horses and bits of harness. I walked down the line of guns and tried the breach of No. 1 gun. It was jammed with earth and dust. There was not a sign of a man anywhere. When I had got two-thirds of the way down the line they started rafaling again and realising exactly why the Major had ordered the men to quit, I ran like a hare for the bottom of the valley. The lane at the bottom was choked with fallen masonry over which I climbed until I reached the wall of the chateau close to the church. Here I turned up the hill through the chateau gardens and eventually fetched up at the corner where the teams had stood and where the cookhouse had been. It was not a pleasant sight and need not be described ...

The 126th Battery of the 29th Brigade RFA also had a hard time from the German gunners on 15 September. Sergeant George King was with the guns that day:

> We commenced firing at dawn and fire about 150 rounds per gun. German high explosive shells fall within 5 yards of our guns. My fellow operator and I seek protection in a hole in the ground. [A] large piece of shell falls between myself and the Major. 'A' sub-section gun limber blown up whilst we are trying to get our guns away. Wheel horse killed and driver badly wounded. We had to get our guns away by sections, the last section being man-handled out as it was too risky to bring horses to the guns. We all get away after a very hard struggle with our guns. Sleep in a hayshed at night.

Mac Robertson's battery was in the thick of the fighting on the Aisne, supporting the 2nd Division infantry. In the afternoon of 18 September his guns came under shell fire from a battery of heavy German howitzers:

> ... we had an awful time [with shells] falling within a few yards of the guns. Finally one blew up a wagon, the body blown 20 yards back and the limber smashed. Looked out of my pit to see two men buried in the ruins, but no one hurt. Got them out just as it caught fire. One's nerves get very bad and the men are very 'jumpy'.

Also on 18 September Captain Josslyn Ramsden, adjutant of the 27th Brigade RFA, watched the German guns open up on the 121st Battery: 'The Germans turned a torrent of fire on to the battery. It was terrible to watch.'

As ever, the gunners had more than just the enemy to contend with. They were also fighting an unequal battle with the elements. During much of the fighting on the Aisne the rain fell relentlessly. Gunner Reeve of the 16th Battery described the effect this had on the battlefield by 20 September:

> ... shifted the position of our guns, which had sunk well into the ground and also through constant digging out the wheels my own gun was 4ft 6 inches below the level of the epaulments, over 6ft high from the

inside. We had a fine job getting out. We had to take down our shelter and of course it started raining and before we could erect a fresh one, got a wetting …

Not everyone endured these extreme hardships. Captain Mackie, with the 30th Brigade Ammunition Column, had found himself a cosy billet back at Braine. On 15 September he wrote: 'Had a fine night's sleep in a bedroom of the chateau. Very hard to leave the sheets at 5.40am. Can get practically everything we require from the old caretaker and his wife.'

Notwithstanding all the physical hardships, Gunner Reeves and his mates eventually settled down in a battlefield routine:

Our usual programme is to get up at 3am, have breakfast, and then go up to the guns about half a mile away, across some very heavy fields. Generally manage to crawl into our shelter and get another hour or so of sleep. Amuse ourselves between spasms of firing by digging. Have our dinner and tea fetched up to us and retire to billets at dusk. There has been a constant battle all round us since we got up here but beyond the rattle of musketry and the boom of guns and bursting of shell we cannot see much.

Captain Mackie had another army ritual to perform, even at the height of the fighting. On 17 September at Braine he paid his men their wages: 'Pouring rain all day. Payed out the men in 5 franc notes, the first pay day since leaving. As they can find nothing to buy in the villages, however, the money is not much use to them.'

The gunners had the support of the Royal Army Medical Corps, whose doctors and nurses worked right up at the batteries and endured much of the same hardship as the men themselves. One such doctor was James Fairley, who on 26 September found himself working with the men of the 31st (Heavy) Battery. The battery had just lost three men killed and five wounded:

September 27th. Up at 5.30am to the guns. The men in the Battery are very sick at losing their men and are very keen to locate the battery that peppered them. They cannot locate it, however. They think it is a heavy howitzer battery hidden behind some hill. The ground round our battery is ploughed up with shells which are some 3 feet deep and 3 or 4 yards in diameter. No shells came our way today as the battery that had caused us trouble has been silenced by the French artillery. Had afternoon tea with the men. They regretted lack of beer. They are a very happy lot but dread the German shells and respect them as gunners.

The gunners had to learn the rudiments of camouflage in order to conceal their batteries from the prying eyes of enemy aviators. On 26 September Sergeant Francis Miller, with the 17th Battery, wrote: 'We were beginning by experience to learn the art of cover from aeroplanes and we had had some rare practice here cutting fresh trees down every morning and planting them around the guns.'

For the men fighting under these miserable conditions, personal comfort and the shortages of useful equipment began to assume the foremost priority. The officers sent off appeals to their families at home to make good the inadequacies of army issue and to improve their physical lot. On 2 October, for example, Austin Bates wrote home to his parents with a long list of needs:

I should like the following ordered:

1. From Messrs Huntsman & Co, Albemarle Street, W, one pair khaki breeches, same pattern as previous (you might get my account there settled through the office – it stands at £3.3.0)

2. A 'tent d'arbri' not less than eight feet long and four feet high with a floor stitched to both sides. To be obtained from the Army and Navy or Junior Army and Navy, most probably the latter. [These] are minimum requirements. I have a small one six foot six inches long and my toes are always out at the end.

3. A Wolsely valise from Harvey Nichols – also a long one, seven feet say.

4. Either a pair of high powered field glasses or a small telescope in strong case. Aitchisons in The Strand make the glasses and I believe the best firm of telescope for my purposes is made by Davidson & Co, 29 Portland Street, W. I have had a pair of the Aitchison glasses once and they were not a success. Am rather inclined to favour the telescope with a small tripod. Power required is about 25 diameters. This is an urgent necessity. On several occasions we have not been able to distinguish German from English infantry owing to lack of powerful glasses.

Could you investigate the merits or otherwise of these or any others you know of, when you are next in town, and have something of the nature sent, labelled OHMS URGENT by post.

The primary need on the British side, however, was for more guns to make good the losses at Le Cateau and for heavier artillery to take on the bigger German guns. On 19 September the first replacement 18-pounders arrived.

Clarrie Hodgson, whose section had had no guns since the disaster on the bridge on 13 September, was waiting at the railhead south of Soissons for his replacement guns to arrive when he had a remarkable chance encounter:

There was a big replacement camp there where all the casualties were being replaced. We were put into decent accommodation, given fresh clothing and food. I was so hungry I could have eaten a ... well, a scabby headed child I think! There was some German prisoners there too, a little way off in a wire enclosure. We were kicking our heels, waiting for the guns to arrive and I was talking to three German officers who were boasting how they were going to win the war. They all spoke rather good English.

I watched a stretcher go past and I could only see this chap's head. Somehow it looked familiar but it didn't dawn on me then. It was quite a while after the stretcher had gone that I suddenly realised that it was Nick, my twin brother. So I legged it to a place they were using as a Casualty Clearing Station – just a sort of barrack room, part of a farmhouse or something. As I went in the doctor was just coming out. He gave a terrific start when he saw me and I said to him, 'Have you seen a chap who looks just like me, coming in on a stretcher just now?' He said 'Good heavens yes! I've just examined him. I thought it was you when I saw you standing there!' We were identical twins and this poor man got a terrific shock because he'd just left Nick and Nick was unconscious.

He took me inside to where he was. After a while Nick came round and he said, quite matter-of-fact, 'Well Clarrie, I'm going to die. I want you to take all my things and see that they get home.' So I took these things – went through his pockets. There was nothing much of course, but there was some money and letters and photos and a few odd personal things. He wasn't wounded so when I went out I said to the doctor 'What's the matter with him?' He said, 'We don't actually know. He might possibly have been poisoned because the Germans have poisoned all the wells around here. But we're not sure.'

When I got back [to the railhead] there was word that the guns had arrived and I knew that meant we would be going into action. I thought to myself, 'What the hell am I going to do with Nick's things? I'll probably be killed tomorrow.' So I took them back to him and said 'Look, it's no good me taking these things. We are going into action at any minute.' So I handed them back to him.

I didn't see him again for about two years. His ailment was a burst appendix. How he survived I don't know because it must have taken more than a day to get him back to England.

The British were in desperate need of more firepower. On the 23rd the first of four batteries of heavy 6-inch breech-loading howitzers began to arrive on the battlefield – the 1st, 2nd, 3rd and 4th Batteries RGA. The first rounds were fired at around midday on the 24th. Getting the heavy guns into position was not an easy task. Major G.B. Mackenzie, commanding the 2nd Siege Battery, recalled that a 'considerable delay resulted from the guns having to be manhandled over a bridge on the Aisne canal which had been half destroyed'.

The heavy howitzer batteries had all been raised in August by splitting up existing siege companies that were employed in the coastal defence role. They, like all other batteries, had experienced a trying time in getting to war readiness. They were short of horses and had insufficient harness. The 1st Siege Battery, for example, saw a steady turnover of Reservists through its ranks as men were posted to one unit, only to be rapidly moved on to another that was equally short of personnel. The battery only received its full complement of horses two days before embarkation for France on 19 September. Few of the men had time to be fully trained on their equipment. Lieutenant Hubert Burke was serving with the 2nd Siege Battery based at Plymouth: 'All the confusion and want of training etc could have been obviated if the War Office had left us to mobilize according to their original orders made out in peacetime. As it was we went abroad with no trained drivers, no senior NCOs as well, owing to the amount of promotions necessary ...'

The 6-inch howitzer was not a particularly effective weapon, and it lacked the range necessary to take on the German guns safely. Nor was it a very accurate weapon. But it was better than nothing and gave the British artillery on the Aisne bigger teeth. The guns were deployed in counter-battery work and on pounding the German infantry in their trenches but were not concentrated into a single force.

Lieutenant Burke described the difficulties his men faced in bringing their guns across the Aisne on 23 September: 'Getting over the bridge was a slow job as the bridge was not strong enough to take teams and guns together so we had to unhook and manhandle the guns across.' The 2nd Siege Battery would eventually take up position on the northern edge of the Bois de Bousy, about 2 miles beyond the village of Bourg. It would take about 36 hours to get the guns ready for action: '[This] was rather a difficult job owing to the softness of the ground into which our heavy guns, with their narrow little wheel treads, sank like a knife into butter.' No sooner were the guns ready for action than they came under shell fire from heavy German guns. Lieutenant Burke takes up the story:

> It was about 9am on the 24th September that the Battery got its first taste of shell fire. Black Maria searching the country lobbed up a chance shell which pitched within 3 yards of number 4 gun. Luckily it did no damage to either men or material except plastering the men with earth. One or two rounds fell into our wood. Our battery opened fire at 10.10am on September 24th – the first time I suppose that these guns had ever fired a round in anger.

The sight and sound of the heavy howitzers in action had a profound effect on morale, if nothing else, according to Burke:

> Our arrival on the scene of action has apparently heartened up our troops a great deal. They care nothing for the German infantry or cavalry, but Black Marias and Coal Boxes have put the fear of God into them. On our march up, passing infantry were continually saying 'Thank God you've come. We've been waiting for you the past three weeks.'

The 6-inch howitzers fired mainly on targets of opportunity rather than to a strategic plan, which diminished their overall effectiveness. There were also other problems to overcome, in particular the poor quality of the ammunition. On 25 September two gunners in the 1st Siege Battery and another in the 2nd were killed when a shell prematurely exploded shortly after it left the gun barrel. The dead gunner from the 2nd was buried that night in a candle-lit vigil, with Major Mackenzie reading the burial service and the men lined up around the grave. The same thing happened again a few days later in the 1st Siege Battery, this time wounding eight men, including the battery commander, Major Ewart. The guns were also liable to break down after only moderate use. One of the cradles of the 2nd Siege Battery's guns split after firing only a couple of rounds and had to be returned to the railhead for repairs.

But it was not all bad news as far as ammunition was concerned. During their time on the Aisne a new heavier and more effective high explosive shell ('heavy' Lyddite) became available for the 6-inch howitzers. Other innovations soon followed. Within a couple of days of arriving on the Aisne, the heavy guns were being guided on to their targets by RFC airplanes using wireless apparatus to communicate directly with the gunners on the ground. This innovation would mark one of the many turning-points in the evolution of gunnery during the First World War.

The ground conditions towards the end of September were appalling and this caused particular problems for the heavy guns of the siege batteries. Major George Birnie Mackenzie, commanding the 2nd Siege Battery, found that the guns would sink several feet into the mud after firing and had to be hauled out each time by men and horses. Men of the 3rd Siege Battery had to work without a break throughout the nights of 24, 25 and 26 September in order to lay down specially designed wooden gun platforms so that their howitzers did not disappear into the quagmire. The labour required to support the heavy guns in action would turn out to be prodigious.

Nevertheless, the heavy batteries of 60-pounder guns proved themselves to be highly effective weapons on the Aisne, and were employed against infantry, enemy batteries and communications. The problem was that there were just not enough of them. Lieutenant Colonel A.C. Wilkinson had four 60-pounders in the 35th (Heavy) Battery RGA, which provided the heavy artillery for the 2nd Division. These guns were a major target for the Germans and as a result were under constant shell fire. His experiences on 24 September provide an informative snapshot of daily life for his unit at this stage of the fighting:

On September 24th, near Viel Arcy, one of the Battery wagons was ignited by a shell – it immediately blazed furiously and the conflagration was carried by the wind to another wagon which also caught fire. As soon as it was possible to approach the wagons the fire was partially subdued and it was thought that no more damage would ensue. Owing to the strong wind, however, the wagons became practically red hot and one of the limbers exploded with a terrific explosion. As the gun appeared now to be in imminent danger of being destroyed, it was necessary to remove the shell and cartridges from the remaining wagons. This was done at great personal risk by Lieutenant Paris and Sergeant Weatherhead – the shell at the time being so hot that they had to be wrapped in cloth in order to handle them …

The battle gradually ground to a halt in the last few days of September, although it would carry on for another two weeks. It ended in a bloody stalemate, setting a precedent for much of the subsequent fighting. The Germans had the enormous advantage of superior positions and a crushing preponderance of heavy artillery which made it impossible for the British infantry to gain any effective lodgement on the heights above the river. The British artillery fought hard and bravely to support the infantry and their fire was frequently highly effective in breaking up German counter-attacks and in counter-battery work. Inevitably, the gun fire was not always as effective as the gunners would have liked. Major William Strong, the battery commander of the 128th Battery, noted in his diary on 29 September: 'Infantry pleased with us shelling enemy's trenches. I don't think we do much harm but it probably annoys the enemy.'

But it was not sufficient to break the resulting deadlock. In a prophetic despatch to the King on 2 October Field Marshal Sir John French wrote:

> I think the battle of the Aisne is very typical of what battles in the future are most likely to resemble. Siege operations will enter largely into the tactical problems – the spade will be as great a necessity as the rifle and the heaviest calibres and types of artillery will be brought up in support on either side.

On the same day Major John Mowbray, reflecting on the lessons the artillery had learnt during the fighting on the Aisne, wrote in his diary:

> It is quite clear that artillery of a Division require much more effective communication arrangements than we have. There should be a signal company allotted for this purpose and able to provide at least 4 stations

with several miles of wire. The CRA would thus be able to communicate direct with his Brigades and fire could be rapidly controlled. Present arrangement by communication through infantry brigades is most unsatisfactory – many delays often entirely nullifying the value of messages, opportunities being lost.

Without air reconnaissance no accurate artillery work at long range is possible. We have had some excellent results with an air observer who controls his machine, observes fire and signals results by wireless. I reported effect of wireless work to Sir Douglas Haig and he has ordered us to apply for more equipment.

These early experiences would help lay the foundations for the evolution of gunnery tactics for the rest of the war. It would take time and the commitment of huge resources to put these lessons into practice. It was also clear that effective anti-aircraft weapons needed to be developed to counter the growing threat from the air. Small pom-pom guns which fired a 1lb shell were sent out to France at the end of September and saw action for the first time on the Aisne. They proved to be almost completely useless. Writing on 30 September, John Mowbray was scathing in his assessment of these new additions to the artillery's arsenal:

Converted pom-poms sent out for anti-aircraft work, which arrived only a day or two ago, already is clearly useless. It is slow, the shells do not readily burst and the 'tracer' only works up to 2–3,000 feet. As the planes generally reconnoitre at 5–7,000 feet this is of little use. Perhaps it does keep the hostile planes a little higher.

It would take another 18 months before a modified 13-pounder gun would be deployed in the air defence role.

As the fighting ground to a stalemate on the Aisne, the Allied and German commands both began looking at ways to break the deadlock and thus open up the prospect of turning each other's flanks. The British had an overriding need to safeguard their supply routes through the Channel ports. The Germans had the obvious objective of denying those ports to the British. Both sides wanted to escape from the static campaign of trench warfare into which the fighting had descended on the Aisne and return to a war of manoeuvre of the sort that had characterised the opening phase of the struggle. Here lay the chance of a quick victory – of getting behind the

18-pounder guns in action at Ploegsteert, 19 October 1914. (*Q51223*)

4.7-inch guns in action near Ypres, 19 October 1914. (*Q50335*)

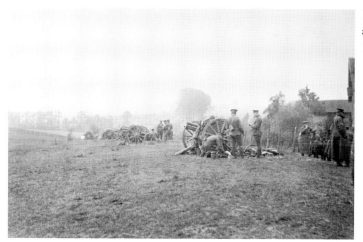

13-pounders of J Battery at Wytschaete, 31 October 1914. (*Q56307*)

J Battery moving up to Ypres, October 1914. (*Q56310*)

J Battery in action near the Messines Ridge, October 1914. (*Q56311*)

Officers of the 6th Siege Battery RGA at Petit Point, November 1914. (*Q56160*)

Horses of the 7th Division artillery using woods as cover near the Ypres–Menin road, October 1914. (*Q57256*)

6-inch shells being produced at the Yorks & Lancs Railway Works, Horwich. (*Q109907*)

Belgian workers at Birtley Munitions Factory, Co. Durham, 1915. (*Q27736*)

The wheelwrights' shop at Coventry Ordnance Works. (*Q30122*)

One of the 13-pounder guns used by L Battery in the action at Nery in September 1914. (*Q68293*)

General Milne, CRA 4 Division, at Chateau Rossignol on Hill 63, near Messines, November 1914. (*Q56717*)

Two photographs of the 61st (Howitzer) Battery RFA, attached to the 11th Division, early 1915. (*MD/1121*)

Some of the new recruits: gunners of the 61st (Howitzer) Battery and their mascot pose for the camera. (*AL 1605271*)

A howitzer gun section of the 61st (Howitzer) Battery RFA. Lieutenant John Wills is standing third from the left. (*AL 1605280*)

Captain David Nelson VC, L Battery, RFA. (*Q80586*)

Lieutenant Mac Robertson, 70th Battery RFA, photographed shortly before his death in 1915. (*MD/1174*)

enemy's front line and cutting them off from the rear. So began the so-called 'race to the sea'. The British would soon be leaving the muddy graveyard of the Aisne and heading north to Flanders to resume their original place on the left flank of the French armies. One gruesome field of death and destruction would soon be replaced by another, and this one would prove to be even more ghastly than the Aisne. The fighting here over the next few weeks would stretch the BEF to breaking point. The name of this place would be for ever associated with the horrors of the First World War: Ypres.

For those serving with the guns, there was little information available about where they were going or what the plan would be when they got there. Austin Bates, with the 31st (Howitzer) Battery, summed it all up in a diary entry for 11 October:

> Marched at 8am through the forest of Compiegne, reaching that town at 11.30am – roads full of French cavalry and guns. Had the best meal of my life at the Cafe de la Cloche – crossed the river by pontoon bridge close to the original stone bridge demolished by us on our retreat south and to the German pontoon destroyed by them on their retreat north. Entrained at 4pm and left at 6pm. Destination unknown …

For Cyril Brownlow, rumours abounded:

> On the evening of 1st October we marched out of Braisne on to the plateau where we had been three weeks before. We had no definite news of what was in progress but we knew that great events were afoot and rumours whispered that we were marching to Antwerp …

Chapter 7

The Landing at Zeebrugge

'By the time we had passed through the streets of Bruges we looked more like a bank holiday crowd than soldiers.'

Major Lord Ralph Hamilton, 22nd Brigade RFA

The German advance through Belgium in August 1914 had, within a few days, swept aside the small Belgian field army, forcing its six divisions back into the area around Antwerp, where they defended both the vital port itself and the King of the Belgians, who had set up his government there. The Germans laid siege to the city, and confined the Belgian Army to its fortified perimeter. But they refused to allow it to distract them from their overarching war plan – the Schlieffen Plan – and the attempt to outflank the Allied armies in northern France.

From the fortress at Antwerp the Belgian Army launched numerous attacks against the Germans, raising a question mark about the security of their lines of communication and supply. On the eve of the Battle of Le Cateau, for example, four Belgian divisions attacked southwards towards Malines and into the gap between Louvain and Brussels, and made good progress before deciding enough was enough and retiring back behind the safety of their line of forts. During the Battle of the Marne the Belgians made another attack on the Germans, which continued for several days. The Belgians even briefly entered Louvain. As a result, the Germans were obliged to keep large numbers of their soldiers in Belgium rather than sending them south to join the fighting in France.

The continued resistance in Antwerp presented the Allies with an opportunity to land a force at the port which could operate behind the German lines, adding to the discomfort and disruption the Belgians were already causing. After the stalemate on the Aisne, both sides sought to break free from the static situation that was developing and each tried to outflank the other. The protagonists began moving northwards, thus commencing what would become known as the 'race to the sea'. In these circumstances the continued defence of Antwerp provided the Allies with a potentially important advantage. A landing at Antwerp would dramatically accelerate the speed at which the Allies might succeed in turning the enemy flank, and would create a major strategic threat to German military operations further to the south. Sooner rather than later the Germans would need to snuff out the vestiges of Belgian and Allied resistance at Antwerp. The scene was set for a significant engagement.

In early September the Germans began to tighten their stranglehold on the city. Heavy siege artillery was brought up and on the 28th the city and its defences were heavily shelled. It was clear that a major effort was being mounted to end the Belgian Army's presence in Antwerp. The German bombardment of the outer ring of fortresses, which provided the first layer of defence, was brutal and highly effective. The buildings could not withstand the blast from the super-heavy German and Austrian guns and were quickly rendered unfit for defensive purposes. After only 24 hours of such devastating cannonade, it was clear that unless significant reinforcements could be dispatched to the city, Antwerp would fall within a few days at best. What could the Allies do to prevent the loss of Antwerp? A small British force of Royal Marines and some cavalry had landed at Dunkirk on 19–20 September but, lacking artillery and a means of transportation, they represented neither an obvious threat to the German operations at Antwerp nor any real practical help to the Belgian defenders of the city.

The British had few remaining troops in reserve. Virtually the whole of the regular army was already deployed in France with the BEF. Only the 7th Division, being formed from units returning from Empire postings, and the newly formed 3rd Cavalry Division could be sent and this would take several days at best to organise. There was, however, a scratch force of surplus naval volunteers being formed into an infantry division that might be able to arrive more quickly. But its members were, for the most part, either very recent recruits with little training or elderly reserve personnel too old to be effective combatants. To make matters worse, the Naval Division was very poorly equipped and had no artillery support, significantly reducing its value as a fighting force against the superbly enabled German forces at Antwerp. But there was no one else available. So this rag-tag unit was duly dispatched on the night of 4/5 October and reached Antwerp on the morning of the 6th, by which time the Belgian retreat from the city was already in full cry.

The Royal Naval Division came under the authority of the Admiralty, not the War Office. It was essentially Winston Churchill's decision to send the naval volunteers to Antwerp. He was determined to get in on the action, whether on sea or on land. In truth, sending the naval volunteers was a largely token gesture to bolster Belgian spirits and demonstrate solidarity with an ally under pressure. By the time the army of sailors arrived, the collapse of the fortress city was inevitable. The German artillery onslaught had blasted a way through the outer ring of defensive forts and the vastly superior German infantry had no real difficulty in pushing on to the city itself.

The War Office, recognising the desperate shortage of artillery to defend the city, had ordered the despatch of two of the experimental 9.2-inch heavy howitzers and eight 6-inch howitzers to Antwerp. These were formidable weapons but they would end up playing no meaningful role in the city's defence. Only six of the 6-inch guns reached Antwerp and they arrived just as the city was being abandoned. The same fate would befall these guns. They were rendered unserviceable and left where they had been unloaded, as it proved impossible to organise the necessary trains to take them to safety. The 9.2-inch howitzer and the remaining two 6-inch guns were mounted on railway trucks and formed the 7th Siege Battery RGA. The armoured train reached Ostend on 6 October and its guns were disembarked and taken as far as St Nicholas, 12 miles south-west of Antwerp. The fate of the city now being clear, the battery was ordered to get the guns away and on the 11th they were re-embarked and sent to Le Havre. They never fired a single round in defence of the city.

The two remaining British divisions in England were a much more formidable force than the plucky but ineffective Naval Division. The 7th Division had been hurriedly rushed to Southampton on the night of 4/5 October. Gunner Charles Burrows was with 10th Battery, 22nd Brigade, RFA:

Sunday 4th October. Reveille at 6.30am. Stables, water, feed our horses and are told to stand by, no one to leave camp. Infantry start marching at 8am. They marched all day long, battalion after battalion with drums and fifes and the Scots with their bagpipes. We are all tensed and anxious to move, ready with the guns and horses to march to Southampton. As we leave Lyndhurst there are thousands of people cheering us as we move off about 1.45am.

Monday 5th October. On reaching Southampton about 4am we are again met by thousands of people, the whole of Southampton is awake to receive us all the way to the docks. We think this is going to be a lovely war. After embarking on a Canadian Pacific liner we found that the ship is already crowded with Scots Guards and Gordon Highlanders and we can only take half the battery on board – 3 guns, 6 ammo wagons and 30 horses. We sail in complete darkness and are cheered by thousands of sailors on destroyers in Southampton Water. After trying to get some sleep on deck we find we are in Dover harbour alongside the destroyer *Cossack*. The sailors join us in a bit of fun. We hear we have to put in to Dover which is full of a convoy (about 15 ships) as a grain ship has been blown up by a mine, just in front of us.

Second Lieutenant Charles Banfield was serving with the 4.7-inch guns of the 112th (Heavy) Battery. They had left Lyndhurst at 8am on 5 October: 'Crowds of people lined the streets the whole way from camp to the docks and overloaded the troops with fruit, cigars, tobacco etc.'

The division had been held up by about 36 hours as decisions were made about where it should land in Belgium. It was now highly unlikely it could make any significant contribution to the defence of Antwerp. It could, however, be of positive assistance in helping the beleaguered Belgian Army, together with the Royal Naval Division, make good their escape to the south, via Ghent, to join forces with the main body of the British Expeditionary Force, which in early October was making its way to Flanders from the Aisne.

During daylight on 6 October the 7th Division crossed the channel from Dover to Zeebrugge. Its orders were to co-operate with French forces with a view to assisting the Belgian Army in its defence of Antwerp. On landing at Zeebrugge, General Capper, commanding the division, wisely determined that it was impossible to do anything practical to save the city. It was just too late. If the guns did move up to Antwerp, they risked being surrounded and captured. Capper decided instead to march the forces under his command to Bruges, from where they would at least be able to help the Belgians make good their own escape from the doomed city. It would also have the added advantage of bringing his force closer to the rest of the British Army, which sorely needed support. The division also had to protect the landing of the 3rd Cavalry Division, which was about to join the war. There was one other thought in General Capper's mind: the imminent fall of Antwerp would release two German army corps which would be free to make for the Channel coast. These powerful units – several divisions, in fact – would be heading straight for him. It was imperative to safeguard and protect the British lines of supply from the threat posed by this dangerous force.

Major Lord Ralph Hamilton, the Master of Belhaven, was serving as an interpreter attached to the 22nd Brigade RFA, part of the 7th Division artillery. Having landed in the morning of the 6th, the brigade marched south to rendezvous with other units of the division. The march lasted the whole of the day. Major Hamilton later recalled:

> The march was one of the most extraordinary experiences I have ever had. The Belgians went absolutely mad at seeing the British troops. We were fairly mobbed and it was with the greatest difficulty that we forced our way through the crowd who pressed cigars and Belgian flags on us in thousands ... by the time we had got through the streets of Bruges we looked more like a bank holiday crowd than soldiers. Every gun and wagon was decorated with large Belgian flags: most of the men had given away their badges and numerals and all were wearing ribbons of the Belgian colours.

Gunner Charles Burrows remembered the affection with which the Belgians greeted their British allies:

> The people gave us a great welcome with flowers, fruit, bread, chocolate and anything they could give us. Marched on to Bruges and had the same great reception, everyone pleased to see us. They were shouting 'God save the English!' We had a fine time. We thought this was a pretty good war up to now. The girls pinched our cap badges for souvenirs. Marched on to a village named Oost, we billeted there and had some sport trying to speak the language.

The 7th Division was ordered to Ostend on the 8th to cover the landing of the 3rd Cavalry Division, which began to arrive there in the evening. Two infantry brigades, five batteries of artillery and the engineers of the 7th Division were despatched on the 9th to Ghent to protect the Belgian retreat from Antwerp.

Charles Banfield of the 112th (Heavy) Battery RGA recalled that: 'About 2pm we moved from Ostend and proceeded to Bruges, a distance of 16 miles. One of my ammunition wagons got into a ditch and it took an hour to get it out. It started raining and we got wet through, properly fagged out and laid down in some passage way [to sleep]. Too cold to sleep.'

The Belgian railway network was, however, collapsing under the pressure and there were very few trains available to help them make this move. Eventually, at 3am on 10 October, the men of the 22nd Brigade boarded a train that they hoped would take them to Ghent. But the fog of war was about to descend. The trains were instead directed back to Bruges, where the brigade had been two days earlier. When the train eventually arrived in Ghent in the morning of 11 October, the enemy were already close at hand. Lord Hamilton takes up the story:

On arriving at the station we were met by a staff officer, who told us to get out of the train as quickly as we could as the Germans were attacking the town on the far side. It did not take us long to detrain and we at once posted off through the streets and out of Ghent in the direction of Melle, where we could hear the guns firing quite close. We took up position at Melle, covering the crossing of the Schelde and facing east. At nightfall we withdrew a mile and billeted ourselves in a deserted chateau.

Before dawn the next morning we returned to our positions and no sooner had we occupied them than two batteries of Belgian artillery trotted up to our flank and immediately started firing. We enquired of the Belgian officers what they were firing at and were told 'At nothing. We always fire in the early morning and late in the evening just to let the Germans know we are here.'

All that day we remained in our positions expecting to be attacked, having no idea what force was in front of us.

Gunner Simpson, with the 104th Battery, described the scene at Ghent: 'When we got to Ghent the Germans were reported to be just outside the town. We did come into action and stayed there all day until dark and never fired a round, although the Belgian artillery were firing all the while.'

By now, the inevitable had happened. Antwerp had fallen to the Germans and it was decided that it was time for the 7th Division to make good its own escape and avoid the danger of encirclement. Lord Hamilton travelled back through Ghent with the 22nd Brigade that night:

I shall never forget that night march. The column, of interminable length, was led by an officer in a motor. No smoking was allowed and no talking as we knew the Germans must be close to us. On the other hand the motor that was leading us could only go at a foot's pace and made enough noise to be heard ten miles off. The men had been in the trenches all day and had stood to arms the whole of the night before. They were thoroughly tired before starting and were marched without halting except for ten minutes at a time from seven in the evening until seven o'clock the next morning.

For the Belgian civilian population, this retreat would herald more than four years of occupation and hardship. Hamilton was caught on the horns of a dilemma:

The people of Ghent, who had received us with such joy as their saviours the previous day, were quite at a loss to understand why we were going back into the town and it was most pathetic the way the townspeople anxiously asked when there was any danger of the Germans arriving. It was very difficult to know how to answer them. I could not say there was no danger and if we had told them the truth – that the Germans would occupy the town within an hour of our leaving – it would immediately have caused a panic and the population fleeing from Ghent would have blocked the roads for us. As a matter of fact, the Germans entered the east side of the town as we left the west.

Hamilton remained diplomatically silent about the proximity of the enemy. By doing so, he allowed his own men to get away safely.

Charles Banfield and the divisional heavy artillery made their way to Coolscamp on 12 October: 'We arrived there in the afternoon at a farmhouse. The men had to sleep anywhere they could but managed to get into a barn. The civilians all along the march were giving us fruit, smokes, and even raw bacon …'.

The 7th Division wisely made its own way south to join forces with the bulk of the BEF, which was by now moving up to resume its original position on the left flank of the French – the position from which they had started the campaign in August. It was a tense journey, as Charles Banfield recalled: 'What a lovely time, raining the whole way and all on the tiptoe of excitement. The Germans were reported to be very close the whole way.'

The Belgian expedition had come to an end. Now the 7th Division would provide a crucial source of fresh manpower and extra firepower for the real challenge that lay ahead: the First Battle of Ypres.

Chapter 8

The Race to the Sea and First Contact at Ypres

'Bombardment terrific – seven Batteries firing hard over my head has given me a terrible gun headache.'

Major Livingstone, 65th Battery RFA

In October the whole of the BEF in France began to shift northwards. The plan was simple enough – to move the British Army from the banks of the Aisne to the banks of the Yser in Belgian Flanders. Executing this plan would be far from straightforward. In order to secure the maximum possible advantage, Sir John French sought to keep the redeployment a secret for as long as possible. Many of the soldiers themselves had no idea where they were moving to. Stealth tactics were used to avoid the prying eyes of German aviators. The troops rested during the day and marched through the night.

However, the road and rail networks were creaking under the strain of simultaneously carrying so many soldiers up to the new front and so many civilians away from it. The Second and Third Corps were the first to arrive in Flanders. The war diary of the 65th Battery, 8th Brigade, RFA, recounts what must have been a familiar experience to every member of the BEF at the time:

October 5th. A horrible night. Did not reach our billet at Pontdron until 5am. Delayed for hours by the infantry of a French Corps who were being moved on hundreds of motor lorries and buses. They streamed past us for hours. One long delay as a bus caught fire and we could not pass until the fire had burnt out.

Major Livingstone Learmouth of the 65th (Howitzer) Battery recalled the conditions he and his men faced as they marched towards the rail station at Compiegne:

October 7th. Marched at 6.30am. Bitterly cold. To Compiegne, about 13 miles, independently. A comfortable march through Forest of Compiegne, a beautiful forest, trees all turning. Halted for 3 hours about 2 miles short of station, had a comfortable meal and got clean at a very nice chateau. Started to entrain at 3pm, train left at 7pm.

October 8th. Bitterly cold journey. Arrived at Noyelle at 3.30am. Sidings and shunting arrangements so bad did not start to de-train until 7am. Had an excellent breakfast at a pub. This is a land of plenty, no troops have been here, eggs, milk, bread, all luxuries to be had. Marched 10 miles to Neuilly l'Hopital, halted for 4 hours and had lunch. Marched again at 6.30pm, arrived at Boufflers at 12.30am.

Lieutenant Fairley, with the 31st (Heavy) Battery, RGA, also encountered severe difficulties in getting his battery into position. On 14 October he recalled:

Up at 5.30am. Battery moved off for Bailleul some 7 miles distant. Road was blocked 3 deep with guns, ambulances and transports of all kinds and as wagons were coming the other way in front the jam was absolute. It was criminal. Waited on road for 5 hours and at 4pm pushed on. At 7pm arrived at Meteren and were again blocked with transport.

The rail network was also coming close to total collapse under the pressure of troops and refugees. Lieutenant Desmond Payne, serving with the 109th (Heavy) Battery, described his experiences that October as his battery sought to move into position. Their journey started at Abbeville at 7am on 17 October. Lieutenant Payne painted a miserable picture in his diary of delay and frustration as the troops crawled slowly across the French countryside:

Passed Etaples on Sunday, 18th October at 9.30am. The train is very much behind time. Four hours late at Etaples. At present, nearing Boulogne, we have at least one train immediately in front of us and another hanging on to our rear van. We stop continually – every 3–400 yards. Reached Boulogne at 2pm (on the 18th). We are now a string of some 8 to 10 trains. It appears that there have been two accidents on the line. The first to one of our troop trains on Saturday, the second to a Belgian refugee train on Sunday.

Progress was slow and difficult. Their journey of 100 miles would only end two days later, in the early hours of 20 October.

Mac Robertson, with the 70th Battery, 34th Brigade, RFA, left the Aisne on 12 October. For him and all the other men in his battery it was a blessed relief to be getting away from the incessant noise and tension of being under constant enemy fire:

> October 13th. Arrived at Loupiegne about 2am and put horses and vehicles into a field and went and got an hour's sleep in a farmhouse. Up at 5.30am and watered and fed the horses. We marched off again at 12pm and got to the station at Fere en Tardenois about 2pm where a train was waiting. Entrained Battery and got baggage in our carriages. Simpson and I together in one. Tea before we left and started at 5.15pm for, where we believe, somewhere near Calais. Was very tired and after a meal about 7pm went to sleep. Very nice to be away from guns and aeroplanes for a bit ...

Major John Mowbray's battery was part of the 2nd Division artillery and was amongst the last of the British units to leave the Aisne at midday on 18 October. Two days later he was in Ypres:

> Arrived Hazebrouck 3.30am. Much delayed on way by accident at Boulogne to train the day before. All traffic hung up for 24 hours. I was lucky on arrival. Had been directed at St Omer by the Railway Transport Officer to the next station where he said I would find the First Corps, the 2nd Division being at some place not known to him. [Instead] the train did not stop until it reached Hazebrouck. I arrived there furious and on enquiry was told 2 Division was four hundred yards away. Got in to [my billet] at 4am. Had time to wash, unpack and have breakfast in time for start at 6am.

The movement north was also an opportunity to undergo some impromptu re-equipping. In 1914 the rank and file of the British Army, with few motor lorries at their disposal, marched on their boots and many of these were in a terrible state after weeks of frantic fighting and tramping over hundreds of kilometres of rough French roads. Unlike many of his colleagues, Major Mackenzie, commanding the 2nd Siege Battery RGA, had a pleasant, uneventful journey from the Aisne to St Omer. In the early hours of 15

October his men reached the town and Mackenzie took advantage of a visit to a local cobbler to remedy the dismal state of his soldiers' footwear:

> We detrained and went into billets at St Martin village about one and half miles out. We were the first Battery to get there and we had the pick of the billets, being very comfortable and well received by the villagers. The men's boots being in a deplorable condition, I bought 49 pairs in a shop in St Omer – fitting them in the shop [which was] a big undertaking. I also took the opportunity of getting my hair cut.

The rationale for this move from the Aisne to the Yser was simple. The Allied commanders had resolved to strengthen the left flank of the Allied front and prevent the enemy reaching the coast and getting behind the French and British lines. This was the immediate task facing the BEF. But there was still the hope of achieving something more dramatic. They would be given the job of attempting to either break or turn the German right flank. This would prove to be a forlorn hope. British plans were based on a lack of hard information on the strength and disposition of the enemy forces in front of them. In this 'race to the sea' the Allies were always one step behind the enemy. In fact, the Germans were arriving in Flanders in considerable strength in the hope that they might be able to outflank the Allies. German numbers in the north had been swelled by almost 100,000 troops who became available once Antwerp had fallen, and an entire new army – the Fourth Army – of four fresh infantry corps of reserve troops about which Allied intelligence remained blissfully unaware. The BEF would be hard-pressed just to hold their own line, let alone breach that of the Germans.

Both sides were thus committed to the same strategic plan. It would lead to a colossal head-on encounter and eventually to the stalemate of trench warfare that would endure until the last few weeks of the war itself, in November 1918. French reinforcements were also being rushed further and further north to meet the growing enemy threat. Enormous momentum was building up for an encounter that would have a decisive bearing on the whole conduct and character of the war. During the first three weeks of October 1914 the British Army would gradually take up a line stretching nearly 50 miles, taking in the area around Bethune, Armentieres, Messines, Wytschaete and Ypres itself.

The fighting during what has become known as the First Battle of Ypres would soon flare up from the southern part of the newly held line and spread rapidly to the north around Ypres itself. The fighting had two distinct phases. From 11 to 20 October the British and French forces attempted to break through the German lines, down the Menin road to the south-east of the city and further south around Armentieres and La Bassée. They made limited progress but would quickly be forced onto the back foot as the Germans began to take advantage of their enormous numerical superiority and exerted remorseless pressure on the Allied line. The second phase of the fighting from the 20th onwards would last for a further three weeks as the British, Belgian and French forces withstood terrific and continuous enemy attacks. The battle ebbed and flowed. Whenever ground was captured, counter-attacks were quickly made to try to recover any lost advantage. The fighting was relentless. For the entire duration of the battle a steady and unprecedented drumbeat of gun, rifle and machine gun fire could be heard on most days. Nothing like this had ever happened before in the history of armed conflict.

The fighting during the battle was punctuated by some absolutely critical days, perhaps the most important being 19/20 and 31 October and 2 and 11 November, when the fighting reached fever pitch. A German victory on any of these days could easily have brought about a very different outcome to the war. The British line itself was thinly spread out on the flat plain around Ypres. The men were exhausted, and there were no more reserves available. More worryingly, the guns were running out of ammunition. The forthcoming German attacks would stretch the British Army to breaking point. For days, the outcome of the war itself hung in the balance. In the end it was the character and resilience of the British soldiers that eventually enabled them to hold the line.

These frantic days would, for the first time, see all three Allied armies fighting together as one force. In fact, this was the first time the BEF had seen very much of their French comrades. Up until now their paths had rarely crossed: to most men in the BEF the French had been invisible allies in the war against Germany, always operating over the horizon on some distant front. All this was about to change at Ypres in the autumn of 1914. The bravery and resilience of the French Army at Ypres in the last few weeks of 1914 would leave a lasting impression on the weary British.

The cavalry and the horse artillery, being the most mobile of all the units in the army, had gone on ahead of the infantry and began to form a new line to the south of Ypres. The Second Corps, together with the newly formed Cavalry Corps, now fighting as infantry, were the first of the infantry units to take up position at Bethune on 10/11 October. The plan was for the Third Corps to move up to Hazebrouck further to the north and form a front around Armentieres and Laventie. The newly established Fourth Corps would extend the British line around Ypres itself. The First Corps would be the last to leave the Aisne, moving up in support of the Fourth Corps at Ypres.

The fighting at Ypres in October/November would come to mark a decisive moment in the evolution of gunnery tactics and deployment. The use of heavy, concentrated and coordinated artillery barrages, which became the basic standard battlefield tactic for both sides, using air observation to bring fire down on to the right targets, was one of the principal lessons learned from the First Battle of Ypres. For example, at the outset, as the Second Corps began to advance, the divisional artillery had been dispersed and deployed alongside individual infantry brigades and so operated with little or no central control.

The deficiency in heavy artillery was a serious impediment. Nearly half of the heavy guns available to the BEF at this time were the 4.7-inch guns developed during the South Africa campaign. Although a quick-firing gun, its 45lb shells were unreliable and the accuracy of the gun itself was highly questionable. These characteristics earned the gun the nickname 'strict neutrality', for its shells were just as likely to land on British positions as on those of the enemy. It was probably something of a mixed blessing therefore that there was very little ammunition available for the 4.7-inch guns. The daily expenditure in 1914 was limited to only eight rounds per day, so in the wonderfully understated words of the Official History, this weapon 'did not count for much'. Lieutenant Colonel W.B. Emery, commanding the 1st Brigade RFA, had some 4.7-inch guns under his command. He wrote in the brigade's war diary: 'A section of 4.7-inch guns was in action under my command at this time but owing to their condition and bad ammunition, I had to stop them firing anywhere near our own lines.'

The ammunition for these guns had a well-earned reputation for unreliability. On 26 October a 4.7-inch gun of the 109th (Heavy) Battery, in action on the Indian Corps front, suffered from a premature explosion as it fired on enemy targets. In what would become a fairly regular occurrence, the shell burst almost as soon as it left the gun barrel. Lieutenant Denys Payne, a subaltern with the battery, recalled: 'A premature – fortunately outside the muzzle – bagged one man of B Section in the arm and another in the backside. The latter remarked that he wondered what his wife would say when she put her finger into the hole! This made us laugh …'

During the first phase of the fighting (11–20 October) the Second Corps, in conjunction with the French 21st Corps, initiated a series of attacks around the La Bassée Canal to try to turn the German flank and on 12 October made an advance of about 8 miles, taking up positions around Givenchy. Men of the Dorset and Bedfordshire Regiments held the area around the village. The BEF was heavily outnumbered on this new front. The 5th Division faced four German cavalry divisions and a number of infantry battalions. Bitter and heavy fighting lasted several days, but little progress beyond Givenchy could be made by the British forces. The village would change hands on more than one occasion. The fighting took place in difficult country, flat and muddy, intersected by deep hedgerows and numerous streams and dykes. Accurate artillery observation was vital, but the best places – church towers and factory buildings – were themselves obvious targets for enemy gun fire. Factory chimneys were a particularly favoured site for observation posts. The Official History describes how: 'For the first time artillery officers were seen looking like chimney sweeps as a result of climbing up the inside of the tall chimney of a brewery …'

The 61st (Howitzer) Battery of the 8th Brigade RFA was in action a mile to the south of Givenchy, beside the La Bassée canal at Pont Fixe, supporting 5th Division's advance. The battery war diary recorded the events of the next few days:

13th October. Pont Fixe was shelled all day, but the battery, being well under cover, only lost 2 men wounded. The observing station (in a factory) came in for a good deal of attention and was shelled out three times. Fired at Cuinchy, enfilading the Germans lining a ditch, which was cleared, several dead being left in the ditch and in the field behind.

The Dorsets and Bedfords heavily attacked in the afternoon. Bedfords retired which necessitated the retirement of the Dorsets. The Battery covered the retirement but was unable to save the Dorsets' heavy casualties (they suffered over 400 men wounded, killed or missing) as they were enfiladed from both flanks. Part of the Dorsets retired past the Battery but one company was at once rallied behind the Battery staff (at the Observing station in front of the guns) and lined the buildings on either side of the factory. At this moment, the Battery finished its ammunition but fortunately more arrived from the Column in about 10 minutes, just as night fell. The position of the Battery at this time was untenable. To the right the Germans were about 600 yards in front. In front, their advance was stopped about 1,500 yards from the Battery. Only one roughly handled company of the Dorsets lay between us. On the left they were in line with the Battery about 500 yards distant. The Battery remained in action until about 11pm, when it received orders to withdraw to billets. The fire from the Battery was, as appeared from the observing station, effective in stopping the direct enemy advance on Pont Fixe but we were unable, in addition, to cope with the attack on Givenchy.

October 14th. Took up position further back. Position on 13th would have been absolutely untenable as by now it was enfiladed from the left at short range and fully visible to hostile artillery forward observers. Fired on Givenchy and Cuinchy and various farms from where the infantry had located Maxims.

October 15th. Shelled Givenchy and the church tower which was hit repeatedly. Captain McClymont fired on the Germans occupying houses and trenches on the west of Givenchy with success, causing them to retire.

The battery remained in this position until 18 October, when it moved forward to support the infantry, who had succeeded in retaking Givenchy the day before. The fighting at Givenchy took a particularly heavy toll on the gunners of the 11th Battery, 15th Brigade, RFA, who had been the subject of such harsh treatment at Le Cateau. It was still common for the guns to be deployed in close support of the troops in the firing line, putting them at direct risk of being captured by enemy infantry assault. This was the fate awaiting the 11th Battery at Givenchy. The battery war diary recounts what happened:

The 11th Battery sent one section along the road from Festubert towards the trenches of the 1 Cheshires who were facing Rue d'Ouvert. The section moved east to a position in two little hollows between Pont Fixe and Givenchy to support the attack by the Dorsets from Pont Fixe. Towards 3pm the enemy made a strong counter-attack from east, north-east and south of the canal driving out the Bedfords from Givenchy. The Dorsets also fell back and the section of the Battery under Lieutenant Boscawen found themselves attacked by close infantry fire from the front and both flanks. Captain Grayson was killed and the guns abandoned, breech blocks being taken away …

Fog on 16 October ruled out any prospect of firing for many of the guns. But around Givenchy the artillery was in continuous action. The 65th Battery, 8th Brigade, RFA, which had until now been supporting the French flank attacks at Vermelles, crossed the canal to the north to lend support to the BEF in the fighting around Givenchy. Major Livingstone Learmouth, its commanding officer, described the scene:

Battery in position south of Pont Fixe. Observing station in a house in Cuinchy about 800 yards from German lines. Enfiladed a trench in front of some railway trucks, making it impossible for them to fire. Got a good many Lyddite into the trench. Many dead of both sides all round the village. French gained a good deal of ground under cover of our fire. A good deal of rifle fire around our house. Have sandbagged my window …

On 18 October the 2nd Siege Battery RGA came into action to support the attacks around La Bassée. Major Mackenzie described the events:

I left at 2am, reconnoitred the position, a very exposed one, and selected an advanced position west of the Estaires–La Bassée road about 1,200 yards south of the crossroads. I put on parties to make cover for the guns in the advanced position. They worked hard, made trenches for men and parapets and felled and transplanted trees for cover. I had an excellent observing station, though very conspicuous in the loft of the distillery. The right section, under Lieutenant Todd, came into action about 150 yards to the west of me in the grounds of the distillery. Fired 32 heavy Lyddite into La Bassée causing great detonations and trying not to hit the fine church, put shell all around it. [I was] asked to put a shell into a house where there was a machine gun which was annoying our men. Fired six rounds, got a hit with the sixth round and was told to stop.
    [I was] ordered to move the Battery to Rue du Marais to come into action there against Auchy with aeroplane observation. The distance

was about one and a half miles. I went off at once myself as soon as I could and the Battery followed quickly. But siege batteries are not well adapted for rapid changes of position. When we left the distillery the enemy shelled it with Black Marias.

We came into action on the Rue du Marais quite close to its junction with the road running north to the Rue du Cailloux. The Brigade Major warned me the Battery might get shelled coming up. I said we must risk it. A staff sergeant came up with the compliments of the Officer Commanding a field battery behind us to say that the enemy had the range to a yard of a house in front of me. We went ahead. Mr Robert Lorraine, the actor, observed for us in the aeroplane or piloted it. The results were meagre but observation was carried out under great difficulties. The Brigade Major was sure we would catch it as we were so exposed. The guns were on the road behind a ledge, but not otherwise concealed. I emptied guns in the evening at La Bassée and set up big fires in the town. An oil store apparently burnt. Billeted in farm on Rue du Cailloux. Proprietor very sad at having been ruined.

Major Mackenzie and his battery saw desperate action the next day also:

Was ordered to get Battery into same position as yesterday by daybreak and open fire on howitzers just south of the canal and due south of La Bassée. Did so. Fired 145 rounds. Second Lieutenant Moriarty went out to Givenchy church to observe from half way up the ruins of the tower. A telephone was run out to him but he could not see the howitzers. I received a message from Count Gleichen [OC 15 Infantry Brigade] begging me if possible to knock down the sugar factory at Violaines which held machine guns which were holding up the Cheshires of 15 Infantry Brigade and the King's Own Scottish Borderers and the Manchesters of 14 Infantry Brigade.

At the same time I got orders from General Headlam [Artillery commander, 5th Division] telling me that the tower of La Bassée church must be knocked down as it was used by the Germans as an observing station. I was to use one gun on this, keeping two others on the howitzers as previously ordered.

Observing myself from a shell hole in the roof of a small house immediately in front of the guns but perhaps 50 yards away I directed fire first of 2 guns on the church and later turned one of these on to the howitzers, whilst Lieutenant Todd fired the other 2 at the sugar factory. We were thus firing at three targets simultaneously. The western wall of the tower and half the spire was knocked down and daylight appeared through the frame of the spire. In shooting at the sugar factory things went well until the aeroplane arrived. It was using a code of red and green signals which were not correctly read and shooting went off the target. Sergeant Smith was sent out to observe from a point 500 yards from the factory and a chain of signallers was established between him and the Battery. Fire was continued, all light Lyddite having being finished and heavy brought up. At 4.20pm a shell dropped into the redoubt outside the factory at which we were principally aiming. A great sheet of flame issued from it and then at half minute intervals about six explosions took place, flames being seen also, then followed an explosion with a cloud of smoke but no flame. It then smouldered with occasional puffs.

The factory was also hit several times and an outhouse destroyed. We fired until the last round of Lyddite was finished. It was then about dark. Fifty more shells came up that evening on a lorry.

The fighting around the La Bassée canal was genuine coalition warfare: British and French forces in action together at times and both working to a common strategy. Coalition warfare involved the need to share resources between the two armies. Some 5th Division field guns were used to support an attack by French forces on the village of Vermelles, south of the La Bassée canal, and the 65th (Howitzer) Battery was also detached from the 8th Brigade to bolster the French attacks. Having spent the day on 12 October firing a few desultory rounds at the enemy at Rue L'Epinette, the battery was moved south the next day to Annequin. Major J.E.C. Livingstone Learmouth, the battery commander, painted a ferocious picture of the battery's new environment in the war diary:

October 13th. Considerable fighting going on. [We are] to support the French in an attack on Vermelles. An awful din: seven batteries are firing over my head, three 18-pounders, one Heavy, two French and my own. Am observing from a horrible slag-heap, so am filthy. Five Battery Commanders observe from a heap behind, two are French so it is like the Tower of Babel. We all plastered Vermelles but the French only took the southern edge. Germans delivered a strong counter-attack just before dark. It was temporarily successful. It was hard to make out what was happening as the French guns did not fire – I don't know why. I fired a good many rounds as near the French as I dared and possibly did some good. A horrible wet cold day.

October 14th. In action again at the same place. 28th Brigade RFA close by. Observing station shelled a lot in the morning, very uncomfortable, smell of shells spoilt our breakfast. French attacked Vermelles in rather a half-hearted way in the afternoon. We shelled it heavily, the whole place was ablaze, fire and dust everywhere, and very heavy rifle fire. Bombardment terrific – seven batteries firing hard over my head has given me a terrible gun headache. Heavy counter-attack delivered by Germans at dusk, lasted until 9pm. Rifle fire terrific. Reached billets very tired and filthy.

October 15th. Left billets at 5am. Reported to French CRA [the artillery commander, 58th Division]. Had some difficulty about my orders as I could find no one who could speak English and it took him some little time to understand me. [He] sent me with one of his staff to the Commandant of two groups near Annequin. Saw a lot of Germans on the west of Vermelles. The Commandant said they were French, but at last he allowed me to shoot. Had a very effective shoot, got well amongst a lot of Germans who bolted from some stacks. A gun from their trenches opened fire but we silenced it after it had fired one round, their teams then bolted and we got at them. Six French Batteries then chipped in and that neighbourhood became most unhealthy. One could see nothing for smoke, dust and flames. We got some hits very close, if not direct on the German guns. Range to all targets about 3,400 yards. Again, strong counter-attack. French have only made good the southern edge of Vermelles. An interesting day …

In the early hours of 20 October – the day on which the Germans would launch their major offensive around Ypres – the 6-inch howitzers of the 2nd Siege Battery were also deployed to render assistance to the French forces at Vermelles. The German defenders of the village were taking advantage of the deep cellars in the houses, which the French 75 guns and even the howitzers of the 65th Battery were not able to penetrate. Major Mackenzie wrote: 'The French sent a working party to dig cover trenches and had a doctor and a lady nurse in attendance. The French fired a few rounds to let me see the line. I opened fire at 1.30pm with all four guns on the north-east section of the town and knocked it to pieces. Fired 100 Lyddite.'

As the attacks developed, it became increasingly obvious that the German lines had been strongly reinforced. On 18 October the Allies got into a position about three-quarters of a mile to the east of Givenchy – the high water mark of Second Corps' campaign – but could make no further progress in the face of stiffening resistance.

Cyril Brownlow was closely involved in the fighting on the Second Corps front. On 18 October batteries of British artillery were in position just to the east of Aubers village and Cyril's job was to replenish the guns with fresh ammunition:

[A]s I was approaching the village of Aubers the enemy started shelling it with field howitzers. Heavy, evil clouds of yellow smoke appeared above the church and house-tops and the detonations struck rudely on the ear. Suddenly from the village down the road up which I was making my way there swept a torrent of panic-stricken refugees who had been sheltering in the village.

From the 17th to 21st October we remained at Fauquissart. During this period our advance was brought to a standstill by the hardening resistance of the enemy, who had turned the tables by launching attack after attack against our exhausted infantry.

His overall assessment of the action was particularly insightful:

The fighting was unique. The enemy were comparatively weak in numbers and artillery but were strong in machine guns. Their defence was most tenacious, for, according to a captured order, they were to delay at all costs the English advance until the arrival of strong reinforcements, which were on the way.

Bombardier P.J. Hillman, 28th Brigade RFA, was also in action on 20 October supporting the infantry of the 5th Division near La Bassée:

We came into action early and fired hard all day. In all we fired about 1,500 rounds, it was a fierce battle. We had not been reached [by enemy artillery] until after dark. We had just had tea and fires were blazing all round us, when the enemy found us lovely. Every man dashed to the pits, but there was not room for us all, so Gunner Cardean and I sat behind our wagon and watched the shells burst and listened to the bullets dropping all around us. Our Captain got hit and a corporal and a gunner were hit in the leg. Two drivers were also wounded and three horses killed. We were very lucky ...

As the fighting drew to a close on the evening of 20 October, Sir John French ordered an end to the effort by the Second Corps to break through the German lines and the troops dug in to await the inevitable German counter-attack. They would not have long to wait.

At the same time that the fighting raged over Givenchy, further to the north the Third Corps and the Cavalry Corps had been busy in and around Armentieres and Messines. The troops had been ordered to advance from Hazebrouck towards the high ground at Messines – a ridge that was to see heavy fighting at several stages of the war. It overlooked much of the ground to the south of Ypres and, in an overwhelmingly flat countryside, would assume totemic strategic significance as an observation point to both sides in the conflict. On this section of the front at least, and at this stage of the fighting, the Germans enjoyed no numerical superiority over the British and were themselves spread fairly thinly on the ground. The enemy were, however, established on the Mont des Cats and in and around the village of Fletre, directly in the path of the British advance.

Bombardier Harry Sprotson saw action at Fletre on 13 October with the 68th Battery, 14th Brigade, RFA: 'We moved again and came into action just in front of the village of Fletre. We have a terrible battle here but we manage to put the Germans to flight. At dusk we leave our guns in action and get to a farm to get a meal and rest. Very wet but the men in good spirits.'

To facilitate the advance of the Third Corps, the cavalry would first have to clear the Germans from the high ground of the Mont des Cats. This task fell to the 3rd Cavalry Brigade. Dismounted troopers from the 4th Hussars and the 5th Lancers attacked from the east, supported from the south by the guns of D Battery RHA and the rifles of the 16th Lancers.

Once the enemy had been cleared from the Mont des Cats, the immediate task facing the two divisions of Third Corps – the 4th and 6th – was to advance eastwards towards Bailleul. The Germans were entrenched across the line of advance of the Third Corps on the far side of the Meterenbecque stream, taking advantage of a long low ridge running down from the main hills of Mont Kemmel and Mont des Cats. The village of Meteren stood in the centre. Its prominent church tower provided excellent observation over the surrounding area – and thus the approach of the Third Corps. British aircraft had spotted two enemy batteries and a battalion of infantry moving towards the village. The Third Corps planned a general advance along a 5-mile front, taking out any opposition in Meteren and elsewhere. At 2pm the attack began. The day was wet and misty, making it hard for the artillery to offer much assistance; the fighting was therefore very much an infantry affair.

Lieutenant Austin Bates was with the howitzers of the 31st Brigade:

Tuesday 13 October. Did not shift until 10am. Marched to near Fletre – heavy firing going on and still heavier rain. At 4.30pm I was sent to the top of Fletre church and laid out lines on Meteren. We had orders to shell this village as soon as we could see it. Luckily it did not clear – I say 'luckily' since we afterwards discovered that there were very few Huns there and the place was full of inhabitants.

Sergeant William Edgington of D Battery RHA saw action on 13 October from the newly captured heights of the Mont des Cats: '[We] came into action on the south slope of Mont des Cats. A fearful day. [It started] to rain early and continued in a perfect deluge all day. We fired a good many rounds but one wonders if fire can be observed in such weather.'

Meteren and the surrounding area were captured after nightfall. The advance continued the following day. The weather, however, continued to make effective artillery fire impossible.

Austin Bates and his men became impotent bystanders: 'Wednesday October 14th. Ready to shoot at 6am but not needed. At 9am marched to Meteren where we halted for some hours and then on to Bailleuil, arriving at 8pm. Vile billets from which we were ejected by fleas early next morning.'

Over the next couple of days the troops of the Third Corps maintained a steady advance eastwards against fairly light opposition. The Germans had withdrawn in the face of the British advance, evacuating Bailleuil in the process, opting instead to take up strong defensive positions behind the River Lys.

On the night of 15 October Austin Bates was moving forward as slowly and quietly as possible with the guns of the 31st (Howitzer) Battery:

At 5pm the Battery left for duty with the advanced guard and billeted in inky darkness at 11pm near the Bailleuil–Lille road. We had been marching with no lights or smoking allowed when a car came up with two enormous headlights which showed up the whole column. He was stopped by an infuriated infantry Major who asked where the —— he was driving to with that damned car. An individual said he was looking for billets! 'Looking for billets, are you? If you go much further you will find billets with the Germans you —— idiot!' It is queer how few brains some staff officers possess.

The Germans were in fact taking up a defensive stance all along the front around Ypres while they awaited the arrival of an entirely new army – the Fourth – which was to be brought into action in order to attempt a dramatic, war-winning breakthrough to the Channel Ports.

For now at least, things seemed to be progressing well on the Third Corps front. On 14 October the Cavalry Corps joined hands with the 3rd Cavalry Division of the Fourth Corps just to the south of Ypres. The First and Second Cavalry Divisions then advanced through to the line Neuve Eglise–Wulverghen–Messines–Wytschaete. On 16 October the Third and Fourth Corps were both ordered to press on with their advance against what were still thought to be weaker enemy forces on the retreat.

The weather conditions during this advance into Belgian Flanders did not permit effective artillery support for the infantry. It was foggy and wet and so air reconnaissance was frequently impossible. As the ground over which the troops were advancing was flat, and the views interrupted by buildings, small woods and tall trees along the roads, without eyes in the air the artillery could render practically no support at all. Austin Bates complained on the 16th that 'we could do no good on account of the mist'.

In a letter to his brother dated 18 October Austin Bates described the difficulties the artillery experienced on this new front:

Dear Percy,

We have shifted a long way since I wrote you last. I wish I could give you the details but I can't. At the moment of writing everything is going as smoothly as possible. We have made considerable advance during the last week against minor opposition.

The country is for the most part flat and it will be interesting to see what the artillery will do when we meet any serious opposition.

The only possible observing stations may be divided into two headings, (1) church towers, windmills etc, (2) the advanced infantry trenches. Number 1 is sure to be subjected to undue attention from every German gun in the country. Number 2 necessitates a long telephone with the attendant chances of having it cut and, usually, a close but limited field of view.

Despite these problems, some batteries did see limited action during this time. Sergeant Edgington described the action of D Battery RHA on 16 October and an unusual (and very one-sided) trade that was being developed with the local inhabitants:

Came into action early, east of the Messines–Wytschaete road. Fired a good many rounds again but the enemy appear to have no guns so between whiles we run races to enliven things up a bit. The natives from the houses just in rear of the gun position kept us well supplied with hot soup and coffee, in exchange for which we gave them all our empty cartridge cases.

Later that evening the guns of D Battery were ordered forward with the Lancers of the 3rd Cavalry Brigade to Warneton, a few miles to the east, across the River Lys. The German resistance here was fierce and deadly:

Came out of action after dark when my gun was ordered forward to Warneton. It was pitch black darkness and I had to exercise my wits to keep in touch as a wrong turn would have landed us slap in the German trenches. However, we clattered into the town alright, having lost half my detachment en route and having never until now imagined what inferno means. A perfect hurricane of bullets from four Maxims simply swept the opposite side of the street, added to which the glare of buildings that been fired by incendiary German shells and also their fire balls made up a scene that is simply indescribable. I was ordered to break through the wall of a house to get my gun through so that we could fire on the barricade which was only 40 yards up the street. It was deemed impractical as we were without searchlights so the Cavalry Brigade were ordered to retire. I felt sorry as I hoped to have a bit of close fighting. We retired to Messines where we found that the remainder of the Battery had been ordered into action again, and we remained so all night ...

Captain Francis Adams with E Battery RHA, supporting the cavalry of the 5th Cavalry Brigade, also saw action on 16 October in and around Warneton. He described some very close-quarter fighting:

Four guns of the Battery, after a long halt near Garde Dieu, came into action and fired at German trenches south-west of Warneton. The four guns were afterwards ordered on by General Gough [CO, 2nd Cavalry Division] to the river bank just west of Warneton where we engaged trenches south of the river and snipers in houses at a range of 700 yards. Major Forman was observing from a building in front of the Battery but had to leave it as rifle fire was too hot and immediately after a German shell fell right into the building setting it on fire. Battery then moved back, coming into action again as guns could not clear the crest at such short range from [our] first position.

Three guns were sent back to billets at dusk. The remaining gun (my own) was taken on by the Major and Lieutenant Walwyn into the town. The gun was unlimbered and run along the street by hand in the dark and fired point-blank at a barricade about 100 yards away. About 10 rounds were fired enabling the 16th Lancers to take it. The gun was then run up to the barricade but was unable to get on owing to heavy rifle and Maxim fire from a right angle street. The place was one great blaze. The Lancers were eventually driven out by greatly superior fire.

Getting his gun away would prove a real challenge:

I met with a series of accidents. First, my wagons and wheelers got stuck in a dung pit in a yard where they had taken cover. On the road back to billets all the ride horses of the gun fell into a ditch. It was pitch dark and one could not see a hand's breadth in front of one. We then took a wrong turning and after discovering the mistake the pole bar of the gun broke. I was very pleased to get back to our billets at the Cafe au Belge at Wytschaete.

On the following day D Battery remained in action throughout the day, but the men of Edgington's section had something to take their minds off the job in hand: '… getting very cold. Had sub-section races during a lull in the fighting – for a tin of strawberry jam. [We] remained in action all night.'

For Austin Bates, the action was beginning to hot up. On 18 October he recorded:

Shifted in a great hurry at 6am through Armentieres to the railway station at Houplines. Came into action observing from a house some 500 yards in rear of our infantry. Shifted observing station again at noon to the church which was promptly shelled [by the enemy]. The Major just got out in time as the next shell removed half the staircase. Again moved observing station back to the house. [Fired a mixture of shrapnel and high explosive] at a range of 2500 yards."

James Fairley, the young, newly qualified doctor attached to the 31st (Heavy) Battery RGA, also noted this increase in the tempo of the fighting. The guns were in action near Neuve Eglise on 18 October: 'Up at 5am. Battery in action at 6am. Fired all day on Warneton and Quesnoy. Aeroplane gave us the range in both cases, although imperfectly as it became very cloudy.'

The next day, the 19th, was another day of heavy activity for the battery:

Up at 4.45am. Battery in action at 5.45am. Shelled an area of 1,000 yards. Waiting for aeroplane to come and give us line and range. Very slow work. Somewhat fed up. One day succeeds another. Still I am feeling very well and am having a great holiday and a splendid open air life although it is not exactly as I pictured it! Ranged with the aid of aeroplane on German battery and were very successful. Also emptied German trenches after having been ranged with aeroplane. Day cloudy and cold. Elaborate arrangements made to protect guns from a night attack.

Sergeant King of the 126th Battery, 29th Brigade, RFA, was in action on 18/19 October supporting the troops of the 10th Infantry Brigade:

October 18th. We go into action with one section [two guns]. This section do some very effective firing. The 9th Lancers and Lancashire Fusiliers suffer owing to enemy machine guns playing on them. We are observing from a roof in a farm. It is shelled by the enemy and a horse is badly wounded, having been hit by a shell entering the stable. I shoot it to put it out of its misery. The farm owner was very distressed but we got them to safety. We move in the early evening and bivouac in a field nearby.

October 19th. We leave our bivouac before dawn and cross the railway line and get into action. The Battery commences firing at a quick rate and our gunners do some fine shooting. Our shells fall right into the German trenches. During the morning I swim across the River Lys with the telephone cable as this is the only means to obtain communication with our infantry. It was very cold and I felt numbed. On returning I am dragged ashore by the Battery Sergeant Major who pulled me through a bunch of nettles! Oh, my legs! The village on the further side of the river is on fire. The Seaforth Highlanders [10th Infantry Brigade] have a bayonet charge which is successful and they gain their objective [Frelinghein]. When it is dark we go to an adjacent farm for the night.

This would mark the limit of the Third Corps advance. In the evening of 19 October they dug in to defend the gains they had made. Any further progress the Third Corps might be able to make would depend on the fortunes of the Fourth Corps on their immediate left flank, which had recently arrived at Ypres. The First Corps was also by now making its way to the front, completing the move of the entire BEF to its new position on the left flank of the Allied line.

The task allotted to the Fourth Corps and the 7th Division was to advance down the Ypres–Menin road, capture the village of Gheluvelt on the high ground to the south-east of the city and then take Menin itself, before fanning out into the surrounding countryside behind. It was an audacious strike designed to turn the German lines. However, it all felt a bit tentative to Gunner Burrows of the 104th Battery, 22nd Brigade, RFA, as he recounted the first couple of days in the new British line:

Thursday 15th October. 3am march out of Ypres, north-east, wait in a field. Received our first mail at noon. Move again about a mile to another field. Thousands of French infantry with us. Would sooner be with our own boys. All quiet. Nothing doing. We billet in a factory which has been closed. No sleep for me – I'm on piquet!

Friday October 16th. 2am. March north about 2 miles. Stop in a lane for about 6 hours. We are getting fed up with all this waiting and arc all anxious to get into action. Weather dull and cold. Heard that the enemy advanced guard was falling back a few miles ahead and had set fire to a village. Billet in a small village.

On the 16th Charles Banfield and the 112th (Heavy) Battery, part of the 7th Division heavy artillery, rode up the Menin road from Ypres:

All turned out at 3am and harnessed up. Had breakfast about 5am and at daybreak advanced about 2 miles towards Menin. We remained out all day and in the evening returned to Ypres. Excitement getting great. All hands had to sleep close by the horses and to be prepared to turn out at any time. Rifle fire had been heard close by during the night …

The division was getting into position to launch its attack. Major Lord Ralph Hamilton was on the headquarters staff of the 22nd Brigade RFA, attached to the 7th Division, and described how the battle plans for the brigade were developed:

[On the night of the 16th] we received orders that the 22 Infantry Brigade, supported by the 22 Brigade, RFA, would take the village of Zonnebeke in an assault before dawn. Other Brigades received similar orders to take villages left by the German advanced guard at the same time. We paraded at 3am on the 17th and in the dead of night marched off down the Ypres–Zonnebeke road. After going about a mile we passed the barricades which had been our advanced post the evening before.

We knew that at any moment we might come into contact with the enemy and in front of us there was nothing but three miles of road before we would reach the German outpost line. The Germans, however, being well served as usual by spies, knew of our attack and the Uhlans who were holding Zonnebeke evacuated it on the approach of our infantry. As dawn began to break we found ourselves in Zonnebeke and news was passed down the column that the village had been occupied without any problem. The artillery halted at the level crossing south of the village, while the infantry proceeded to take up a position on a line from Zonnebeke station in a south-easterly direction.

It was a case of so far so good. The Germans had fallen back in the face of the British advance, but it was only a tactical feint and a precursor to an enormous attack they themselves would shortly launch against the British and French. The locals were, in the meantime, taking it all in their stride, as Lord Hamilton found out that evening: 'We billeted in Zonnebeke that night. The town was full of its inhabitants, shops were open and life going on in the normal manner. Little did the townspeople imagine that 24 hours later they would be flying for their lives, with shells bursting all around them ...'

As the troops settled down for the night, plans were drawn up for the next stage of the advance, which would take place the following morning. The 22nd Infantry Brigade, on the left flank of the division's front, would continue its march east and take the village of Dadizeele. The 21st Infantry Brigade would march down the Menin road and capture the village of Gheluvelt and the 20th Infantry Brigade would pass through Zandvoorde, covering the advance from the right flank. Having secured these objectives, the division would assault Menin itself, which it expected to take with little opposition.

The forward movement was, however, already blighted by a misunderstanding. General Capper thought he was under no pressure to advance quickly. There had been some confusion over the precise nature of the orders from GHQ and General Rawlinson, the Fourth Corps commander, had interpreted them to mean the division should move forward carefully rather than launch a full frontal attack. This probably saved the 7th Division from catastrophe. If the men had pushed forward more rapidly they may well have found themselves isolated and exposed at the apex of a dangerous salient, as they were, unbeknown to them, moving straight into the clutches of the German Fourth Army. This was moving up like a bulldozer, intent on smashing a hole through the British lines on its way to the Channel Ports.

The British line around Ypres was reinforced by the arrival of the First Corps, which began de-training at Hazebrouck on 18 October. On the 19th the 2nd Division was ordered to move towards Ypres and billeted in the area around Poperinghe, Cassel and Mont des Cats. The first elements of the Indian Corps were also arriving at about this time. They would all be joining the fray soon.

Sergeant Fred Reeves arrived in Ypres on 20 October with the 70th Battery, 34th Brigade, RFA:

I well remember that afternoon when we arrived [at Ypres]. The square was crowded with refugees fleeing from the Germans. Also another thing that impressed me mostly was with all the commotion going on, workmen were still decorating a large building opposite the Cloth Hall at the end of the square. They little thought that the whole town would (soon) be a heap of rubble …

On the 20th Mac Robertson was with Reeves as the battery arrived in Ypres. He was up early:

Ordered to move at 4.30am. Up, dressed and got off on time. Marched via Goedvaersvelde, Berthen to Ypres in Belgium. Could hear guns all day about 15–16 miles. A dull march. Near Ypres we met lots of refugees from Roulers – poor wretches – it's the rotten side of war. They came past in carts, on foot and bicycles. C'est terrible. Got to Ypres and halted for two and a half hours on the road. Moved into billets on a wharf at 3.30 – quite a good place. We got an excellent billet in a private house. Guns sounded closer. The 7th Division under Rawlinson on the job …

The 7th Division had in fact begun its movement forward in the early hours of the 18th. There was sporadic contact and some exchange of fire between the opposing guns and infantry. For the gunners much of the morning was spent getting into position and being ready to support the troops if necessary. Gunner Burrows experienced more boredom than anything else: 'Stayed in a lane for 8 hours from 3.30am. Got paid 10 francs near a small village named Frezenburg. Received mail. Very quiet. No sign of the enemy …'.

Charles Banfield and the 112th (Heavy) Battery moved forward to Hooge on the Menin road:

At 4am we moved towards Hooge and halted. Heavy firing is heard on our right, left and front. Considerable rifle firing is also heard on our front. The refugees still continue to come in, being driven from their homes by the Germans. It makes one's blood boil to see the poor devils. In the afternoon we moved forward about a mile and again halted for the night.

Reports began to trickle in indicating a stiffening German resistance and the imminent arrival on to the battlefield of large numbers of enemy soldiers. The advance of the 7th Division was running straight into the tracks of the advanced guard of the German Fourth Army. Early in the afternoon Major Hamilton began to realise that things were not going as planned:

> At about 2 in the afternoon heavy gun fire broke out on our left, in the direction of Moorslede and Rolleghem–Cappelle. This being the flank on which my own Brigade was operating, I thought it was my duty to return to them and see what was happening. With some little difficulty I found the Batteries which were occupying positions in the immediate neighbourhood of Dadizeele. I had scarcely reached them when news arrived that we were being attacked in tremendous force on our left flank, where the cavalry were [3 Cavalry Brigade] ... [they] had been driven in and that our flank was exposed.
>
> Colonel Fasson [Brigade Commanding officer] returned to the Batteries and ordered them to limber up and move as quickly as possible to Strooiboomhoek. Before we could reach the place the German attack had developed and our infantry were being driven back. I thought the guns must inevitably be cut off. I remained behind to bring on the Brigade staff and telephone cart and as we were passing through Dadizeele I asked an infantry officer how near the Germans were. At that moment firing broke out at the far end of the village and the officer told me that the Germans were then entering the village some three hundred yards away. Our infantry fought magnificently and disputed every inch of ground but were fairly overwhelmed by numbers. Their stand enabled us to take the guns away.
>
> At Strooiboomhoek it was obvious that if the guns could do anything it would only be as single batteries: there would be no time or opportunity of going into action as a Brigade.

The fighting caused complete panic among the villagers. Gunner Burrows moved off at about 4pm: 'Passed hundreds of refugees. All seemed terrified. They blocked the roads and we cannot move until they get back towards Ypres. Heard plenty of rifle fire to our front ... we expect to be busy soon.'

Major Hamilton was having similar trouble in getting away:

We arrived at Zonnebeke just before dark. The roads were blocked by the whole civilian population of the district who were flying before the Germans. It was an extraordinary sight to see them – farmers with their carts containing the women and children with all their movable goods piled up inside, people on bicycles, cattle being driven along the road and even an old woman of 80 being trundled along in a wheel barrow by her husband of the … same age. Panic had got hold of these people and it was only with the greatest difficulty that the troops were able to move on the road with them.

On the 19th the Germans began a heavy infantry and artillery assault, using the newly arrived regiments of the Fourth Army, on the ground held by the 7th Division. Hamilton spent most of that morning with Major Bolster, commanding the 106th Battery, whose guns were already in position near Zonnebeke:

We were on the crest of a small ridge and thirty or forty yards in front of us, on the forward slope, was the line of our infantry trench, at that point held by the South Staffordshire Regiment. We had an excellent view of the country to our front. [The enemy's infantry] came into view at 3,400 yards but they were in very open order and came on in rushes. They did not present much of a target to artillery and owing to the farms, woods and trees we could only see them here and there …

For Charlie Burrows, 19 October was a confusing and frustrating day of manoeuvre as they tried to avoid enemy artillery fire. They never managed to fire a round at the attacking Germans:

We moved off at 5.30am. Stay in a large field for two hours and heard sharp rifle fire to our front. Move on two miles ahead, passing the 106th Battery in action. We wait in small village, all deserted, move forward at 11.30am, take up position in a field, advance again. A shell bursts about 550 yards from the Battery. We go back to another field. Shells burst in the next field to us. We go further back and take up position in a turnip field. All the people are running for their lives. The village is burning just in front of us. Wagonloads of wounded pass us as we wait on the Menin road. We have to go back again so they are pushed into a field on our right to clear the road. As we move on the Germans start shelling again and we see the shells are falling all among them. Poor things! We go back to another village and billet there. It is completely deserted.

Charles Banfield, with the 112th (Heavy) Battery RGA, had a similar set of experiences on 19 October:

We started about 3am and advanced to a position about 5 miles from Ypres, protecting Becelaere. Got into position and fired about 12 rounds of Lyddite but could not hold the position. Limbered up and retired rapidly to another position about 3 miles in rear. Again dug trenches but before firing a round had to again retire. We kept marching until about 10pm, having a hell of a time. The infantry retiring have been terribly cut up. Heavy firing was carried out all day ... a very hard day, all fagged out.

On the 20th the full force of the German attack hurled itself against the British line on the Menin road. Hamilton, by now back at Brigade HQ in Zonnebeke, described what he saw and heard that day:

All day the Germans continued to shell our trenches. The loss amongst the infantry was very heavy but the guns, being well concealed, and not having been yet located by the aeroplanes, suffered comparatively lightly. About midday the enemy began to bombard Zonnebeke for some hours. They fired in bursts, six or eight shells arriving together and the air was thick with flying lead, fragments of steel, slates from the roof, glass and bricks. The noise was appalling ...

About 3 in the afternoon the high explosive shells started. The German gunners, knowing that our HQ was in the town, were using the church steeple as a target. This bombardment in the streets of a town by high explosive shells was, I think, the worst part of the whole experience. Everything in the town shook when one of these shells burst: the whole ground appeared to tremble, as in an earthquake, even when the explosion was a hundred yards away.

Our infantry were, all this time, being subjected to appalling fire by both shrapnel and Black Marias, the trenches in many parts being completely blown in and the men in them buried. They dug out as many as they could but when the cover was gone the survivors were exposed to view and as nothing can live under fire unless entrenched, I fear many of the men were buried alive. It was becoming obvious that our position was becoming untenable and it was decided to withdraw as soon as it was dark. By this time we had no reserves, all having long ago been sent up into the trenches. Even the General's own HQ guard had gone up too. The only men available were some belonging to a company of the Royal Engineers. They hastily threw up a little shelter trench at the level crossing and if the worst came to the worst we hoped to be able to hold the crossing until the remains of the infantry got through.

Unfortunately, we had no position prepared for the guns in rear and it seemed quite likely we should have no chance of digging in at a fresh place. The same thing had been happening on the right and the other Brigades were compelled to withdraw also …

Charlie Burrows was close by, his battery in position near the level crossing outside Zonnebeke:

we go into action at 7am in a turnip field near a farm. Heavy artillery fire to our right. The Battery starts firing again at 9am and we fire at intervals for about 6 hours all told. Heard that the enemy's infantry were attacking very fiercely. We keep firing until dark, then retire to a small village and billet there. All the houses are deserted. Move off again at 10pm for a night attack and go into action at the same place.

Charles Banfield described 20 October as 'another hellish day':

Turned out at 3am and moved off at 4 to take up position near Zonnebeke. Got into position and dug trenches. We then opened fire and kept in action throughout the day. Heavy artillery firing going on from all directions, one continuous roar. Infantry and Maxim fire being kept up continuously. A terrible fire is being dealt to the Germans and they soon found our position. The German shrapnel began to fall near our position and the Jack Johnsons were falling over. Everyone tried to take cover. No casualties. The horse and field artillery retired from positions near us during the afternoon and took up new positions. At dusk the Battery moved back to Frezenberg and billeted. The horses were kept harnessed and tied to vehicles on the road. The guns were in a bad position as the ground was soft and after a few rounds the guns sank to the axle trees. A very hard day …

Bombardier Thomas Langston of the 114th Battery, 25th Brigade, RFA, was in action on the front held by the 1st Division to the north of the Menin road on 20 October:

At 5.30am the enemy commenced to shell our position. [A round] dropped under a tree directly in the rear of number 3 gun and killed four and wounded seven. Under great difficulty we managed to dress the wounded and bury the dead. Still the shells continued to fall around us and do great damage to the wagon line. Altogether, the casualties number around sixty. We are ordered to withdraw – a very difficult procedure owing to the number of horses being injured. I assist in getting three guns and one wagon out of action.

During the fighting on the 20th Major Moloney, the CO of the 104th Battery, was seriously wounded. Major Hamilton went to his rescue:

About 5pm news came down that Major Moloney had been seriously wounded. He was observing from the infantry trenches some 800 yards in front of his guns at the foot of the windmill by Zonnebeke station. I rode up to see if I could help.

When I eventually reached the windmill close to Moloney's observation post I found a young officer, of I think The Queen's, sheltering under the mound of the windmill with some twenty men. He told me that he and his men were all that were left of a company of 250. He also told me that Moloney had been dragged out of his trench and was lying behind a cottage on the other side of the road. On reaching this, I found that he had already been moved back towards his Battery. I could see him being carried on a stretcher. He was now under cover from rifle fire and it was much better to let them continue across the 800 yards intervening between where he was hit and the Battery than take him all the way round through the streets of the town which were being heavily shelled. I found an ambulance at the level crossing and took it up to the farm, where we were joined by the Medical Officer. Moloney had just arrived at the farm and was lying on some straw in the kitchen with some other wounded men …

Elsewhere on the 20th, heavy German attacks were launched along the whole section of the British and French lines around Ypres.

James Fairley was with the 31st (Heavy) Battery RGA near Neuve Eglise:

> Up at 7am. Cold and rainy morning. We are situated right on the crest of a hill and the wind comes whistling along at a great rate. A great battle began today about 10am. Germans attacked our lines vigorously and have driven us back in parts. What with the shells of 8 heavy and 6 field guns sending shell over our heads, and the German shells bursting upon us we had a pretty rotten time. Then at 3pm 8 German Black Marias [heavy howitzer rounds] burst within 100 yards of our Battery and although they had the line perfectly they did not send anymore. If they had increased their range by 100 yards they would have given us a rotten time. We fired an enormous number of rounds all day – 280 – and the ammunition man does not know how we will keep the supply up. One can hear rifles and Maxims crackling away in the valley below us. We are all wondering how the battle is going …

The artillery of the 6th Division was also heavily engaged on 20 October, supporting the 17th Infantry Brigade in the line to the east and south-east of Armentieres. The war diary of the 2nd Brigade RFA describes how the batteries were employed:

> 21st and 53rd Batteries in action shelling various objectives with the aid of observing officers. Heavy shell fire in the evening. Both batteries searched behind woods in the direction of Funquereau and (hostile) fire ceased.
>
> Received information that the Royal Fusiliers were about to be attacked at about 4pm. 53rd opened heavy fire on the enemy's trenches at Epinette and checked the attack before it was developed.

The 86th (Howitzer) Battery of the 12th Brigade RFA fired off 667 rounds of 4.5-inch ammunition on 20 October from a position just to the north of Bois Grenier, assisting The Buffs in repelling heavy enemy infantry attacks on Radinghem.

The task facing the 7th Division on 21 October was to hold its ground as the First Corps moved up on its left to ease the pressure. Major Hamilton was convinced that his positions were being spied on by the enemy, using abandoned houses in the village as vantage points:

At dawn we took up a position extending roughly from the level crossing west of Zonnebeke to the vicinity of Veldhoek. This line passed through a thick wood and it was in this wood on succeeding days that our losses were heaviest.

Owing to various suspicious happenings the GOC (General Capper) instructed me to go with the Provost-Sergeant and search the houses for spies. This was as unpleasant a task as one could well hope to perform. By now, the eastern part of the town where I was searching was being subjected to heavy and continuous shell fire. The street was also enfiladed by rifle fire. All the doors had been locked by their owners before leaving and I think this part of Belgium must make a peculiarly strong form of lock and bolt. I never could have believed it so difficult to break in doors. At last we found a forge and in it a large bar of iron, so heavy that it was as much as two men could do to carry it. Our task now became easy. One blow was almost invariably enough.

We searched dozens of houses in this manner. At last we came to one house where, on rushing in, we were met by a man in plain clothes with a rifle who immediately fired and shot the Provost-Sergeant practically through the heart. His assailant was immediately killed ...

The gunners were in action alongside the infantry and had to contend with the attentions of German snipers as well as the menace of shell fire. On 21 October Gunner Edward Childs was with the 12th Battery, 35th Brigade, RFA, at Kruiseecke on the right flank of the 7th Division: 'Snipers caused great trouble. Lieutenant Dennis killed. Terrible time. 7 men killed. Made crosses and put names on graves.'

Charles Banfield and his fellow gunners of the 112th (Heavy) Battery were also the subject of the snipers' attention that day:

A continuous sniping was going on and the Battery, through being as near the infantry lines, were under fire of the German infantry. Spent bullets were whizzing and dropping around us all day. Two men in the Battery got wounded and a few also of the ammunition column. One bullet struck the ground only about 2 inches from my side while chatting with the Colonel.

It was not only sniping that Banfield had to contend with:

The German shrapnel is bursting just beyond the Battery and the Jack Johnsons are dropping just to the right. It's like being in hell. The whole ground shaking. Everyone had to keep in the trenches. I thought my last day had come. My gun went out of action during the afternoon – the extractor failing to extract the empty cartridge cases. We ceased fire about 6pm and retired to Frezenberg to take up billets.

The infantry of the 2nd Division were all in position and ready to launch their own attack on 21 October on the line Zonnebeke–St Julien. The troops made steady progress and by 2pm had advanced between 1–2,000 yards from the Zonnebeke–Langemark road (the start line for the attack), although they had been under steady artillery and machine gun fire. The 9th Battery, 41st Brigade, RFA, came into action supporting the 3rd Coldstreams at a range of only 1,200 yards, from where it fired a colossal 1,400 rounds of ammunition.

Gunner Albert Reeve was with the 16th Battery, 41st Brigade, RFA:

[A]t present we are in reserve ready to support the Guards who are attacking a village in front. Moved off to support the infantry and dropped into action behind a hedge and immediately came under shell fire. I had some [land] as near as I want any to come and got rid of 100 rounds at my gun. Enemy's trenches only 1,000 yards away from our position. As it was getting dark they made an attack and we were under heavy fire for half an hour …

The First Corps artillery was in fact presented with abundant targets that day. The 46th Battery, 39th Brigade, RFA, for example, had the target the gunners dreamed about: thick waves of enemy infantry advancing in close formation in the open at a range of only 1,000 yards. They could not fail to inflict hideous casualties on the German soldiers. The advance of the 2nd Division gradually ran out of steam as neither the 1st Division on the left nor the 7th Division on the right could get forward. The French further to the north were in fact being pushed back by a strong infantry counter-attack that presented a serious risk to the 1st Division. The 2nd Division therefore halted its attack and that evening entrenched on a line stretching about a mile and a half from just north-west of Zonnebeke to a point on the St Julien–Poelcappelle road. Here its troops would stay for the next couple of days as they sought to beat back the heavy infantry assault on their new line.

The attack against the left flank of the 1st Division presented a serious threat to the British line. A fresh German division began to move forward against the open left flank of the division between Langemark and the Yser canal. Initially a battalion of Cameron Highlanders and the 46th Battery were able to check the advance of an enemy force of brigade strength. Facing the main thrust of this enemy division was the 2nd Infantry Brigade, supported by the 25th Brigade RFA and a couple of battle-weary battalions of the 1st Guard Brigade on the outskirts of Ypres itself. In fact the German force never pressed home its attack and a new defensive line was established that night without any meaningful interference.

Major John Mowbray, on the staff of the 2nd Division artillery HQ, wrote home on 22 October, describing the first day's fighting:

> The fight yesterday evening ended in quite a dramatic sunset. The fire of our Lyddite shells set quite a number of places in the enemy's lines alight. One of them was a large farm. This was blazing brightly at sunset and lighting up a considerable extent of ground held by the enemy. Our Batteries took advantage of this to fire quite a number of rounds. It all made a remarkable picture.

On the front held by the 7th Division the day began with a heavy barrage of enemy artillery fire followed by another wave of infantry attacks. The Germans had largely failed to identify the positions of the British guns and the batteries supporting the 7th Division were able to render tremendous assistance to the beleaguered infantry. The fighting was intense and the defensive line on the left around Zonnebeke had to move back in the evening. The 7th Division was also pushed back along the Menin road. The enemy, pressing home a fierce attack at the point where the flanks of the 2nd and 7th Divisions met, got as close as 200 yards to the British line. The British trenches, dug in very sandy soil, were almost completely battered in under the weight of hostile gun fire, and practically the whole village of Zonnebeke was ablaze. The 22nd Infantry Brigade was given permission to pull back and form a new line joining up with the 21st Infantry Brigade at Reutel. As darkness fell, it seemed as though a further attack was imminent. Lieutenant W. Evans of the 25th Battery, 35th Brigade, RFA, takes up the story:

> During the afternoon columns of the enemy appeared on the Terhand Ridge and I fired several series at them as they moved down the ridge

[towards us]. As it got dusk we saw some Germans wearing white arm bands standing by one of the houses in Becelaere so my Colonel [E.P. Lambert] suggested that as I hadn't been spotted all day, I should run a section up on to the crest and be ready to take the Boche on over open sights when they topped the rise just west of Becelaere. We did this just in time to see Germans appearing on the ridge, shoulder to shoulder, and engaged them at 1,000 yards.

It was too dark to see what effect we got on those who came over the crest but I know we killed a good many as I saw their bodies lying there from my observation post near Gheluwe the next day …

The Germans attacked along the whole front on 21 October. Sergeant George King, with the 126th Battery, 29th Brigade, RFA, was in action on the 4th Division's front near Frelinghien:

We resume position as yesterday but have to evacuate owing to the heavy shell fire upon us. We retire about half a mile into a much worse position. We fire 641 rounds and the whole line of guns is surrounded by shell holes caused by the enemy's heavy artillery. We have 12 men hit and one gun smashed to pieces by a German high explosive shell. This is our worst position up to date. The staff observe from Le Touquet station. We are fired upon by snipers as we climb into railway trucks to observe. Machine guns also play upon the trucks. When night falls everywhere seems to be alight. A terrible battle is raging on our front and the appearance is hell at its worst. This continues until the early morning …

Captain Francis Adams of E Battery RHA saw plenty of action on 21 October from his position near Oostaverne, on the eastern flank of the Messines Ridge:

[S]tarted at 5am and was in action all day. Right and centre section on the west of the village and my section on the east. Battery fired over 500 rounds in checking strong infantry attacks supported by heavy artillery fire on line held by 2 Cavalry Division which, with 1 Cavalry Division, was holding a gap between our Corps. The village of Messines was shelled by Germans and they succeeded in setting church on fire. Battery went back to billets at Wytschaete after it was dark, at 6.30pm

Chapter 9

Ypres – Breaking Point

'At daybreak the enemy commenced sending Jack Johnsons across, clouds of smoke and earth being thrown around us. One of my gunners shot himself through the foot.'

Charles Banfield, 112th (Heavy) Battery RGA

On the night of 21/22 October Sir John French placed the whole of the BEF on the defensive. Any hope of a breakthrough towards the Belgian coast was put on hold.

For the next few days the German infantry kept up a series of heavy attacks – through the night as well as during the daytime – against the rapidly depleting ranks of the British infantry. A steady but deadly rhythm descended on to the battlefield. Their prime focus was on the line around Ypres itself but they did not lessen their operations against the La Bassée–Armentieres section of the line held by the BEF. But it was the First and Fourth Corps that bore the brunt of the fighting. The British trenches were, in the main, insubstantial constructions, often no more than 3ft deep, usually disconnected from each other, with no defensive wire or dug-outs to provide protection against the heavy shelling. For the gunners, matters were equally precarious. The gun lines were often sited in the open and, despite the best attempts at camouflage, frequently came under shell fire. It was crucially important to deny the enemy effective observation. For some officers this meant making the difficult decision to destroy church towers and steeples. Major John Mowbray recalled one particular incident on 23 October when a brigadier with the 2nd Division wanted the church tower at Poelcappelle demolished as it was being used by German artillery observers. Religious sensitivities had to be observed:

General Fanshawe [commanding 6 Infantry Brigade] wanted Poelcappelle steeple downed but would not give the order. Remarked he was glad it was going to be done without it. But Brierley [a 6-inch howitzer Battery commander] presently demanded orders before touching its 'sacred edifice'.

The enemy fire was relentless. In fact, the Germans seemed to have an endless supply of artillery ammunition, particularly for their heavy guns. Charles Banfield remembered what it was like to be under continuous shell fire and the strain this had on some of the men under his command: 'At daybreak [on 22 October] the enemy commenced sending the Jack Johnsons across, clouds of smoke and earth being thrown up around us. One of my gunners shot himself through the foot …'

For the next few days the British and French held on grimly to their barely defensible line. D Battery, in action along the Messines–Wytschaete front, had taken up a new position on 22 October in order to avoid the heavy artillery fire from the German guns. Sergeant William Edgington saw action with the battery over the next few days:

October 22. Took up a new position before daybreak, dug in and planted a forest around the guns, even our own planes stating that they could not see [us]. Fired during the day and retired to the Chateau at night but were suddenly ordered into action about 7.30pm owing to a German attack and remained in action until the 30th. Firing night and day, cooking our meals in an estaminet about 10 yards in rear of the guns and sleeping when we could alongside them.

October 24th. Much the same. The cavalry are holding a very extended line in front of us and are doing the work of the infantry. Night attacks very frequent and sustained, nights getting very cold now. Sleeping in pits.

October 25th. Nothing fresh – we shell individual farms as soon as it is reported that the Germans are in occupation, with excellent results.

Targets of opportunity were fired on whenever possible. On 25 October, for example, Major W.E. Rudkin, commanding the 80th Battery, 15th Brigade, was in action at Le Plantin, directing the fire of his battery by telephone from an observing station in a house along the canal 700 yards to the east of Pont Fixe. His guns were firing a mile and a half to his rear:

About 2pm I observed parties of Germans assembling behind some houses at Canteloux. This was outside my area but I switched the Battery on to them, 12 degrees from my line. About 2.30pm numbers of Germans began to double in batches of about 50 each along a path towards a newly made trench about 150 yards from the French trenches. It was easy to get Battery on at once as I had the range absolutely. I fired rapidly varying my ranges from 3,000–3,200 yards. The enemy was advancing straight into the line of fire of my guns in sections of four. Those that did not fall under fire turned left–handed into the trenches which was enfiladed by the fire of the Battery. I do not think very many of the Germans who took part in the attack survived. I was about 700 yards from the trenches and could see them throwing bodies on to the top of the bank. Two men stood up on the bank and held up their hands but were hit.

About this time, 2.55pm, my house got a shell through it and was knocked about and the telephone wire was cut. The Battery went on firing and I sent the Battery Sergeant Major back to explain the situation and to get more telephone wire. I and the rest of my staff took cover in the trenches for a bit as we were getting heavy rifle fire from both sides of the canal. Later on we ran back to the factories near Pont Fixe to our houses and rejoined the Battery ...

On 23 October the gunners of the 24th Brigade RFA, part of the 6th Division artillery, found the perfect target. The brigade's war diary recalled:

An enemy battery was discovered in the open. 110th Battery fired a few ranging shots whereupon the detachment took cover in a trench in rear of the guns. The 43rd Battery soon put them out of the trench with Lyddite and soon they appeared running across an open space towards cover, some distance from the guns. The 110th Battery at once turned on them with timed shrapnel and many were left lying on the ground ...

After a couple of days out of the firing line, George King was also back in action again with the 126th Battery that same evening:

At night we take over the 17 Brigade gun pits. Just as we are getting into action the enemy make an attack and rifle bullets pass over our heads. Our horses get away safely and our gunners do splendid work firing on targets unknown to them. The Germans are trying to break through our lines but are held back by our infantry and artillery fire. When the attack has subsided the staff proceed to a farm cottage nearby to observe. On reaching this place, which is in total darkness, I discover one of our men who has been badly wounded. He has been lying there for hours without attention. We get him away to safety and daybreak comes shortly afterwards.

Bombardier Arthur Baxter of E Battery RHA was also in the thick of things on the Armentieres front on 23 October:

In position at 5am with Major Walwyn. Ran out 1,000 yards of telephone cable. Shells burst very close, one scrap went by me with a very loud buzz. Went back 500 yards in trench. At 7pm heavy firing began. Bullets were hitting and passing by the stack I was behind. Shells burst amongst our wagon lines, killing two horses and wounding two men.

It was touch and go for most of the time. On 24 October Lieutenant Colonel Geddes of the 42nd Brigade RFA wrote home to his wife and described his experiences in trying to defend the front line on the Second Corps front:

Messages keep coming in every few minutes – artillery fire was required here, there, everywhere. Things looked so black that baggage wagons and mess wagons were all sent to a village some miles back. Shell and rifle fire going fast and furious. This was one of the occasions when it is hopeless to imagine the worst though preparations for it have to be made. Horses harnessed up for a sudden retreat. All these precautions had the desired effect, like unfurling one's umbrella to stop the rain.

Further to the south Major Livingstone Learmouth, commanding the 65th (Howitzer) Battery, found himself under heavy fire near Festubert. There were few safe places for him to observe from:

In action north-west of Festubert. Church and brewery apparently only observing stations. Hunted about and broke open the door of a school, got into the loft under the tiles and cut some loopholes. Saw little of the Germans in the morning but they shelled us heavily. Knocked the houses about all around our station and put bits into our house so I went on to see if the brewery was tenable. Found it very much knocked about and everyone cleared out. Very unhealthy. Had a lot of shooting about Le Quinque Rue … was hit in the head about 5pm.

To the north, Mac Robertson of the 70th Battery, 34th Brigade, RFA, was in reserve supporting the 2nd Division outside Ypres on 23 October. His battery was being moved about to provide back-up if necessary to the forward troops. It was a difficult waiting game and the pressure was steadily mounting on him and his men as they awaited orders to come into action:

Up at 4am. Breakfast. Moved Battery back to a hollow to be ready to advance if required, then went to 6 Infantry Brigade HQ. Roads blocked with cars. A lot of Generals and staff officers turned up, including the Duke of Westminster. At 9am, as we were no longer wanted, we returned to our farm at St Jean. Lots of French passed through – infantry and guns. Spent the rest of the day in billets with false alarms.

Both sides were using aircraft to spot battery positions and great care was taken by the gunners to conceal their weapons. The sight of a low-flying aircraft usually heralded counter-battery fire. There were, however, some lucky escapes, as Lieutenant James Fairley with the 31st (Heavy) Battery recorded on 23 October: 'German aeroplane came over at 8am, flying at 2,000 feet. It must have seen all the Batteries. I got my dressings ready etc as I was sure we would be heavily shelled. It was a rotten morning, expecting shells to be coming at any moment. None came.'

Lieutenant Denys Payne of the 109th (Heavy) Battery had only recently arrived on the battlefield on 24 October. The battery, equipped with four far from reliable 4.7-inch guns, was attached to the Lahore Division of the Indian Corps, and had followed the 18th Brigade into action in a ploughed field in front of Laventie. Payne too suffered from the activities of German aviators: 'Sunday October 25th. Moved in the morning to a much better position and began digging. Had only been there an hour before Black Marias – helped by an aeroplane which hovered nearby and dropped two white lights – opened on something not very far off.'

Austin Bates was in action with his guns at Hill 63, just behind Ploegsteert Wood, south-east of the Messines Ridge. On 24 October he was directing the fire of his battery:

Out to advanced trenches at 6am. Found a cottage roof eventually which seemed to offer a chance of seeing … shot from 7am to 4pm using one gun at a time with Lyddite. The houses I wished to hit were, on the whole, about 300 yards from our own infantry trenches. Some contained Maxims and others snipers. Owing to their being so close to our own men and incidentally to myself (having had to shift into the trench to get a better view), one had to be very careful not to put a round short. In one case the house was a bare 200 yards from me and the guns 4,000 yards behind. It was most interesting work – I took on 5 separate houses spread over 800 yards. Results were – 9 direct hits – one Lyddite is enough for most houses here but one always hopes they will burn. Two did today. The shooting at the last house was very gratifying, firstly because it contained a Teuton who had two quite good snipes at me, and secondly, because the gun used shot so well …

The intense fighting made supplying the guns extremely difficult and hazardous, and sometimes the logistics failed altogether. As a result, the gunners sometimes needed to take matters into their own hands. On 24 October Captain Francis Adams was in action with E Battery RHA at Wytschaete; he recalled how his men often had to improvise in order to keep themselves fed: 'Had to stop out all night with the centre section guns so we appropriated a few chickens from a farm for supper as we were doubtful about any grub being sent up to us.'

Adams' men were in constant action in and around the Messines front at this time and had no break from the fighting. On 26 October, a typical day for the battery, he noted:

Left billets at 4.45am – in action and supported a counter-attack on enemy's position. About 3pm my section was ordered to advance and support an infantry attack. As we had not to open fire until 4pm we dug ourselves well in as we knew that our position would be given away by flashes as soon as we opened fire. [We] did some good work but were heavily shelled by field guns and howitzers and unfortunately lost Bombardier Dickson, whom we took in and buried at the Orphanage where we billeted. Fired about 300 rounds during the day. Two of our guns were lent to D Battery as they only had one left.

Bombardier Sprotson of the 68th Battery, 14th Brigade, RFA, was in action near Le Bizet, just to the north-east of Armentieres, on 26 October:

> I was sent to the centre section [of guns] to work the telephones and keep communication with the 4 guns and the observing station. This section is only 1,250 yards from the German trenches and the snipers are very busy. It is very dangerous to show one's head above the trench. I built myself a nice hole, 6'x6'x9' deep. At the bottom it is hollowed out underneath the ground so as to permit 8 men to sit comfortably around a small wooden table which we made out of a ration box. A few sleepers from the railway station covered by about 4 feet of earth makes it very safe from splinters of shells – we are getting plenty of these.

It was one of Major John Mowbray's jobs at 2nd Division artillery HQ to ensure that the guns were kept fully supplied with ammunition. Not only was there a growing shortage of ammunition, but the logistical supply chain was coming under growing pressure for another reason – the supply columns were being kept too far back:

> We were today allowed to move ammunition columns a little closer up. They have hitherto been at Vlamertinghe and Reninghelst, with the consequence that ammunition wagons were making a round journey of 18 miles for a refill of ammunition – instead of 2 as contemplated in the book [Field Regulations]. This treatment of horses is impossible. But staff officers not of mounted service do not seem to appreciate that.

The Allies had, by and large, successfully resisted the weight of the German advance, so much so that on 25 October the Allies attempted to take the initiative themselves. Starting with an attack by the French to the north, it was hoped that, as their attack gained momentum and ground, the troops of the First, Fourth and Cavalry Corps would also be able to press forward. The Second and Third Corps, now reinforced by the Indian Corps, would stay put and keep the German defenders busy and unable to render any assistance to their comrades to the north. Everything therefore depended on the French attack being successful. Success would, however, prove elusive.

As a prelude to this operation, the 70th Battery, 34th Brigade, finally came into action on 24 October, just to the south of Zonnebeke. For the next couple of days Mac and his men would be fully engaged in lending assistance to the French:

> October 24th. We were just sitting down to lunch at 3pm when orders came to move. We advanced to a position south of Zonnebeke and occupied it, and dug pits. My section very good at the game now. Fired a few rounds but it got dark soon. A big fight going on in front: the noise infernal. We are all amongst the French here – it's quite a good position. After dark, when the firing died down, withdrew to a farm house and got a meal, horses came to a field in the rear. Slept in a loft.
>
> After 3pm got orders to move my section in close support of the infantry. Got them forward but no good place available. Dropped them in action and went up into the infantry firing line to observe but found it impossible to shoot as ridge flat and covered with houses so went back to the guns. About 7pm got orders to withdraw and we billeted in a cottage loft. Bought a shotgun and cartridges from a farm and hope to have a shot at pheasants and partridges: lots here …
>
> October 25th. Rose at 4am and had breakfast. Then got teams further back and took post at guns. Soon had orders to move to a position on ridge in front, which we did. I went forward with the Major to reconnoitre and got a place in a farm yard with some pits already dug. Major observed from a farm house. I have visits at intervals from goats and pigs. We fired several rounds to the interest of some French cavalry. After lunch I went up to the OP and saw the French advance. They got badly shelled by Black Maria – it wasn't a pleasant sight.

The French attacks ground to a halt against stiffening German resistance and the follow-on attacks by the British never really gathered any momentum. Major Mowbray provided a brief running commentary on the difficulties faced by the French and British as they tried to press home their attack:

> October 25th. Our attack began too late today. Did not develop until 3pm and was then too late. 7 Division co-operated on our right but darkness came on before they got very far. Enemy was heard improving his position afterwards.
>
> October 26th. French attack on Moorslede continued but made little progress.

October 27th. Attack again pressed all along front. Little progress made except 6 Infantry Brigade which gained 1,000 yards.

October 28th. Attack again made after bombardment. 6 Infantry Brigade made good a wood east of Becelaere–Passchendaele road, otherwise no progress. It seems likely that they will now have made good their line here and our attack has missed its chance.

Major Newcombe's battery of howitzers, part of the 44th Brigade RFA, was also supporting these attacks from a position about a mile to the south-west of Zonnebeke:

October 25th. Lovely morning. Found a good observing station about 1,000 yards in front of the Battery on the Zonnebeke road. Watched the French advance on our left and shelled a wood in front of the 6th Infantry Brigade. [We] located a German battery and fired on it. Were then told the battery had departed. I reconnoitred for a more advanced position and found one about one mile south of Zonnebeke and occupied it.

October 26th. A lot of stray bullets coming over and I got hit in the leg by one about 9am. Sent for Captain Crozier [the second-in-command] who came up and took charge. He could see the German trenches. [We] shelled them out of their advanced trenches and then knocked out two machine guns. [I] was helped back to Battery HQ about 12 noon and then Dr Sexton came and extracted the bullet – much more painful than when I was hit. Dozed quietly all the afternoon.

October 28th. No advance made. [Our trenches] under heavy rifle fire for most of the time …

The constant wet weather had also created a further problem for the gunners: mud. The guns were sinking into the ground and the constant heavy rate of firing only made matters worse. Gunner Albert Reeve of the 16th Battery recorded on 26 October: 'In action in a cultivated field – nice sticky mud makes it hard work to move the guns.' The mud also made it hard to keep the guns firing accurately on their targets: 'October 28th. Did an enormous amount of firing at my gun and hard work keeping the line on the soft ground.'

Bombardier Phillip Hillman of the 28th Brigade RFA was in action on the Second Corps front at La Bassée on 27 October:

> As it got dark we retired for the night but were awakened by the guard who told us the Germans were making an attack. We at once ran to the guns and opened fire at 2,500 yards range and after a quarter of an hour silenced them. During that time we had shells falling about 30 yards from us and they smothered us with earth. They were shells from what we called 'Dirty Dickie', rather a large gun. They also had a gun of large calibre which fires at 10,000 yards and we cannot reach it with our guns. We could also hear rifle bullets dropping around us from German snipers …

Sergeant George Smith was acting as a signaller with the 126th Battery on the Third Corps front around Armentieres. On 28 October George and one of the battery subalterns paid a visit to the trenches held by the Durham Light Infantry in a small salient south-east of the Rue du Bois and east of the La Bassée–Armentieres railway. George would be stuck there for over 24 hours as the German attack gathered ferocity:

> A short time after we arrive an attack was made. The enemy tried to break our line but are repulsed. I have a narrow escape from being hit with snipers. Three successive attacks are made during the night but each one is driven off by the infantry.
>
> October 29th. Still in Durhams' trenches. I am acting as telegraph operator for the guns from the forward observation post. Lieutenant Ellis controls the fire which is very effective. I am very cold and cramped but the Durhams are good fellows and are very kind in sharing their rations and comforts with me. When night falls I am relieved by another signaller and am not sorry either.

For the gunners, the fighting had by now taken on a familiar pattern. On 28 October, in a letter to his wife, John Mowbray wrote:

> These battles are desperately slow. We have to find where their strength is and gradually beat it down. This means the expenditure of thousands of shells before the infantry can get forward. When they do, it is perhaps

only for a field or a wood. At night the enemy move their guns and then we have to find them again. There is little to be seen. That is the great difficulty: it is only by feeling at each point that one finds it out. It is gradually found that certain points cannot be passed, some can, and air reports mark down guns and movements. It all takes long …

But the dangers the gunners were exposed to were real and obvious. Lieutenant Austin Bates of the 31st (Howitzer) Battery RFA had a narrow escape from death on 29 October. He was acting as observation officer for his battery in the trenches of the Somerset Light Infantry at St Yves, near Ploegsteert Wood:

I was crouching with my back to the parapet so as not to be sniped, waiting for a gun to fire. My glasses were lying on the top of my cap on the floor. While waiting for this and thinking of many things – notably the absence of any grub since 5.15am (it is now 4pm) – a shell from one of the German horse artillery guns arrived with a shriek and a bang and hit the parapet behind which I was sheltering, exactly in a line with my back. For a few seconds I was not quite sure what was going to happen. I got a big heave from the parapet which was lifted when the shell burst and was covered in smoke and earth. However, I very soon realised that there was no damage bar the loss of temper and proceeded to look for my glasses. These I eventually discovered after digging away the earth, undamaged, like my hat …

At Ploegsteert the artillery rendered as much assistance as possible to the British infantry units when they tried to move forward, and provided vital help in breaking down enemy counter-attacks, which often took place after dusk. The enemy forces were immensely strong on this front and continued to enjoy a great preponderance of artillery, enabling them to bring down a crushing weight of shell on any attackers. Making any significant gains under these circumstances was simply too much to expect from the battle-weary French and British soldiers. There was also another factor at work. By now, the losses amongst the British regiments were at catastrophic levels. The 7th Division, for example, had lost almost half of its officers and more than a third of its other ranks by nightfall on 26 October. Some battalions were only at company strength. A similar story could be found in all of the other divisions of the BEF. The old Regular Army was, quite simply, bleeding to death on the battlefield of Ypres. It was only the influx of some Territorial battalions and the arrival of the Indian Corps that would allow the line to be successfully defended.

British intelligence assessments of the fighting, which had always leant towards the optimistic, were by now beginning to diverge dramatically from the reality on the ground. On the evening of 26 October Sir John French telegraphed Lord Kitchener and expressed the view that the Germans were 'quite incapable of making any strong and sustained attack' because of the enormous losses that had been inflicted upon them. The following day he was of the view that it was only necessary to press the enemy hard and complete success and victory would follow. Orders were therefore issued for another day of offensive operations on the 29th.

General Haig, now in command of both the First Corps and the 7th Division, planned his attack for 9.30am. It would become largely academic. At 5.30am a heavy German attack began to the north and south of the Menin road. A huge barrage crashed down on the exposed British trenches, which were little more than shallow scratchings in the sodden ground, blasting out of existence whole companies of men and their vital machine guns. In the sudden stunned silence that followed the crescendo of fire, wave after wave of German infantry poured forward and quickly overran the thin line of dazed defenders, drawn from the Black Watch and the Coldstream Guards of the 1st Infantry Brigade. The Grenadier Guards to the south of the Gheluvelt crossroads were also forced back in confused close-quarter fighting in the fog. There was little artillery support available to the defenders. As the Official History rather dryly noted: 'No artillery support had been given to the 1st Brigade this morning. Only some nine rounds per gun were available and instructions had been given that if the German attack should materialise, fire was to be directed on the enemy's artillery rather than on his infantry …'.

This was an unfortunate order of priorities that would have serious consequences for the conduct of the fighting. By 10am the Zandvoorde ridge was in German hands and they would soon take Hollebeke. Major Mowbray was watching with alarm the enemy's rate of progress: 'Enemy attacked repeatedly today on the front of 6 Infantry Brigade and they also advanced in strength to Zandevoorde and Hollebeke. They also advanced out of Gheluvelt and massed at Pozelhoek. [Ammunition] park was exhausted of 4.5-inch Lyddite shell this evening …'

Mac Robertson was not having an easy time of it either:

> Rose about 5am and had breakfast. Then went up to the Major's OP
> where I stayed all day. We were shelled continually and had to take
> refuge in a pit dug for such an emergency. Shooting has to be done off
> the map as it is impossible to see. The Germans are making deterined
> counter-attacks on the whole line.

Not for the first time in the battle, the Germans failed to realise the
advantage they had secured in forcing the British line back and did not
employ sufficient reserves to take advantage of the breakthrough. British
reinforcements, small in number but strategically placed, began to appear
and the line, apart from the losses at Gheluvelt, was held. But the British
had sustained very heavy casualties, which could not be easily made good.
Many infantry battalions were by now completely mixed up and after a heavy
day's fighting had to begin digging a new line of trenches in the evening to
establish a new defensive position along the Menin road.

During the night fresh German reserves were brought into the line and
on the 30th they resumed the attack on the British lines along the Menin
road, which was now the flashpoint in the battle for Ypres. The British were
digging in but still hoped at some point to resume their own offensive. This
was not to be. The fighting on the 30th would resemble the previous day's
action: an initial German advance, preceded by a heavy bombardment,
penetrated the British line along the Menin road but then ground to a halt
under dogged infantry and artillery fire.

Gunner Childs, 12th Battery, 35th Brigade, RFA, was in action supporting
the 7th Division near Hooge on 30 October:

> Terrible time. 4 killed, 15 wounded. Guns simply smashed. Had orders
> to get away as best we could. We waited for shells to burst and then
> made a dash for it. Men ran as they had never run before. Going back
> at night we succeeded in getting the guns out, it taking 10 hours to drag
> one gun, it having both wheels blown away.

But the battered and depleted ranks of defenders kept up a determined,
ferocious resistance. The 12th Battery was pushed right up into the firing
line to support a counter-attack to retake Zandvoorde and became embroiled
in close-range combat, losing most of its officers. Three of its guns were put

out of action and all the rest were rendered incapable because of enemy fire. The artillery may not have been able to inflict significant losses amongst the hordes of advancing German infantry, but the men in the trenches, using their rifles with extraordinary skill and expertise, had certainly done so. Having made these initial gains, the Germans did not press home their advantage and settled on their new lines to await further reinforcements. They too had sustained heavy losses and felt the need to gather their own strength again before moving further forward, not least as they were uncertain about the whereabouts of the British reserves. They were not to know that the British had, in fact, already used up their reserves.

The 105th and 106th Batteries, in action to the west of Gheluvelt, had provided valuable assistance during the day by opening up a deadly fire on the German guns on the Zandvoorde ridge at a range of 2,500 yards, eventually driving the German gunners into their shelters with shrapnel.

Elsewhere, the British front came under a continuous wave of attacks on 30 October. Along the Messines Ridge the Cavalry Corps came under ferocious assault, as described by Captain Francis Adams of E Battery RHA, whose guns were in action near the village of Wytschaete:

> Started at 5am and came into action. Enemy put up very strong attack. The two guns west of Oostaverne gave out (springs and pistons). Had to leave the position as no guns available to shoot with. The Major was very upset about it. My section under Major Walwyn had to fall back from its position to St Eloi where we took up position until nearly dark. Battery fired about 900 rounds during the day.

William Edgington, who was with D Battery near Wytschaete, likewise recorded:

> October 30th. A very violent cannonade started early in the morning from the enemy, and all our guns were firing on our different targets … the whole Brigade was ordered back, my section remaining in action all night close in front of St Eloi. We lost about a mile and a half of ground.

Further to the south the guns of the 3rd Division, under the command of Brigadier General Short, were marshalled in such a way as to bring down concentrated fire whenever the enemy appeared. However, right from the beginning of the campaign the British were out-gunned by the Germans.

The BEF were short of heavy guns in particular, and this deficiency came into stark relief as the fighting at Ypres reached its climax. At this stage of the fighting the first of the super heavy British howitzers arrived at the front. The 9.2-inch howitzer, which had been test-fired for the first time in July 1914, was deployed to the Second Corps front, where it was given the nickname 'Mother'. But one gun could not make a difference to the outcome of the fighting, however effective it might eventually prove to be. As with any new equipment, 'Mother' inevitably suffered teething problems. The task of bringing it into action was given to Major Mackenzie of the 2nd Siege Battery RGA:

> At 10.40am I received a message to report myself to 2 Corps at Hinges. I rode there. There met General Lindsay, artillery adviser to Sir John French, General Mercer, artillery adviser to the Indian Corps, and others. Was ordered to take charge of a 9.2-inch howitzer which had arrived from England under Captain Stevens, a special reserve RGA officer, and to reconnoitre a position somewhere near Vieille Chapelle. The howitzer was part of the 8th Siege Battery and I was sent for as I was the only Major who had mounted and fired it, having done so at its experimental trials at Rhayader in July 1914.

Getting this enormous gun into action was a big challenge. It was heavy and cumbersome. On the road, it broke down into three separate loads, carried on different wagons. The barrel and breech, weighing more than 5 tons, made up the first load. The carriage, gun cradle and recoil system formed the second load, also weighing more than 5 tons. The third load, the gun platform itself, weighed more than 4 tons. When 'Mother' arrived in France it was hauled by a number of heavy steam-driven tractors – machines that added additional operational challenges to the gunners. But the gun had actually been designed to be as light as possible in order to be drawn by horses. The main consequence of this was that the gun carriage had a distinct tendency to rear up when it was fired. To prevent this problem, the gun had a metal 'earth box' fitted to its front, which the gunners had to fill – with shovels – with 9 tons of earth. Every time the gun changed position, this box had to be emptied and refilled. In action, the gun fired a 290lb shell to a maximum range of 10,000 yards.

On 31 October 'Mother' came into action for the first time:

Owing to the tractor weighing 18 tons and the weight of the Foden lorries (12 tons loaded), we went a roundabout way by St Venant and Bethune to get to Lacouture so as to avoid weak bridges. Was anxious about some we went over. Started digging hole for platform baulks about 7pm, had a three-quarter hour break for tea and finished, that is to say were ready to open fire at 5.15am.

Paraded again at 6am. Transplanted a big tree and made cover trenches. Laid out a line of fire on distillery chimney by lining a director from Lacouture church spire. Opened fire at 12.45pm on heavy battery target near Lorgies, range 7,530 yards. Observation by Captain Lewis RE in aeroplane by wireless. He reported two hits (in 8 rounds). Then switched on to a battery near 'Les 3 Maisons', bracketed it well enough but did not get a hit except with a fragment. This was the first time 'Mother' was in action and the result gave great satisfaction. The gun worked perfectly and a battery was believed to have been put out of action. Lieutenant Tod, who was observing from Beuvry church tower, saw rounds causing tremendous detonations falling in an enemy's battery the whole of which was enveloped in smoke for about a quarter of an hour.

Owing to the advances made by the German assaults of 1 November, 'Mother' had to be hurriedly moved that night. Mackenzie was ordered to move it to the west side of the Aire–Bethune Canal, and conceal it from air and ground observation. This was no easy task, with the steam tractors eventually proving to be the weakest link in the logistical chain. The narrow muddy lanes were not ideal surfaces for the ponderous steam engines. After receiving a bewildering number of orders as to where to move the gun, Mackenzie was finally ordered to take 'Mother' to Merville:

All went well until we got on to the small side road near Les Lobes when the tractor and some lorries got stuck. With great difficulties we got out the Foden lorries but nothing would move the 18-ton tractor. 200 men of the East Surreys and also a party of the Duke of Cornwall's Light Infantry came to try and help the tractor out. It was in a perilous position and nothing we could do availed to shift it. I therefore determined to abandon the tractor and hooked each of the three pieces which composed its load on to a Foden lorry and to go on with that.

Mackenzie was bitterly frustrated by the inadequate transport arrangements for 'Mother' and reported his concerns directly to the Chief of the Imperial General Staff. The tractor was too heavy for the conditions it was being asked to operate in, and the Fodens emitted huge clouds of white smoke which immediately gave away the position of the gun to the enemy. Despite these initial problems, the 9.2-inch howitzer would prove to be one of the most important weapons in the artillery's arsenal. Hundreds of these monsters would serve on the Western Front over the next few years.

On 31 October the Germans, mustering all the reserves of men and munitions they could lay their hands on, launched an all-or-nothing, do-or-die attempt to break through the British lines. A heavy attack went in along the Menin road and at Messines, using newly arrived troops from the reserves. It was one of the most critical moments of the campaign to date.

Profiting from the clear moonlight, they heavily shelled the British trenches on the high ground to the east of Gheluvelt. Making use for the first time of observation balloons in directing the fire of their heavy artillery, the enemy managed to lay down a withering and accurate fire on the British trenches and gun positions. At the first approach of daylight the infantry attacked and very quickly began to make threatening inroads into the British lines along the Menin road. Gunner Burrows of the 104th Battery was once again at the very forefront of the fighting that day on the Menin road:

Any sleep we had the night before we had standing up. We are stiff, exhausted. The Germans have been shelling since daybreak and about 10am they begin to shell our teams and we have to shift to another position. Hundreds of shells fall around us. A few drivers are wounded and we are lucky to get away. Heard our infantry are hard pressed. One driver and eight horses are killed. We take our teams back another half mile and we hardly get there before we have to go back at the trot. Our infantry are being pressed back and the enemy are not far from our guns.

The German artillery searched for the British guns and shelled them heavily. Arthur Wilkinson and the 35th (Heavy) Battery had a rough time on 31 October:

About 10am the German shells were falling all over the place ... the wood in which the horses were concealed was shelled by high explosives and I got a message to say that our horses were in a bad plight. I went over to see them and found that 2 drivers were dead and 3 wounded and 10 horses were severely wounded. I had to shoot 6 of them with my revolver as they were torn to bits …

Around midday the 116th and 117th Batteries came under direct rifle fire at a range of about 500 yards, but somehow managed to maintain a steady fire on the Germans. The sight of the gunners in action at such close range served to galvanise the infantry. The 54th Battery covered the exits from the village, while the men of the 1st Battalion, Gloucestershire Regiment dug in around them to provide a protective barrier. Here they fought all day.

The German advance posed an immediate threat to the British guns given their proximity to the forward trenches. Major John Mowbray noted the evacuation of the artillery from the 2nd Division's front: 'At 11am our Siege Battery and one section of heavies and two 18-pounder batteries were ordered to Reninghelst to meet possible eventualities on our right flank.'

Mac Robertson's battery remained in action for most of the day, getting finally away as night fell:

[U]p about 5am after a very cold night. Were bombarded all day by all sorts of guns and rifles. We had some very near shaves but luckily, my corner untouched. We got the telephone to work last night so I observed fire of the 70th Battery on a hostile battery which I could only locate by sound. There was some talk of withdrawing the line, but orders cancelled. Got orders to withdraw guns tonight at dusk. It was rather difficult as bright moonlight and part of my way exposed to view and enemy only 1,000 yards off, but all went well and we got back to our billet. Very glad to be out of that place …

For Gunner Burrows it was much more difficult:

We pass through a perfect hail of shells up the Menin road. Awful time! It's a wonder we are not blown to bits. We pass the infantry in reserve digging trenches as fast as they can. We get to the guns at last. They are all ready to be removed. Our gunners are very cool. The German infantry are not far from them. We can see them coming over the hill. There are not many of our infantry left.

We get the guns out just as the enemy come over the hill in full view, and away we go. How we got out of it is a mystery. Shells are bursting all over the place. My off-horse is wounded and nearly drops down with exhaustion but we go on – we have to – along the Menin road. I never expected to get out of that alive. We go back about a mile and stop in a field. We lost an officer, 2 NCOs and one gunner in that affair and several drivers wounded. Even so we are lucky.

Corporal J. Bremner was serving with the 4.7-inch guns of the 115th (Heavy) Battery, attached to the First Corps. On the night of 30/31 October the battery took up a new position just to the east of Ypres. Bremner and his team worked all night to get ready for the coming battle:

... we dug ourselves in, dug all night and started firing about 5am and kept firing all day until 6pm when we got the order to retire and that was great. All sorts of regiments retiring and the Germans kept peppering us. We retired to a small village and slept there for the night.

There were some extraordinary acts of bravery that day, from gunners and infantry alike. Three companies of the 2nd Battalion, Worcestershire Regiment launched a bayonet charge from Nonne Boschen Wood under the protective fire of the 41st Brigade RFA to retake Gheluvelt from the astonished and momentarily bewildered German infantry. This famous attack helped to stall the enemy advance and stabilise the faltering British lines.

For the gunners, the task was to support the infantry for as long as possible under continuous fire from guns and rifles alike. Lieutenant Ralph Blewitt would win the DSO for his actions on 31 October. He was in action with the guns of the 54th Battery, 39th Brigade, part of the 1st Division artillery, and his battery was positioned almost directly in the path of the main German advance along the Menin road. The 2nd Battalion, Welch Regiment, which had been holding the infantry line ahead of Ralph's guns, had been effectively annihilated under the weight of the enemy bombardment. A battalion that had begun the war over 1,000 men strong now numbered no more than twenty-five, under the command of a young captain, H.C. Rees. He reported to Blewitt's commanding officer for further instructions, and his men were placed in a turnip field a few hundred yards in front of the guns to give them a modicum of infantry protection. At this point Ralph sought and obtained permission from his battery commander to manhandle one of his guns onto the Menin road itself to fire at a German gun that had been placed on the outskirts of the village of Gheluvelt in a barricade across the road. Rees described what happened next:

> Lieutenant Blewitt of this Battery came up to say that the Germans appeared to be bringing up a gun to the barricade in the middle of Gheluvelt and asked permission to take an 18-pounder on to the road and have a duel with it. Having got permission he manhandled the gun into position on the road. The German gun fired first and missed, and Blewitt did not give them a second chance. He put a stop to any trouble from that quarter for the rest of the afternoon.

Ralph Blewitt himself only wrote about the incident a few years later:

> Rees came over to the Battery. I had rarely seen a man in a more pitiable state, he was muddy and unshaven of course but barely able to walk for sheer weariness. His equipment had for the most part been shot off him and he was absolutely stunned and speechless. By good luck we happened to have some hot tea going in the Battery and a cup and a slice of bread and jam and a cigarette worked wonders. His regiment had apparently been in a sunken road through the other side of Gheluvelt. They had been shelled constantly from dawn and he and the men were the remains. After profuse thanks for the first meal (!) he had had that day, on the Major's suggestion he took his command forward to a half-dug trench which was on the crest about 200 yards in front of the Battery and manned it much to the satisfaction of the Battery. I did not see Rees again that day as far as I can remember.
>
> Just at this time there were one or two shells bursting among the trees round about but not very close, but on putting up my glasses to observe the next round I saw a flash over the barricade and realised at once that it was a gun – at the moment I had the impression that it must be a howitzer – even before the crash which followed a few seconds later. However, as is so often the case … it was all noise and smoke and no damage was done. However, no time was to be lost and we shot down the road all we knew, high explosive, shrapnel and occasionally a timed round, about 14 rounds in all I should think after which, in the absence of any hostile obus [shell] arriving to prove the contrary I thought one

might stop for a moment to see the result, as at the moment it was all smoke. When it cleared there was the joyful sight of the barricade with a hearty hole in it through which one could see a gun down on one wheel and no sign of life at all.

Earlier in the day another young subaltern and his 70th Battery gun crew also distinguished themselves with a similar display of courage and enterprise. The battery was in action in close support of the 6th Infantry Brigade, which was holding a salient along the eastern and southern edges of a large wood to the east of the Passchendaele–Becelaere road. A forward observing officer had spotted an enemy gun in action just behind the German trenches on the southern edge of the salient. Second Lieutenant T.J. Moss, who had his guns in an orchard in the village of Molenaarelshoek, was ordered up to reconnoitre a forward position to enable one of his guns to move up and take on the German field gun.

Orders were sent at the same time for the newly issued high explosive 18-pounder shell ammunition to be sent up immediately. Moss decided to take a gun and team forward to the road itself and then, hidden behind a hedge, to manhandle it to within 500 yards of the enemy gun, which was plainly visible. The plan worked well and, once the gun was in position, its muzzle was poked through a gap in the hedge. Moss, carrying a reaping hook, then crept on all fours through a field to another hedge, where he cut a hole in the direct line of fire between the muzzle of his gun and the enemy position.

Moss then took over the job of laying the gun on its target over open sights. Just as a group of German soldiers jumped up in front of the gun, he fired, and saw shell hit the gun and detonate. When the smoke cleared the enemy gun could be plainly seen lying on its side, wrecked, with three heaps of dead Germans lying in front of it. Moss fired off several more rounds to finish the job, and also fired at neighbouring houses and trenches suspected of containing machine guns. Having fired all twenty-four of the high explosive rounds at the enemy, he withdrew his gun and men to a nearby house. But their own position had been given away, and the gunners remained under heavy and continuous fire for the rest of the day. They finally made good their escape when night fell, taking the gun with them.

Charles Banfield was with the 112th (Heavy) Battery, and the range at which his guns engaged enemy targets gradually reduced as the German attack progressed. The 4.7-inch guns started firing at a distance of over

7,500 yards but this would reduce to just 5,000 yards in the afternoon. By early evening Banfield was ordered to pull his guns out altogether. It would be a dramatic withdrawal:

> After dinner we got orders to open fire with timed shrapnel at 5,200 yards. Got off 35 rounds in about 15 minutes when suddenly orders came to retire. Everything got in great disorder, everyone shouting and nothing done. I got all the men together and pulled the four guns out of the firing positions. A large number of stores were left on the ground, also some fused shrapnel shell. We retired towards Ypres and proceeded about three miles south-west beyond Ypres to Dickebusche. After the hard firing and such a rush to get the guns away we were all sweating and now stood in the perishing cold for two hours, properly fagged out. We took up a position about 9pm and immediately began to entrench ourselves. We finished about 12.30am and turned in …

The British lines had buckled but somehow they held. Casualties had once again been horrific and important ground had been lost, especially the high ground around Ypres itself, which would spell misery and suffering for hundreds of thousands of British soldiers over the next four years.

Further to the south the Germans gained a strong lodgement on the Messines Ridge. Supported only by I Battery RHA and the guns on Kemmel Hill, the twelve weak squadrons of dismounted cavalry defending Messines could not hold out against a German infantry division supported by heavy artillery and trench mortars. British counter-attacks later in the day, in which the first Territorial battalion to enter the fighting (the London Scottish) participated, allowed some ground to be retaken but the British grip on the ridge had been fatally compromised.

A very heavy German assault was also made against Wytschaete. Captain Francis Adams of E Battery RHA experienced the fury of the next few hours:

> Very heavy attack and very heavy shell fire, especially on the battery commander's observation post at the top of the hill. Later in the day it turned on the battery without effect, the nearest being about 10 yards in front of Sergeant Steel's gun on the right. One of the right section guns gave out early in the day. Battery fired about 300 rounds from remaining three guns. Had to take cover under the bank on the road late in the evening owing to heavy shrapnel and howitzer fire. Teams

and carriages went into billets about one mile north-west of position. Horses remained saddled all night. All three guns remained in action and heavy attacks continued after dark.

Owing to these heavy attacks our line became broken in front of the guns which had to be withdrawn under heavy rifle and Maxim fire about midnight when we fell back to Groote Vierstraat, where we went into action in observation. Guns fired on known points, roads and enemy infantry which were only 500 yards away from the guns before we were ordered to retire. General Sir Philip Chetwode [commanding the 5th Cavalry Brigade] said it was a fine piece of work getting the guns away from that position and much praise was due to Sergeant Major Lane, who built a ramp from a steep bank on to the road by which means we got the guns away ...

Bombardier Arthur Baxter was serving alongside E Battery's commanding officer in the observation post near the windmill at Wytschaete on 31 October:

Moved off at 5am. Took up positions in gun pits. I was at a windmill at Wytschaete with the CO. Black Marias were bursting quite handy. I saw one hit a house and bring it to the ground. This was opposite the convent we had stayed in. Heavy fighting all day. Left guns in action and returned to billet. Kept saddled up. At 10pm heavy firing commenced and had to turn out. After half an hour [we] returned and lay behind our horses.

On 1 November the Germans sought to maintain the momentum of their attack. Once again, the defenders held on grimly but it would be another close call for the British. All the reserves that could be found to strengthen the wavering British front were marshalled together and put into the firing line; cooks, engineers, lorry drivers, even headquarters staff were all pressed into service. Anyone who could hold and fire a rifle was needed in the trenches. Reserves of French infantry and cavalry were also pushed into the seething cauldron of battle. Frantic struggles took place on the right flank and centre of the British lines as the 7th Division came under heavy attack once again. Messines was finally abandoned after bitter close-quarter fighting.

William Edgington of D Battery RHA was in action all day trying to stem the German advance at Messines:

A big fight going on in front, in which we eventually took part, coming into action about 9am, and saw H, K, J and E Batteries were all in action. About midday a Jack Johnson [heavy howitzer shell] fell just in rear of our guns killing two men of J and 6 horses. We shifted our position about 200 yards to the left. Shifting is alright but it means making a fresh pit each time and digging in is a very wearying task in the heavy soil.

Gunner Arthur Baxter of E Battery had a fairly torrid time on 1 November at Groote Vierstraat:

At 2am we quickly retired under rifle fire to Groote Vierstraat. Guns entrenched. [I] ran out wire to a barn 500 yards in front. Laid with [telephone] receiver strapped to my head all night. Bitter cold. The Germans had the main army trying to force its way through … Our fellows stuck it well. We withdrew to allow the French to relieve us.

Elsewhere, the German artillery kept up its remorseless fire on the British trenches. Gunner Childs, still shaken from the events of the previous day, was in reserve at Zillebeke: 'Standing by. Heavy firing still going on. Reinforced by French cavalry.'

On the 1st Division's front Gunner Reeve and his 16th Battery endured a ferocious barrage of enemy shells for most of the day:

Had shells round us as soon as we got to the guns so I started another trench, nipping into the flooded hole when anything came along thinking that wet and mud were preferable to a bullet. This constant cannonade, screaming and whistling of shell and their burst is getting chronic. It is one continual bang, bang, weeeeeee, crack, crash. I tried to count a second without hearing one or the other, far or near, but without success …

On the 2nd Division's front Major Newcombe, commanding the 47th Battery, remembered:

… very heavy shelling and rifle fire all day. A lot of Black Marias coming over, some very near the Battery and two right into the wagon line. Sergeant Cramer, Drivers Woodley, Pitters, Rudge killed, Corporal

Jeffs, Bombardier Diehl, Bombardier Jones, Drivers Crosby, Keay and Waldron wounded. 5 horses killed. A bad day for us.

In John Mowbray's view, the situation was, if anything, easier than on the previous day. The enemy did not make any strong infantry advance anywhere on the divisional front. After the failure to make a decisive breakthrough the previous day, the German tactics were designed to keep up the pressure on the British on as broad a front as possible while new troops were brought up for a renewed attack. Mac Robertson was confused by the fighting. On 1 November he wrote: 'I don't know what this blooming battle is about but the Germans seem to attack somewhere every day and the rifle fire is incessant.'

Corporal Bremner, with the 115th (Heavy) Battery, was mainly concerned on 1 November to ensure his position remained hidden from German observation as the gunners kept up a steady fire with their 4.7-inch guns:

6am: off we go again to take up our old positions of yesterday. We have started firing again and kept it up till 4pm. The only thing that has affected us is aeroplanes and they are hovering about in dozens. We have concealed the Battery so well that we have not been found out yet.

On 2 November the British faced another day of hard fighting. Fresh German infantry units were pushed into a renewed attack all along the front, with artillery fire even heavier than that of the preceding days. Wytschaete was finally lost as the Allied grip on the last part of the Messines ridge was wrested away.

Lieutenant James Fairley, with the 31st (Heavy) Battery was increasingly despondent: 'November 2. Things looking very serious. We must either attack or give ground. Germans in Messines and our infantry are getting no rest at all. Shelled all day and night …'

Further to the south, at Armentieres, the German bombardment showed no signs of easing up. The city had been under constant gunfire for days as the German artillery searched for new targets. The few remaining church spires were a magnet for enemy shells. Lieutenant Denys Payne, with the 109th (Heavy) Battery RGA, was in action near Laventie south of Armentieres on 2 November:

Black Marias had a go this morning, with three others, but was never within 200 yards of us. Seemed to be doing an area shoot as she did not stick to any particular range or line. About 10am a heavy attack was developed on the Meerut Division [Indian Corps].

Black Maria again attacked Laventie church this morning with incendiary shell and set it on fire. It is now a ruin. Several houses are still burning also. It was a most unpleasant sight to see our farmers while it was going on. A shock to their better feelings which turned them almost into mad things. Poor people – for they live entirely for their homes and lands and they are so wonderfully, divinely one might say, resigned and patient in their troubles. Always bravely dignified. The church episode was horrible.

Bombardier Sprotson, 68th Battery, 14th Brigade, RFA, could see the damage being done to Armentieres itself at this time:

It appears as if Armentieres has been on fire, for the sky has been lit up for the last three days and it has been shelled heavily. At dusk, when getting the guns out, the snipers were very busy and a hail of bullets pass over our heads. We had to leave [the guns] until it was properly dark as it was very dangerous to bring up the horses …

Around Ypres the gunfire was heavy and the fighting ebbed and flowed once more around Gheluvelt, although by the evening the ground held by the 1st Division which had been lost in the initial German attack had been recovered by British and French counter-attacks in the later part of the afternoon.

Gunner Childs, 12th Battery, 35th Brigade, RFA, was on the receiving end of harassing German artillery fire:

November 2. Large shell burst in camp. One man killed, one wounded. On guard at 18.30. Around a cosy little fire under cover of an outhouse, our boys are singing all the latest songs and cracking jokes as the shells of the Germans burst near. The enemy continued to shell us all night and made our lads shift their beds more than once. Fragments of shell dropping everywhere. I was showered by dirt flung up by a shell so was told by an NCO of guard to come under cover. A silent funeral for a man of the Wiltshires – he was blown to pieces by a shell called a 'coalbox'.

Major Newcombe of the 47th (Howitzer) Battery RFA fired his battery's guns in support of the French counter-attacks at Gheluvelt:

Quiet night but heavy bombardment began at 7am. Very heavy firing all day, especially on our right where the French attacked. We supported the attack: continuous bombardment all day. We turned out again at 11pm as heavy firing coming from the direction of the Guards' trenches. Put some Lyddite into the spinney in front of their position.

Major Mowbray witnessed another failed counter-attack: 'The French made an attack in the direction of Gheluvelt between us and the 1st Division, but got no further than our own trenches.' During the rest of the day there were moments of high anxiety about the progress of the German attack. Major Mowbray recorded:

Severe attacks all day. Our HQ moved to a small house half a mile west of Frezenberg [from Westhoek]. This was as well for the houses at Westhoek were much knocked about during the day. On the way, a high explosive shell fell in the middle of the road 20 yards in front of our car – a narrow margin as we were travelling fairly fast.

At one o'clock the 71st Battery (Major Scott) reported enemy had broken our line on the Menin road. About same time, 6 Infantry Brigade reported enemy advancing in force on their front and that the French on their left were retiring. Gave what artillery support we had. About three o'clock was ordered to prepare notes for retirement if ordered. Fortunately all attacks repulsed. HQ moved again to chateau a quarter of a mile east of Potije ...

Gunner Reeve of the 16th Battery had a narrow escape on 2 November: 'It rained during the night and everything muddy and sloppy to handle. Had a shell burst in front of my gun and a shower of bullets fell. Luckily only myself and Number 3 there – both on seats behind shield and no damage done.'

Mac Robertson's battery also came under heavy fire that day:

Up at 4.30am, breakfast, and then I rode over to Brigade HQ to find out what was on, but not much news. Got back and then went up to Battery

OP. Got on to a road where I could see the Germans walking down, and hope I hit them.

About 12 our house was shelled and we retired into the 'funk' pits. Suddenly it burst into flames and we had to rush to the road and take shelter in some dug-outs there. They then shelled the road and one passed just over my head and burst a few yards behind. A few moments later another fell right on top of the dug-outs where the whole of the staff were and buried them all. Macdonald and Wallbank killed and Laming's leg broken. Heneage was buried but we dug him out unhurt. I was in the next one, luckily. It was very horrible. We heard that the Germans were attacking our front heavily, and shot for an hour continuously off the map. After supper the Major, Moss and I went out to try and find another OP. A very difficult task as ridge very flat and the whole place has been shelled.

By 2 November the 112th (Heavy) Battery had moved up from behind Ypres to a position near Frezenberg. Here the guns came under accurate enemy shrapnel fire and Charles Banfield was lucky to escape injury:

We had just got the guns unlimbered when several shrapnel burst among the guns. Five men got wounded in Number 1 detachment, two of them seriously. The Major got hit in the hand. We were lucky that many more were not hit. Everyone took cover. Luckily we had our trenches to dive into as several more shrapnel came over and burst in the Battery. Many horses were killed – at least 30 could be counted lying on the ground just near the Battery. It was a terrible time. The earth vibrating as each shell burst and terrifying us all. The bursts are deafening.

Some French infantry just on our right had an awful time. They were awaiting orders to reinforce and were sitting about under the hedges when the Jack Johnsons intended for our Battery fell among them. Seventeen of them were blown to atoms and many others wounded, a most awful sight. It's the worst day we've had and [makes] one thank God to be still alive.

The British were hanging on by their eyelids. Two weeks of fighting had seen the line gradually pushed back to within about 2 miles of Ypres. Losses amongst the infantry had been horrendous. Battalions, brigades and divisions were now a fraction of their original strength. The Regular Army was slowly but surely bleeding to death. Fresh drafts from the home depots and Territorial army reinforcements were beginning to arrive but could not make up the losses that had been sustained in holding back the Germans in Flanders.

Over the next few days the enemy artillery bombardment increased in its intensity as Ypres and Armentieres continued to be heavily shelled. German infantry attacks continued all along the front. The horrors mounted. However, these attacks were principally designed to hold the British and French to their ground as the German High Command gathered its resources for one last attempt to break through the British lines before the winter set in and made further campaigning impossible. This time the elite Prussian Guard regiments would be thrown into the attack – and they very nearly achieved a decisive victory.

The gunners were under increasing pressure. Instead of being concentrated for greater effect, batteries were often split up and placed piecemeal in or close to the front-line trenches in order to provide as much fire power as possible for the infantry. Mac Robertson complained bitterly about these tactics: 'November 3rd. Got orders tonight to send 3 guns to separate places in firing line to blow up houses. It is absurd to prostitute the field guns like that.' But in the absence of trench mortars, such deployment was inevitable. Other than the field guns, there was nothing powerful enough in the British arsenal of weapons to take on such a role.

Gunner Charlie Burrows and his mates in the 104th Battery RFA were under constant fire for the next few days:

November 4th. 5.30am. We are being shelled again heavily, mostly by light guns. We shelter in a wood. Weather is dull again. The enemy attacked very strongly towards dusk and we reply with every available gun and shell them heavily until about 10pm. Their attack failed. The infantry fire all the night. Plenty of shells coming over but no damage to us. Another stand up sleep in the rain!

November 5th. After trying all night to get some sleep we are wet through – still pouring! Plenty of firing on our right but a bit quiet on our front. Our Battery starts firing at 9am. A big shell burst amongst us about 2pm. And we are again lucky. Only a trumpeter wounded (he was about 15 years old), three drivers wounded and some horses hit. Dozens of those heavy shells, which we call Jack Johnsons, burst all around us. Awful time! Never thought any of us would get out alive.

Three men and six horses killed. We managed to get away with this slight loss, but what a scramble. It was like being in hell. There are great holes in the ground made by the heavy shells. We go to another field but they spot us and shell again. We shift to yet another field. A bit better here but they still send them over nearby all night and we have some narrow shaves. Try to get some sleep on some wet straw in a ditch. The hottest Guy Fawkes night I ever had …

On 5 November Lieutenant Cyril Brownlow, who had until now been attached to the 40th Brigade Ammunition Column, was posted to a field artillery battery dug into an orchard on the Second Corps front to the south of Ypres. After a couple of days with the battery, he had settled down for the night as best he could when he too came under direct shell fire:

Wrapping a blanket around me and thrusting my feet into a sack, I lay down on the straw in the bottom of the short length of trench which served as my dug-out, and in a few minutes I was asleep.

A heavy concussion which shook the earth and vibrated the air, and a sudden pandemonium of explosions which seemed like the beating of the drums in hell, brought me with a start to consciousness.

I saw the shadows of gunners scrambling up from out of the earth and grouping themselves around their pieces, and I saw the sky to the east flickering with vivid flashes.

Having received his instructions from the front-line infantry, Brownlow gave the orders to his guns to open fire:

Cones of dazzling light leaped from the gun muzzles and a crashing roar filled the orchard. I could see that the batteries on the left were firing also. For some minutes the noise on both sides continued and then gradually died away until all was peace again. The infantry professed themselves satisfied and we turned in.

The 114th (Heavy) Battery's 4.7-inch guns were in action near Neuve Chapelle on 5 November. Major F.C. Poole was the battery's commanding officer:

At 12.30pm a heavy howitzer located near La Hue found the range of our Battery and shelled it vigorously. The shooting was excellent, four rounds being right into the Battery. Thanks to our trenches no casualties occurred but two shots over killed three, wounded twelve and killed four horses belonging to the ammunition column ...

The rhythm of the battle was remorseless, and the pressure and strain on the gunners were continuous. On 7 November Gunner Charlie Burrows, 104th Battery, noted:

Again being shelled about 5am. Still misty. The infantry are very busy. Expect we soon will be also. The enemy attacked strongly on our right. Horrible smell caused by dead men and horses which are lying everywhere. Ypres burning furiously – flames and smoke reach a great height. We expect a big attack soon. Heavy artillery duels all day and heavy fighting all night on our left. We are still being shelled. No damage. Another stand up sleep by our horses. 19th day of battle.

For Charles Banfield 9 November marked the end of the fighting. His guns were in action near Zellebeke, engaging enemy targets with shrapnel at a range of just over 5,000 yards:

About 6.30pm as I was just going to load the ammunition wagons, I was struck in the left side of my neck by a bullet. When the bullet struck it seemed to knock me stiff for a moment and then I seemed to go round rapidly and then fell down. The detachment tied my neck with my field dressing and then carried me on a stretcher to a French dressing station.

Charles was eventually sent back to England for surgery. Once fully recovered, he returned to the front. He was eventually commissioned from the ranks and ended the war as a captain in a field artillery battery.

The weather was steadily deteriorating and the constant shell fire made it hard to maintain telephone contact between the forward observation posts and the guns. Major John Mowbray observed on 10 November: 'Great difficulty in keeping up communications owing to continual shelling and wet weather. Ground is now deep in mud.'

The following day would mark the last great German attack of the battle. Nearly 20,000 fresh troops, many of them elite Prussian Guards, were hurled against the front held by the 1st Division between the Menin road and Polygon Wood. The morning was grey and the air was heavy with a cold, wet fog. As soon as there was light, the heaviest German bombardment of the campaign crashed down upon the British front line. The right and centre of the line held, but the left flank, thinly held by only a few hundred men, soon ran into difficulties. The trenches provided practically no protection against this kind of battering and the section of the front line held by the 1st Black Watch and the 1st Cameron Highlanders, and Scots Guards of the 1st Infantry Brigade, began to give way under the hail of shell and rifle fire. The Germans advanced about a mile into the British position; passing through Nonne Boschen Wood they came close to the British gun line itself. Having broken through the British lines, all that now stood in the way of a significant advance were two weak battalions of infantry, a field company of Royal Engineers, assorted cooks, mess staff and stragglers, and the gunners of the 41st Brigade. Behind them the way was open to Ypres itself and the victory that could spell the end of the war. But the German thrust had suffered huge casualties and was, in fact, already beginning to lose direction and momentum.

The three batteries of the 41st Brigade RFA – the 9th, 16th and 17th – were all in position just to the east of the small village of Westhoek, together with a battery of French 75mm guns. Brigade HQ, under Lieutenant Colonel Lushington, was situated in a dug-out at the side of the chapel to the south of the crossroads in the village. The guns of the 16th Battery were in action in a grass field under some apple trees. The guns were slightly sunk and deep trenches had been dug alongside them for the gun crews. At about 8.30am, having seen the British front line retiring between the southern end of Polygon Wood and Nonne Boschen Wood, Major W.E. Clark, the battery commanding officer, opened up a heavy fire on the southern end of the Nonne Boschen Wood in order to hold up the advancing German infantry. By 9am the situation appeared serious. German infantry were approaching within a few hundred yards of the guns themselves. The mess staff of the 16th Battery, four or five men in total, armed with French rifles, rushed up to help defend the battery. From their position in a sunken lane to the left rear of the battery they immediately engaged the Prussian Guards. The 16th Battery and its men now made up not just the gun line but also the infantry line on this part of the British front.

Major Bond, commanding the 17th Battery, was also forced to arm some of his gunners with rifles. With two bandoliers of ammunition wrapped around their shoulders, they went to occupy a wooden barn that lay about 100 yards from the guns, and Second Lieutenant R.T.W. Glynn deployed the gunners with rifles at wide intervals along the hedge running around the barn. Almost immediately the men opened up on German soldiers at a range of about 400 yards. Some of the enemy advanced to within 150 yards of the guns before being hit. None came any closer. On the right flank of the brigade a small party of cooks, signallers and servants, armed with rifles and under the command of the brigade veterinary officer, were rushed up to hold a position around a few cottages 400 yards in front of Westhoek crossroads. There they linked up with a dozen or so British infantrymen and together this scratch force began to pour a steady fire into the oncoming Germans.

A party of gunners from the 35th (Heavy) Battery, in action a few hundred yards away to the west of the Estkernest crossroads, was dispatched to provide further rifle fire protection to the defence of the 41st Brigade. Under the command of Lieutenant Hyde Clark, the officer commanding the battery ammunition column, they rendered valuable assistance in holding the line. Hyde Clark himself was seriously wounded by a rifle bullet.

Throughout the morning the guns of the 41st Brigade were under direct rifle fire; in addition, the 9th and 17th Batteries were subjected to continuous and heavy shelling from the German artillery. Casualties would have been higher were it not for the cover provided by the gun shields, which were peppered by bullets.

The rifle fire from the various parties of gunners, together with the shrapnel fire from the guns, which were targeting enemy troops in the open as well as those sheltering in various cottages and farmhouses, finally began to break up the German thrust, which in truth had already lost considerable momentum, and eventually halted it altogether. Batteries in action on the flanks of the German penetration cooperated by enfilading the German positions. The howitzers of the 44th Brigade, for example, on the left of the 41st Brigade, were able to give some support by shelling concentrations of German infantry who were preparing to join in the fighting. This helped to disrupt the strength of the German thrust. Major Newcombe, however, recalled how precarious the situation looked at one point during the day:

Heavy attack on our right, where the Germans got through and were at one time in a wood a mile to the rear of the Battery. They were eventually driven out but there was a lot of shooting all day in the direction of Westhoek. Went on until 6pm when things quietened down. We got through a lot of ammunition. A very strenuous day. I slept with the Battery that night.

By the middle of the afternoon the British front line was recovered after a counter-attack by the 2nd Oxford & Buckinghamshire Light Infantry.
    Gunner Albert Reeve was with the 16th Battery on this fateful day:

November 11th. Got a warm reception on going to the guns from the enemy's shells. As soon as it was light they commenced a regular bombardment and we had to lay low. Our infantry began coming back and before we knew where we were the enemy were upon us. We had a very busy hour, especially at my gun. Some of them got to within 30 yards. They didn't go back. We plonked the shrapnel into all the farmhouses all round our front, at point blank and soon had several going back and tried to entrench – but we got them nicely and those that got out of the trenches were popped off by our spare gunners with rifles. Accounted for several hundred. Our reserve infantry came up and finished off the job. Got a fine message from the GOC congratulating us on our work and in saving a critical situation.

Major John Mowbray had been up early that day and had seen the shelling of Westhoek:

November 11th. Rode out with General Perceval [Artillery Commander 2 Division] to see 41 Brigade but seeing Westhoek very heavily shelled [at 8.30am] suggested he should not go there. At 9am 41 Brigade sent an officer to report that the enemy had advanced against 1st Infantry Brigade. They were told to stick tight. At 11.45am … 41 Brigade had repulsed enemy who had penetrated line and got into Nonne Boschen Wood and advanced through it. It had appeared that they caught one or two stragglers and with their own rifles, formed a firing line of about 25 men, aided by a few men from 35 Heavy Battery. This successful work checked the advance and gave time for the reserve to come up. At 3.30pm it was reported that the wood was cleared and trenches re-occupied.

The fighting that day was the last serious attempt on the part of the Germans to break the line at Ypres. They maintained a heavy artillery fire against the British line but made no further serious infantry attacks. The fighting had been horrendously costly on both sides. The original BEF had, to all intents and purposes, been reduced to a tiny rump. The 1st Division, for example, which had borne the brunt of much of the fighting at Ypres, on 12 November could muster only 68 officers and just over 2,700 other ranks – roughly a tenth of its original fighting strength. The Official History describes in a telling and understated way how, at the end of the First Battle of Ypres, 'the old British Army was gone past recall'. Of the infantry battalions that had fought at Mons, on the Aisne and at Ypres, few had more than one or two officers and maybe thirty men left of those who had landed in France in August. The losses amongst the artillery had also been heavy. Batteries were kept up to strength as far as possible by a constant supply of fresh drafts from home. During October and November 1914 the BEF suffered over 58,000 casualties.

Chapter 10

Winter

'We hope for a few days' rest.'

Lieutenant Mac Robertson, 34th Battery RFA

Just as the battle of Ypres was petering out, the 8th Division arrived to bolster the depleted ranks of the BEF, although it was far from being in perfect fighting condition. It was made up almost entirely of old soldiers and was barely trained to take the field. Its artillery was not up to strength either. It had no howitzer brigade at all, and one of its brigades was made up of horse artillery 13-pounder guns. One of these horse artillery units was G Battery, 5th Brigade, RHA, under the command of Lieutenant Colonel H.M. Davson. At 3am on 15 November, in the freezing darkness, Davson's battery took over the gun pits of the 29th Battery RFA. Its baptism of fire was about to begin:

> We found later, when dawn broke, that it was not an ideal position. Except for the Aubers Ridge, which appeared to overshadow us, the country was flat. The guns were concealed behind a blackthorn hedge and, owing to water, the pits could not be dug deep. Our first night was enlivened by an enemy attack. It was probably only a raid and was easily beaten off. On the following night he shelled us vigorously at 6.30, 8.15, 10pm and at 5am. It was unpleasant but not damaging. Then the frost came and afterwards the snow. Shelling continued at night but there was little during the day …

As the British Army settled down for the winter, the first requirement was for more men to help hold the line until Kitchener's New Armies could enter the field of battle in the new year. By the end of the year no fewer than twenty-three Territorial infantry battalions had arrived to stiffen the front, but the position was still far from secure. The desperate losses and the continuing shortages of ammunition were major causes of alarm at GHQ. Fortunately winter was descending. The battleground was now an ocean of mud. Fatigue and exhaustion, together with the enormous casualties, had combined to impose an uneasy stasis across both sides of the battlefield. From time to time, fighting flared up as one side or the other sought some tactical advantage, but for now at least, both sides began to dig in, to await reinforcements and to bide their time until the weather allowed the fighting season to open again in the spring.

From 15 November, and over the next few days, the battered British troops began to leave the Ypres front and were replaced by French units. By the 22nd the British held a much shorter and more compact front, stretching from the La Bassée canal at Givenchy to Wytschaete. Here they would dig their trenches, gun pits and dug-outs, and begin a new battle with the elements as well as the enemy.

Mac Robertson left Ypres with his men on 16 November. They marched to Locre: 'We hope for a few days' rest. Of course, the roads were impossible. The pavement, the only place on each side, mud inches deep. We had a most damnable march, halting continuously, being passed by the French the whole time.'

Major Newcombe of the 47th Battery had a very similar experience:

November 15th. Got orders at 2pm to move at dusk as we were being relieved by the French. Moved out at 4.30pm after considerable difficulty in getting the guns out of their pits and through the mud. Fearful confusion on the road, our columns and the French all trying to pass in opposite directions and road two feet deep in mud. Marched through Ypres and arrived at a farm four miles west of Ypres by midnight.

Sergeant King of the 126th Battery left the front line for some well earned rest and recuperation on 18 November: 'Leave Houplines at 3am. March to position for rest. The roads in a very bad state. We get into camp about 9am. So glad to be at rest as we have been in action so long. Sleep in hayloft at night …'

The fighting continued in fits and starts over the next few weeks but it would not become active again until the following spring. A winter survival routine began to establish itself. In letters home on 22 and 28 November Major Ernest Tyrell of the 108th (Heavy) Battery RGA wrote:

One gets a good deal of time at this game for writing letters for it is often too misty or dark to make it worthwhile shooting. One may have to wait hours for orders or for targets to appear. One is in a half frozen state all day and one's feet and hands are perfectly numb sitting still in a trench. Luckily I can retire at frequent intervals to the adjacent farm house and get thawed. There is a farm house also down close to the guns where the men can go in and get warm by relays when we are not actually shooting.

Really things are getting a bit monotonous here …

As winter took hold and the fighting subsided, officers and men were allowed some well earned leave. Mac Robertson left with a party of sixty officers on 20 November. He travelled up to Victoria rail station in London and then caught the 3.55pm train to Hayling in Hampshire. Here he would meet up with his younger brother Alec, a newly commissioned infantry subaltern. Mac made the most of his trip, and his family and friends all gathered around to see the returning warrior. He had a game of tennis with his father and played the piano in the evening. He, like all the others, did not know whether this would be the last time he would see his family and friends. On the 24th he went up to London for the day: 'Went and left luggage at Brook Street, then ordered table for lunch and seats at the Coliseum, then to Selfridges to do some shopping. Lunch at the Trocadero. A very good lunch and after it the Coliseum – a very good show.'

Mac would live to see his family once more, in February 1915. On 22 May that year he was killed when a shell exploded outside the house he was using as an observation post near Givenchy.

Mortars

Once the fighting at Ypres had shut down, the front line in France and Belgium became a static line of defence as both sides fought the elements rather than each other. It was during this time that the British Army in France began the development of a particularly important new type of equipment – the mortar – and it fell to the artillery to bring this new weapon into service. The BEF had gone to war that August with no mortars in its armoury and the onset of trench fighting had exposed the clear deficiency in the equipment needed for that kind of warfare. Mortars (along with grenades) were perhaps the most vital requirements. A small group of gunners – quickly given the nickname 'the Suicide Club' – were brought together on 26 November at Pont du Hem near Estaires by Brigadier General Holland, who commanded the artillery of the 8th Division. Two artillery officers, Captain Grosvenor and Lieutenant Churcher, and nine other men from Z Battery RHA and the 119th (Heavy) Battery formed the first British mortar battery of the war.

Their equipment was ancient and rudimentary. The mortars with which they were to practise were relics of a bygone age. Indeed, the weapon handed to Lieutenant Churcher had been cast at Toulouse in 1842 and had seen action in the Crimean War. The bomb itself was the original cast-iron sphere filled with black powder. A wooden sabot about 9 inches long was attached to the bomb, and an ancient fuse was screwed into the fuse hole. Once the weapon was armed, there was nothing scientific or modern about aiming it. The tube was elevated and fixed into position by means of a wedge. An element of modernity did, however, creep into the firing process. The detonator was electrical and the weapon itself was fired from a safe distance. This was just as well. Once fired, the mortar itself would leave the ground and become a deadly hazard to anyone nearby. The weapon naturally had little accuracy or not much range – at most the ancient devices might be able to project a bomb a couple of hundred yards. Its effect would be largely on morale. But given the lack of equipment, there was little option but to improvise and make do. There was a predictable price to be paid for this process of trial and error. Just after Christmas 1914 more than thirty men from V Battery RFA were killed when a bomb exploded prematurely inside a mortar. The development of this new equipment – which was to play such an important role in future operations – came at a terribly high price in human lives.

Lieutenant Churcher described a variation in methodology, and the Heath-Robinson nature of the early developmental stage of mortars in the British Army in the First World War becomes readily obvious: '[We would] load [the mortar] with a sabot the full size of the interior of the mortar. By means of delicate work with old bricks, bits of iron or anything that came in handy, an 8-inch bomb was balanced outside the mortar and the contraption [fired off] again.'

* * *

The onset of Christmas brought some surprising developments at some parts of the front line, with some troops crossing no man's land to fraternise with the enemy. For a brief and extraordinary moment, enemies became friends.

Gunner Herbert Smith, 5th Battery, 45th Brigade, RFA, was a witness to the famous Christmas Truce:

> On Christmas Eve there was a lull in the fighting, no firing going on at all after 6pm. The Germans had a Christmas tree in the trenches and Chinese lanterns all along the top of the parapet. Eventually the Germans started shouting 'Come over, I want to speak to you.' Our chaps hardly knew how to take this but one of the 'nuts' belonging to the Regiment got out of the trench and started to walk towards the German lines. One of the Germans met him half way across and they shook hands and became quite friendly. In due time the 'nut' came back and told all the others about it. So more of them took it in turns to go and visit the Germans. The officer commanding would not allow more than 3 men at a time.
>
> I went out myself on Christmas Day and exchanged some cigarettes for cigars and this game has been going on from Christmas Eve till midnight on Boxing Day without a single round being fired. The German I met had been a waiter in London and could use our language a little. He says they didn't want to fight and I think he was telling the truth as we are not getting half so many bullets as usual. I know this statement will take a lot of believing but it is absolutely correct. Fancy a German shaking your flapper as though he were trying to smash your fingers and then a few days later trying to plug you. I hardly know what to think about it but I fancy they are working up a big scheme so that they can give us a doing, but our chaps are prepared and I am under the impression they will get more than they bargained for …

That Christmas Lieutenant Cyril Drummond was serving with the 135th Battery, 32nd Brigade, RFA, near Ploegsteert Wood, the scene of the famous football match between German and British soldiers:

> On Boxing Day we walked up to the village of St Yvon where the observation post was. I soon discovered the places where we were usually shot at were quite safe. There were two sets of front trenches only a few yards apart and yet there were soldiers, both British and German, standing on top of them digging or repairing the trench in

some way, without ever shooting at each other. It was an extraordinary situation.

In the sunken road I met an officer I knew and we walked along together so that we could look across to the German front line which was only about 70 yards away. One of the Germans waved to us and said 'Come over here.' We said 'You come over here if you want to talk.' So he climbed out of his trench and came over towards us. We met and very gravely saluted each other. He was joined by more Germans and some of the Dublin Fusiliers from our own trenches came out to join us. No German officer came out, it was only the ordinary soldiers. We talked, mainly in French, because my German was not very good and none of the Germans could speak English well. But we managed to get together alright. One of them said 'We don't want to kill you and you don't want to kill us so why shoot?'

They gave me some German tobacco and German cigars – they seem to have plenty of those and very good ones too – and they asked whether we had any jam. One of the Dublin Fusiliers got a tin of jam which had been opened but very little taken out and he gave it to a German who gave him two cigars for it. I lined them all up and took a photograph.

Sergeant William Edgington of D Battery RHA did not enjoy any home leave before Christmas. He was given a commission in March 1915 but his time as an officer would prove to be short. On 8 May 1915 he and nine other men were killed in an explosion during a heavy enemy bombardment in the second battle of Ypres.

Mac and William were just two gunners among many who fell in those first few months of the war. The human costs of the fighting were almost incalculable, but the lessons learnt were real and enduring. Most of the lessons the BEF needed to learn about the effective use of artillery in modern warfare – developing new techniques of observation, new tactics in the deployment and use of the guns, more effective command and control of artillery, meeting the need for heavier equipment and more ammunition – were learnt and digested during the critical first few months of the campaign. Guided by the surviving veterans of this period, the task of applying these painfully learnt lessons would effectively pass to a new generation of artillery men, the amateur soldiers being trained up in England to replace the experienced men lost in that first feverish period of fighting. The regulars had, however, performed miracles within the limits of their capabilities and equipment. They were outgunned by the enemy, but they were nonetheless able to lay down a devastating quantity of accurate fire when it was most needed at Ypres, and in so doing prevented a German victory that would undoubtedly have heralded an early end to British involvement in the war and perhaps resulted in an entirely different outcome to the hostilities. The German accounts of the fighting at Ypres bear testimony to the power of the British guns: 'Advancing columns were under accurate fire at long range … all roads leading to the rear were continually shelled for a long way back. It was not possible to push up reserves owing to heavy artillery fire. Any regular transport of supplies became impossible.'

The victory that would come later, after four more years of violent struggle and catastrophic losses, would be built on the shoulders of these first few gunners of the British Expeditionary Force.

Chapter 11

The Shortage of Munitions

'Our effort was futile ... one round every now and then.'

Lieutenant Denys Payne, 109th (Heavy) Battery,
29 November 1914

Guns, however good they are, and however well served by their crews, are fundamentally useless without ammunition. From the outset of the campaign in August 1914 it became apparent that British supplies of gun ammunition were completely inadequate for the task in hand. Given the emerging significance of artillery as a decisive battle-winning weapon, the consequences of any failure in supply would be felt directly on the battlefield. Almost as soon as the fighting had started in France, ammunition supplies came under intense pressure. The shortages came to a head during the First Battle of Ypres in October, when, at the height of the fighting and when they were needed the most, shells were strictly rationed to a few rounds per gun per day. How had this happened? How could the British war effort have been laid so low by such a fundamental failure of planning?

Military planning is not, unfortunately, an exact science. Risks are inevitably taken in predicting both the precise nature and location of future conflict and the equipment needed to conduct an effective campaign. In the years leading up to August 1914 British strategic planning for a European campaign rested on two important but exceptionally risky assumptions. First, that a British Expeditionary Force to be deployed to the continent would consist of no more than six divisions, i.e. the whole of the Regular army based in the UK. Accordingly, supplies of equipment – including ammunition for the artillery – were organised to meet the needs of a force of this size and no larger. In the event, the fighting in France demanded massive additional numbers of troops far in excess of pre-war expectations. By November 1914 the BEF consisted of fifteen divisions, of which ten were infantry divisions. In these circumstances the supply of ammunition, intended to meet the needs of a force roughly half this size, very rapidly and inevitably came under enormous strain, particularly given the fact that dozens of additional guns of heavier calibres were being pressed into use at the front. The need to supply increased amounts of this type of ammunition had not been foreseen and therefore no preparations had been made for its manufacture and distribution.

The second assumption was that any war in Europe would not last very long and therefore supplies of ammunition would not become a major issue. The British were not the only ones to make this mistake. This was also the view of the German High Command. General von Moltke, Chief of the German General Staff, thought that one decisive battle would be sufficient to bring proceedings to a close. The British anticipated that a European war against Germany would be wrapped up after only four great battles in two months. The French had a similar view.

These two assumptions had a direct and obvious effect on the crucial issue of supply: provision of reserves and supplies would only be sufficient for a brief campaign involving a limited series of engagements. No thought or allowance had been made for a war of attrition or for the needs of large-scale industrial mobilisation. Thus their strategy gave the British military commanders little room for adjustment when events on the battlefield took a dramatically different course. There was, quite simply, no margin for error. The war would either be over in a short while, in which case supplies would be ample, or the war would last for longer, in which case supplies would rapidly begin to dwindle and there would be an inevitable time-lag before supplies could be produced in sufficient quantity. In truth, none of the parties to the conflict had laid the right foundations for winning the other war that events would reveal to be as important as the fighting itself: the war of materiel. With the considerable benefit of hindsight, pre-war military strategic planning appears naive in the extreme. But this naivety was compounded by a serious flaw in military assumptions about the nature of any European campaign. As already noted in Chapter 1, the British Army began to be equipped with the new quick-firing guns from 1908 onwards. This should have changed the underlying thinking about the supply of gun ammunition. If a gun could fire more quickly, it was not unreasonable to assume that the gunners would use the guns in this way and more ammunition would be required. It was, after all, what they were designed to do. But no changes to the logistical plans surrounding the provision of gun ammunition were made, and the supply chain continued to be modelled largely around the experience of the artillery during the South African War. In this conflict the army had fought with old-fashioned guns with a much slower rate of fire. This failure to take into account a factor as blindingly obvious as the basic dynamic of artillery when planning sufficient supplies of gun ammunition is rendered more extraordinary by the fact that the army did increase, in 1912, its estimate of the amount of small arms ammunition needed to fight a European war. As the Official History tartly remarked: 'There seems to have been disinclination on all sides to face the expenditure involved by the increase of gun ammunition and of the additional transport required to carry it.' This observation confirms a depressingly familiar feature of defence procurement throughout the ages.

Shells are more expensive than bullets, and guns and howitzers are more expensive than rifles. Money, especially that belonging to taxpayers, is a finite resource and there are always competing claims for its use. This fundamental principle of public finance held true in the early part of the twentieth century just as much as it does today. Pre-war economies and budget cutting in the run-up to the First World War left the artillery cruelly exposed when the fighting began to take on the characteristics of siege warfare. This was certainly the view of many gunner officers. Major Ernest Tyrell, serving with the 108th (Heavy) Batter RGA, probably spoke for many when, in a letter home to his uncle from France on 28 November 1914, he wrote:

> This war has shown, like every other, that we have not enough heavy guns and, of course, now the supply cannot meet the demand. Everyone who thought about it knew this was the case long ago and yet the revelation always comes on us as a surprise again ...

The army had gone to war in 1914 with a pitifully small supply of artillery ammunition. The reserve stocks of gun ammunition maintained in the UK at the outbreak of hostilities was sufficient to provide only 1,500 rounds for each 18-pounder gun, 1,900 rounds for each of the lighter 13-pounder guns of the Horse Artillery, 1,200 for each howitzer and 1,000 rounds for each of the heavy 60-pounders. Most of these supplies of ammunition went out to France with the BEF in August 1914. A small reserve of 500 rounds for each of the main equipment types was kept in store in the UK, but this too would be hurriedly dispatched to the front. The estimated manufacturing capacity to replenish these meagre stocks looked highly suspect. For example, there was only enough industrial capacity to supply 30 rounds for each of the

18-pounders per month – a tiny fraction of the amount of ammunition being expended. Only 100 rounds per month of 60-pounder ammunition could be supplied from the ordnance factories – the equivalent of 4 rounds per gun per month – a ridiculously inadequate situation given the increasingly important role these guns were playing on the battlefields of Flanders. The heavy 6-inch howitzers of the siege batteries, which were beginning to play a crucial role with the BEF, were in an even worse position. These guns were never intended for active service in the European campaign and there was therefore no strategic reserve of ammunition to speak of. These batteries were getting through their stock of ammunition at an alarming rate. The four howitzers of the 2nd Siege Battery, for example, fired nearly 700 rounds of high explosive shell in twelve days of fighting on the Aisne – a significant portion of the entire national stockpile.

The supply of manpower to provide the extra fighting troops the army needed was not proving to be an issue, as recruitment to the New Armies exceeded all expectations. But it became rapidly apparent to everyone in government that something had to be done immediately to increase the supply of both guns and ammunition. Lord Kitchener, the Secretary of State for War, told the House of Lords on 17 September, during the height of the fighting on the Aisne, that, 'Our chief difficulty is one of materiel rather than of personnel.'

Accelerating the production of shells for the artillery was, however, complicated by one substantial obstacle. The armaments manufacturers had most of their industrial capacity tied up in contracts to deliver shells for the Royal Navy, meaning that there was little extra help that could be immediately provided to the Royal Artillery, even though their need was more urgent. At the end of September the Cabinet approved the provision of £20 million to help the armament companies increase the capacity of their factories. A few days later a special Cabinet Committee on munitions was established. All of the key ministers were represented, including Kitchener, Churchill and Lloyd George (Chancellor of the Exchequer). The Committee met five times in October 1914 and then again in December to address the issues of gun and ammunition supply, manpower shortages and industrial capacity. Enormous contracts for new supplies were placed, with both British and overseas manufacturers. As part of these new deals the British Government secured the output of the Bethlehem Steel Corporation in the United States for five years.

Progress was also made in another vital area. Pre-war reluctance to commit large amounts of taxpayers' resources to the military was swept away and the Committee substantially increased the amount of new equipment on order. For example, the Master General of Ordnance, General von Donop, had already placed contracts for nearly 900 new 18-pounder guns to be delivered by June 1915. The Committee increased this number to 3,000. It was assumed that if the guns could be provided, then so could the ammunition for them, but in fact this would prove a harder nut to crack. The established armament manufacturers, such as Vickers, Armstrong Whitworth, Beardmore and the Coventry Ordnance Company, all assured the ministers that, provided the right financial provision was made, then production targets could be met. An Armaments Firms Committee was set up and given the powers to distribute the various munitions orders to individual firms, each company entering into contracts directly with the War Office. By the spring of 1915 the War Office had contracts with more than 2,500 firms for the supply of new equipment.

Kitchener, however, remained fearful that the establishment of this Cabinet Committee represented an encroachment upon his ministerial authority and after the Committee met in December he declared that he would not attend any further meetings. Unfortunately, the real work of providing sufficient supplies of war fighting materiel was far from complete, as subsequent events would confirm.

Despite all of these difficulties, the War Office managed to oversee a nineteen-fold increase in gun ammunition in the first six months of the war – an extraordinary achievement in the circumstances. Even this, however, would not be enough to keep up with the insatiable demand for more supplies.

The position was slightly better for the howitzers and the horse artillery guns but even here the gap between expenditure and resupply was dangerously wide. To make matters worse, the arms factories were short of skilled men. Ten thousand skilled engineers had enlisted by the end of August 1914 alone, leaving machines and workshops idle when they should have been working at full capacity. At the start of the war the Woolwich Arsenal – the centre of gun ammunition manufacturing – employed only half the numbers estimated to be necessary to keep production up to the levels needed to meet wartime requirements. By September 1914 the Vickers armaments company, in an effort to keep its skilled workforce intact, proposed to the War Office that armaments workers should wear a special badge to protect them from pressures to enlist. Men of fighting age were often accosted in the street if they were not in uniform. No one wanted to be accused of cowardice and this was therefore a pressing issue. Inertia, however, prevailed and such a scheme would only come into existence in March 1915, by which time the shell shortages had reached epic proportions.

The consequences of these manpower shortfalls were entirely predictable. At the high point of the fighting at Ypres in October 1914, when the British Expeditionary Force faced the real prospect of strategic defeat, the guns were limited to an average of 4 rounds per gun per day. Some batteries fired very much more than this. Careful husbandry, a willingness to plunder deep into the reserves and strict allocation of resources allowed some batteries to use much more than this pitiful amount. Captain Francis Adams of E Battery RHA thought that the guns of his battery had fired over 1,500 rounds at Wytschaete between 19 and 22 October during the height of the fighting for the Messines Ridge. The 86th Battery, in position at Bois Grenier, fired 667 rounds on a single day (20 October).

On 23–24 October, as the German Fourth Army attempted to press home its attack on the wafer-thin British lines, the 2nd Brigade Ammunition Column provided 2,566 rounds of 18-pounder ammunition to the four batteries it was supporting; in fact, all the ammunition columns would have been providing a similar, almost miraculous, level of resources. From 1 to 20 November, at the moment of greatest danger to the British lines at Ypres, the 35th (Heavy) Battery fired 2,125 rounds of 60-pounder ammunition. On one critical day alone, 11 November, when crack units of Prussian Guards threatened to break through the British lines along the Menin road, the battery fired 224 shells.

But it was frequently a case of 'touch and go' and the reserves inevitably came under serious strain. Major Dane, commanding the 4th Division Ammunition Column, recalled how, at the peak of the fighting south of Ypres in October, he managed to keep the guns supplied with ammunition:

> … on the 20th October, there was an enormous demand for ammunition all day from nine in the morning until seven at night. The whole column was soon emptied and we had lorries filling up at all the railheads right back to Arques. Considering that the drivers had no maps, did not know the country and could not speak the language, it was wonderful how they found their way about and always turned up in the nick of time with a fresh load. Theoretically an Army Service Corps officer

was supposed to be in charge of each party, but practically, owing to the rush, each lorry either went on its own or in small convoys of 3 or 4.

But these resources were necessarily finite and the stocks were being progressively reduced at a far quicker rate than they were being replenished. The quality of the ammunition for the heavy guns was also far from adequate, leading to premature explosions that often caused more damage to the weapons themselves than to the enemy. This could only have one consequence. As the fighting progressed into November, and new German attacks developed, the shortages of gun ammunition began to pose real problems on the battlefield that even the most careful husbandry of supplies could not conceal.

Major John Mowbray, on the artillery staff of the 2nd Division, noted in his diary on 25 October: 'Certain shortages in 18-pounder and 4.5-inch Lyddite ammunition: our arrangements do not contemplate battles lasting a month! Most inconvenient at this time.' Likewise, the 11th Battery RFA was in action at Neuve Eglise to the south of Ypres on 30 October. Its war diary recorded dolefully: 'Guns short of ammunition – limited to 20 rounds per gun per diem …'

Major Rudkin, the commanding officer of the 80th Battery, 15th Brigade, RFA, wrote in his war diary on 2 November: 'The Battery was daily in action at Neuve Eglise. Not firing many rounds owing to shortage of ammunition.' Private William Collins, with the 7th Brigade RHA, remembers being told by the gunners of his brigade at about this time that 'ammunition was in very short supply after the large expenditure of the Ypres battle and that they were restricted to only 4 rounds per gun per day'. On 30 October, at the height of the fighting along the Menin road outside Ypres, John Mowbray again commented on the problem: 'Shortage of howitzer and field gun ammunition is serious.'

On 1 November Lieutenant Colonel Arthur Wilkinson, commanding the 35th (Heavy) Battery, wrote:

During the month of October we had fired 1,044 rounds which was considered a lot in the early stages of the war. Later on it was equivalent to about the expenditure of a battery in one day during active operations. Our guns by this time were getting out of order and we had continual misfires due to defective shells. The Ordnance did all that was possible to help us but ammunition, stores, spare parts etc were almost unobtainable as there were none in the country …

On that day the field artillery of the 1st Division, defending the Menin road against the German onslaught, was restricted to a mere nine rounds per gun.

The 4.7-inch batteries, which were rushed into service in the autumn of 1914 to make good the serious deficiency in British heavy artillery, were in an even worse position. Lieutenant Denys Payne was serving with the 109th (Heavy) Battery. In October and November 1914 the battery was in action near Neuve Chapelle supporting the infantry of the Indian Corps. The supply of this type of gun ammunition was seriously constrained from the beginning of the campaign and the heavy expenditure of shell in the battle of Ypres would lead to a predictable crisis. On 29 November Payne wrote: 'We have been restricted again to three rounds per gun of [high explosive] shell.'

This was not the first sign of shortages of supply. On 4 November, during a frenzied night attack by the Connaught Rangers at Neuve Chapelle, Payne's battery was reduced to the role of an irrelevant by-stander when it should have been drenching the enemy lines with heavy gunfire: 'Our effort was futile. One round every now and then. This cannot have encouraged our people, nor have discouraged the enemy. We probably wasted some good ammunition.' The 4.7-inch shells were also poorly made and were liable to premature explosion; the fuses were also untrustworthy. As a result, Payne was convinced that 'we are likely to cause a fat lot of damage to the Hun'.

The problem was real and apparent. The issue was what to do about it. Both Lord Kitchener at the War Office and Maurice Hankey, Secretary of the Committee on Imperial Defence (CID), had been studying the problem of supply from the very outbreak of hostilities. Action had already been taken, as noted earlier, to increase production and hundreds of new contracts had been issued for rifles, guns and ammunition. But from the first days of the war leading figures in the armaments industry were pressing the government for a new and much more radical strategy – one that might address the needs of both the French and the British armies for more gun ammunition. On 2 September 1914 Sir Charles Ottley, a former Director of Naval Intelligence and Hankey's predecessor at the CID, and now a director of Armstrong Whitworth, one of the largest armaments companies in the country, wrote to Hankey suggesting that the government should appoint an official with extraordinary powers to oversee the development of the additional military supplies needed to prosecute the war effectively. He proposed that such a person should have 'plenary powers to commandeer the entire manufacturing potentialities of the Empire and more particularly of Great Britain. By adopting this policy England will merely revert to her time-honoured role as the main prop of the struggling European nationalities.' Sir Charles proposed Sir Percy Girouard for this new role of armaments supremo. A railway engineer and former colonial civil servant, in 1914 Girouard was in charge of Armstrong Whitworth's Elswick armaments factory on Tyneside.

Attracted by the boldness of such a move, Hankey and Winston Churchill endorsed Ottley's proposals and both made efforts to get the War Office to support it. But feathers were being ruffled in Whitehall and a territorial turf war broke out in which Kitchener, anxious not to lose overall control of the war effort, held out against such an appointment on the grounds that it might undermine and cut across existing efforts to increase supply. In reality, this was nothing more than the old Whitehall tactic of patrolling and defending departmental boundaries. Sadly, it would prevail until the shortages of munitions boiled over into a full-blown political crisis in the spring of 1915.

In the meantime, Lloyd George, sensing that the issue was assuming greater significance than Kitchener would admit, had been pressing Asquith to establish a new, more powerful committee to oversee increased munitions production. Kitchener threatened to resign if the new committee were given any executive authority, while Lloyd George felt it would be a pointless exercise if it were not. Asquith eventually brokered a form of compromise between the two antagonists but, as in the case of many such attempts at conciliation, neither party felt that the outcome, in the form of a new Munitions of War Committee, was worth a candle and it never really got to grips with the fundamental challenges.

Events at the front would give the whole issue a dramatic new momentum. The failure of the first major British offensive of the war at Neuve Chapelle in March 1915 to achieve the intended breakthrough was a bitter disappointment for Sir John French and he attributed this failure to the shortage of gun ammunition. This was certainly a factor in the battle, but it was only part of the explanation for the failure to convert an initial breach of the German lines into a major breakthrough. French himself, driven by personal insecurity and vanity, was no fan of Kitchener, and was determined not to be landed with responsibility for the unsuccessful outcome at Neuve Chapelle. In a serious breach of military propriety from which his career never recovered, French provided a briefing to *The Times* war correspondent Colonel Tim Repington, which eventually exploded on to the front page of the newspaper a few days after the fighting at Neuve Chapelle had ended. The headlines proclaimed that British soldiers had died at Neuve Chapelle as a direct result of the shortage of shells.

This was not French's first indiscretion. A few weeks before Repington's article appeared, he had given two interviews to journalists complaining about the shortage of shells, and his comments had caused real anxiety inside the government. Kitchener had assured Prime Minister Herbert Asquith that his allegations were untrue, that the supply would increase over time and that the stocks of shells were sufficient for present military requirements. On this basis the Prime Minister himself made a speech in Newcastle on 4 April saying that everything was under control. Having been assured by Kitchener that the problem had been exaggerated, the Prime Minister commented, 'I have had a talk with French. He told me I could let you know that with the present supply of ammunition he will have as much as his troops will be able to use on his next forward movement.'

It was a carefully crafted assessment that made no reference to previous military operations and gave virtually no real commitment of any kind about the medium to long term munitions supply position. Asquith read far too much into Kitchener's reassurances and as a result went on to make perhaps one of his greatest blunders as war leader. He began to look complacent and out of touch.

In his Elswick speech he made an even more serious mistake, for which he would pay a very high political price, saying:

I do not believe that any army has ever either entered upon a campaign or been maintained during a campaign with better or more equipment. I saw a statement the other day that the operations of our army were being crippled, or at any rate hampered, by our failure to provide the necessary ammunition. I say there is not a word of truth to that statement ...

The Times ran its story on 14 May under the headline 'NEED FOR SHELLS. BRITISH ATTACKS CHECKED. LIMITED SUPPLY THE CAUSE.' This was the final straw. Asquith, already weakened by the obvious failure of the munitions policy and in the aftermath of the sudden resignation of the volatile Sir John Fisher as First Sea Lord in a row with Churchill over the conduct of the Dardanelles operation, had been effectively manoeuvred by Lloyd George and the Tory leader Bonar Law into forming a wartime coalition government. One of the key issues for the new government would be getting to grips with the munitions crisis. Kitchener finally caved in under the overwhelming political pressure and a new Ministry of Munitions under the Chancellor, David Lloyd George, was formed; it would take over from the War Office complete responsibility for the supply and production of military materiel. Kitchener had by now lost face and credibility over the whole issue of munitions, and could no longer resist the demands for 'something to be done'. Sir Percy Girouard was duly appointed as the senior official in the new department, although his tenure as munitions supremo was a brief one. He resigned just six weeks later, finding it impossible to work with the politicians.

Lloyd George's energy and momentum proved the decisive factors in the success of the new ministry, enabling it to help Britain to win the war of materiel. The transformation brought about by the new ministry was truly remarkable. The scarcity of shells that had reduced the British guns almost to impotence, firing just a handful of rounds per day, would be replaced by an astonishing abundance. By the summer of 1916 the British Army had a prodigious supply of shells. In the week-long preliminary bombardment ahead of the start of the Somme campaign in July 1916, the British guns fired over 1,500,000 rounds at the German trenches – more than all the shells fired by the British in the first twelve months of the war. A further 250,000 shells were fired on the first day of the battle alone. Over the next four months of fighting several million more shells would be fired. All talk of shell shortages would cease.

There were several critical factors underpinning this successful national drive to increase the production of munitions. First, more labour was clearly needed. Skilled workers were replaced by semi-skilled workers, who took on the job of production. Secondly, Lloyd George himself persuaded the reluctant trade unions, anxious about preserving their firm grip on the supply of labour, to agree to a national arrangement whereby traditional demarcations were to be relaxed for the duration of the war effort.

Many of these additional workers were women, who were entering the labour market for the first time. The numbers of women employed in Britain rose from just under 6 million before the war to over 7.3 million by 1918. Much of this extra labour was devoted to armaments production of one kind or another. British metal and related industries employed a total of just over 200,000 women in July 1914. By the end of the war this figure had risen to almost a million. These jobs paid more than the jobs most women had previously occupied, in domestic service or factory work in textiles. But it was not easy. Much of the work involved handling toxic chemicals. The skin of these workers would often turn yellow through exposure, earning them the nickname 'canaries'. Lilian Miles, one of these women munition workers, had beautiful black hair that was turned green by her workplace exposure to chemicals: 'You would wash and wash and it didn't make no difference. Your whole body was yellow.'

Thirdly, Lloyd George ensured his new ministry was run by those he called 'men of push and go'. This was nothing short of a revolution in the workings of government. These key figures were not, in other words, traditional civil servants. He recruited experienced businessmen and entrepreneurs to manage the affairs of his new department of state. They were men of action not bureaucrats steeped in the intricate ways of Whitehall. They got things done and on time.

Fourthly, the network of production contracts was expanded and new production methods employed to boost manufacture. The results, although impressive, resulted in an inevitable lowering of overall standards as quantity took precedence over quality. During the battle of the Somme in 1916, for example, a quarter of the British guns were put out of action by faulty ammunition. These problems were not, however, unique to the British. Both the German and the French armies suffered equally from the same problems. The increase in quantity had come at a price.

But slowly and surely the problem of supply was addressed and overcome. Lloyd George's triumph with the Ministry of Munitions would ultimately serve as his springboard to success, and he became Prime Minister in December 1916. More importantly, it would also pave the way for the ultimate victory over Germany in November 1918, by which time British weaponry and ammunition finally held sway over the battlefields of France and Belgium.

References

The following references are to archive material in the Royal Artillery Museum, Woolwich. All the directly attributable quotes contained in the text of this book are drawn from these notes and diaries.

MD/233	War diary of Captain William Brown Mackie, 30th Brigade Ammunition Column
MD/425	Typescript account of the service of Lieutenant Charles Schreiber, 115th Battery, 25th Brigade, RFA
MD/625	Extracts from the diary of Lieutenant Eric Brooke, describing the actions of 108th Battery, 23rd Brigade, RFA
MD/657	A note written by Sergeant William Collins, RAMC, recounting his service with 7th Brigade, RFA
MD/931	War diary of Major John Mowbray, artillery staff officer with 2nd Division. Mowbray was killed in action in 1916.
MD/1116	Papers of Second Lieutenant Cecil Tyndale-Biscoe, RFA
MD/1121	War diary of Lieutenant John Wills, 61 (Howitzer) Battery, RFA
MD/1150	Journal of Colonel Roderick Macleod, 80 Battery, RFA
MD/1447	Account of the service of Lieutenant Colonel George Mackenzie, with 8th Siege Battery, RGA
MD/1667	Transcript of the diary of Gunner Job Drain VC, relating to his service with 37th Battery, RFA
MD/1668	War diary of Gunner Charles Burrows, 104th Battery, 22nd Brigade, RFA
MD/1758	Notes written by Sergeant Frank Reeves, 70th Battery, 34th Brigade, RFA
MD/2006	Notes from a commemorative book relating to the service of Captain William Rait-Kerr, 57th (Howitzer) Battery, 43rd Brigade, RFA. Rait-Kerr was killed on 10 November 1914 during the fighting in the first Battle of Ypres.

MD/2157	Account of the war service of Lieutenant Ralph Blewitt, 54th Battery, 39th Brigade, RFA
MD/2201	Letters of Captain Josslyn Ramsden, 27th Brigade, RFA
MD/2241	Diary of Gunner Walter Harrison, 27th Battery, 32nd Brigade, RFA
MD/2337/348	Diary of Battery Sergeant Major Philip Hillman, 28th Brigade, RFA
MD/2383	Service diary of Battery Sergeant Major Harry Sprotson, 68th Battery, 14th Brigade, RFA
MD/2399	Account of the action at Landrecies by Lieutenant Harold Willcocks, 44th Brigade, RFA
MD/2563	War service diary of Lieutenant James Fairbairn, RAMC, attached to 31st Heavy Battery, RFA
MD/2608	Diary of Gunner E. Childs, 12th Battery, 35th Brigade, RFA
MD/2736/3	Account of the war service of Major Denys Payne, 109th Heavy Battery, RFA
MD/2808	Diary of Second Lieutenant John Leigh, 122 (Heavy) Battery, RGA
MD/2851	Diary of Sergeant George, 126th Battery, RFA
MD/2960	Diary of war service of Robert Francis Foljambe MC, 120 Battery, RFA
MD/3285	Typescript diary of Bombardier Arthur Baxter, O Battery, RHA
MD/3295	Diary of Sergeant Francis Miller, 69th Battery, RFA
MD/3341	'My four and a half years of Army life', Gunner Herbert Smith, RGA
MD/3551	Notes by Lieutenant Colonel Onslow, 27th Brigade, RFA
MD/3900	Diary of Lieutenant Austin Bates, 31st Battery, RFA
MD/3966	Diary of Captain Charles Banfield, 24th Brigade, RFA
MD/4254	Manuscript diaries of F.J. Adams, E Battery, RHA

Index